W9-DIR-462

THE ANNALS

© 1996 *by* The American Academy *of* Political *and* Social Science

Editorial Office: 3937 Chestnut Street, Philadelphia, PA 19104.

For information about membership* (individuals only) and subscriptions (institutions), address:

SAGE PUBLICATIONS, INC.
2455 Teller Road
Thousand Oaks, CA 91320

From India and South Asia,		*From the UK, Europe, the Middle*
write to:		*East and Africa, write to:*
SAGE PUBLICATIONS INDIA Pvt. Ltd		SAGE PUBLICATIONS LTD
P.O. Box 4215		6 Bonhill Street
New Delhi 110 048		London EC2A 4PU
INDIA		UNITED KINGDOM

SAGE Production Staff: ERIC LAW, KELLY GUNTHER, DORIS HUS, and ROSE TYLAK
*Please note that members of The Academy receive THE ANNALS with their membership.
Library of Congress Catalog Card Number 95-71933
International Standard Serial Number ISSN 0002-7162
International Standard Book Number ISBN 0-7619-0298-8 (Vol. 545, 1996 paper)
International Standard Book Number ISBN 0-7619-0297-X (Vol. 545, 1996 cloth)
Manufactured in the United States of America. First printing, May 1996.

The articles appearing in THE ANNALS are indexed in *Academic Index, Book Review Index, Combined Retrospective Index Sets, Current Contents, General Periodicals Index, Public Affairs Information Service Bulletin, Pro-Views,* and *Social Sciences Index.* They are also abstracted and indexed in *ABC Pol Sci, America: History and Life, Automatic Subject Citation Alert, Book Review Digest, Family Resources Database, Higher Education Abstracts, Historical Abstracts, Human Resources Abstracts, International Political Science Abstracts, Managing Abstracts, Periodica Islamica, Sage Urban Studies Abstracts, Social Planning / Policy & Development Abstracts, Social Sciences Citation Index, Social Work Research & Abstracts, Sociological Abstracts, United States Political Science Documents,* and/or *Work Related Abstracts,* and are available on microfilm from University Microfilms, Ann Arbor, Michigan.

Information about membership rates, institutional subscriptions, and back issue prices may be found on the facing page.

Advertising. Current rates and specifications may be obtained by writing to THE ANNALS Advertising and Promotion Manager at the Thousand Oaks office (address above).

Claims. Claims for undelivered copies must be made no later than twelve months following month of publication. The publisher will supply missing copies when losses have been sustained in transit and when the reserve stock will permit.

Change of Address. Six weeks' advance notice must be given when notifying of change of address to ensure proper identification. Please specify name of journal. Send address changes to: THE ANNALS, c/o Sage Publications, Inc., 2455 Teller Road, Thousand Oaks, CA 91320.

THE ANNALS

of The American Academy *of* Political *and* Social Science

ALAN W. HESTON, *Editor*
NEIL A. WEINER, *Assistant Editor*

─────────── **FORTHCOMING** ───────────

THE MEDIA AND POLITICS
Special Editor: Kathleen Hall Jamieson

Volume 546   July 1996

THE FUTURE OF HONG KONG
Special Editor: Max J. Skidmore

Volume 547   September 1996

THE HOLOCAUST:
REMEMBERING FOR THE FUTURE
Special Editors. Franklin H. Littell, G. Jan Colijn,
Marcia S. Littell, and Irene G. Shur

Volume 548   November 1996

───

See page 2 for information on Academy membership and
purchase of single volumes of **The Annals.**

VOLUME 545

MAY 1996

THE ANNALS

of The American Academy *of* Political
and Social Science

ALAN W. HESTON, *Editor*
NEIL A. WEINER, *Assistant Editor*

CHALLENGES IN RISK ASSESSMENT
AND RISK MANAGEMENT

Special Editors of this Volume

HOWARD KUNREUTHER
University of Pennsylvania
Philadelphia

PAUL SLOVIC
Decision Research
Eugene
Oregon

SAGE Periodicals Press *THOUSAND OAKS   LONDON   NEW DELHI*

Origin and Purpose. The Academy was organized December 14, 1889, to promote the progress of political and social science, especially through publications and meetings. The Academy does not take sides in controverted questions, but seeks to gather and present reliable information to assist the public in forming an intelligent and accurate judgment.

Meetings. The Academy occasionally holds a meeting in the spring extending over two days.

Publications. THE ANNALS is the bimonthly publication of The Academy. Each issue contains articles on some prominent social or political problem, written at the invitation of the editors. Also, monographs are published from time to time, numbers of which are distributed to pertinent professional organizations. These volumes constitute important reference works on the topics with which they deal, and they are extensively cited by authorities throughout the United States and abroad. The papers presented at the meetings of The Academy are included in THE ANNALS.

Membership. Each member of The Academy receives THE ANNALS and may attend the meetings of The Academy. Membership is open only to individuals. Annual dues: $51.00 for the regular paperbound edition (clothbound, $74.00). Add $12.00 per year for membership outside the U.S.A. Members may also purchase single issues of THE ANNALS for $15.00 each (clothbound, $19.00). Add $2.00 for shipping and handling on all prepaid orders.

Subscriptions. THE ANNALS (ISSN 0002-7162) is published six times annually—in January, March, May, July, September, and November. Institutions may subscribe to THE ANNALS at the annual rate: $197.00 (clothbound, $229.00). Add $12.00 per year for subscriptions outside the U.S.A. Institutional rates for single issues: $34.00 each (clothbound, $40.00).

Second class postage paid at Thousand Oaks, California, and additional offices.

Single issues of THE ANNALS may be obtained by individuals who are not members of The Academy for $18.00 each (clothbound, $28.00). Add $2.00 for shipping and handling on all prepaid orders. Single issues of THE ANNALS have proven to be excellent supplementary texts for classroom use. Direct inquiries regarding adoptions to THE ANNALS c/o Sage Publications (address below).

All correspondence concerning membership in The Academy, dues renewals, inquiries about membership status, and/or purchase of single issues of THE ANNALS should be sent to THE ANNALS c/o Sage Publications, Inc., 2455 Teller Road, Thousand Oaks, CA 91320. Telephone: (805) 499-0721; FAX/Order line: (805) 499-0871. *Please note that orders under $30 must be prepaid.* Sage affiliates in London and India will assist institutional subscribers abroad with regard to orders, claims, and inquiries for both subscriptions and single issues.

Printed on recycled, acid-free paper

CONTENTS

BOOK DEPARTMENT CONTENTS

PREFACE

During the past two decades, our society has grown healthier and safer on average and has spent billions of dollars and immense effort to become so. Nevertheless, the public has become more, rather than less, concerned about risk. We have come to see ourselves as being exposed to more serious risks than we faced in the past, and we believe that the worst is yet to come.

A second dramatic trend is that risk assessment and risk management, like many other facets of our society, have become much more politicized and contentious. Polarized views, controversy, and overt conflict have become pervasive. The public has lost faith in the ability of science, industry, and government to manage the risks from many important technologies, such as nuclear power and chemicals and their wastes. In addition, the conflict is exacerbated by sharp differences between people as to who should and does benefit or lose as a result of specific decisions—for example, siting a noxious facility.

Difficulties in managing risks from technology are compounded by the fact that there is often great uncertainty associated with estimates of those risks. This uncertainty is sometimes due to a sparse database from which to derive risk estimates. Knowledge of the ways in which accidents, illnesses, or other forms of harm result from exposure to a technology may also be lacking. If the hazard is latent, then it may be even more difficult to determine the potential harmful consequences. In addition, there may be many factors triggering a particular disease (such as cancer), making it difficult to determine the responsibility of a particular technology or event (for example, groundwater contamination).

In addition, each party concerned with a particular problem involving risks to health, safety, or the environment has its own goals and agenda, often framed around how risky a particular activity is likely to be. Scientific experts frequently disagree on the nature of the risks, so that each interested party can typically find someone to support its position. Given the lack of adequate theoretical models and data for many of these risks, it is often difficult to evaluate the differences between these estimates.

The U.S. Congress has also been concerned with risk assessment and risk management. Several recent bills have proposed detailed risk assessments and benefit-cost analyses as a basis for determining appropriate regulations and standards. It is not easy to forecast the impact that this proposed legislation might have on the treatment of risk in our society.

THE NEED FOR A NEW PERSPECTIVE

The conflicts and controversies surrounding risk are not due to public irrationality or ignorance but, instead, may be seen as a side effect of our remarkable form of participatory democratic government, amplified by certain powerful technological and social changes. The technological change allows the electronic and print media to inform us of bad (trust-destroying) news from all over the world, often right as it happens. Special interest groups, well funded and sophisticated in using their own experts and the media, effectively communicate their viewpoints and influence risk policy debates and decisions. All of this is blended into an adversarial legal system that pits expert against expert, contradicting each other's risk assessments and further destroying the public trust.

The young science of risk assessment and the techniques of benefit-cost analysis and decision analysis face numerous challenges in addressing questions about how society should manage its health, safety, and environmental risks. Scientific analysis of risks cannot allay our fears of major accidents or delayed cancers unless we trust the system.

It is essential that we understand the complex psychological, social, cultural, and political forces that dictate success and failure in risk assessment and risk management. Understanding the root causes of conflict and ineffective action gives hope for improvement. As we come to understand the complexity of the root causes of risk conflict, we also recognize the need for radically different approaches to risk management.

ORGANIZATION OF THIS VOLUME

The articles in this volume of *The Annals* provide a perspective from leading scholars on the challenges in risk assessment and risk management. Each of the articles addresses a set of key topics in the authors' field of expertise. The questions raised provide a blueprint for action as well as an agenda for future research.

Uncertainty and risk assessment

John Graham and Lorenz Rhomberg's article reviews the types of scientific data that can be collected to assess risks. Such data range from real-world observations to controlled clinical trials. The power and limitations of these different approaches are illustrated with empirical examples. Graham and Rhomberg conclude with a set of cautionary notes on the difficulties of settling value differences with risk assessments due to uncertainties in the estimates and the possibility that the assessment may exacerbate conflicts between potential winners and losers.

The principal message from Robert Pollak's article is that risk assessment today cannot be viewed as scientific because too little is known about the relationship between exposure to certain substances and contraction of diseases. Hence he is somewhat skeptical of proposals that attempt to achieve uniformity of risk assessments across federal agencies. He concludes his article by pointing out that the government needs to be concerned with issues of trust, public perception of risk, and value differences in developing risk regulations.

Dale Jamieson's article focuses on the high level of uncertainty associated with many societal problems and suggests that people can thus find or create risk data to support their own agendas. He points out that uncertainty is more than just an analysis of scientific data, being determined also by the degree of trust that people have in the institution providing the data and the ways in which people are likely to behave in the future. He thus concludes that we need to bring science into closer contact with the public and our policymakers in order to improve the decision-making process under conditions of uncertainty.

William Freudenburg also focuses on the challenges in using risk assessment by focusing on the difficulties that scientists and technologists have had in dealing with the public. He argues that risk assessors are often overconfident, frequently overlooking or underestimating the unknowns. He introduces the word "recreancy" to depict our reliance on scientific experts who we fear will not do their job. The inability of scientists to recognize or admit their blind spots has created a sense of distrust in experts on the part of the public.

Valuation and risk

Robin Gregory, Thomas Brown, and Jack Knetsch point out that valuations of environmental risks are often contentious because people focus on different dimensions of the risk and weigh them differently. Gregory and his colleagues indicate some of the challenges in obtaining valuations such as loss/gain differentials and varying rates of time preferences by individuals. The absence of prices makes assessment of environmental values difficult and may require the use of new approaches such as value trees and citizen juries.

The importance of understanding the sociocultural system associated with any problem is the principal theme of Roy Rappaport's article. Using the example of an oil spill's impact on fish and other marine life, he points out that for some individuals, the loss may be viewed as economic, while for others it is seen as a threat to their culture. Many values such as integrity and equity cannot be expressed in quantitative terms but need to be recognized when evaluating specific risks and strategies for dealing with them. The article contends that one must take into account these apprehensions of the affected public even if the experts view the risks as much lower.

Baruch Fischhoff addresses the issues of eliciting values from the public and using them to establish trust. He indicates that one can use focus groups, citizen juries, and public opinion surveys to do this. Fischhoff also makes the case that people are anxious to understand the models being used to estimate risk and to know how good they are. By sharing their knowledge with the public, it may be possible for scientists to become trusted by citizens.

Risk communication

William Leiss addresses the questions of how to improve the dialogue on risk between experts and the public and how to achieve a higher degree of social consensus. He first reviews two earlier phases in the evolution of risk communication, where quantitative risk estimates and comparative risk estimates determined priorities (Phase I) and where an emphasis was placed on characteristics of successful communication (Phase II). He feels that the current phase, which emphasizes social interrelations between players in the risk management game, has a better chance of successfully addressing his questions than did the other two phases. Two case studies illustrate how this third phase has been operationalized.

The importance of risk communication in the amplification and attenuation of risk is highlighted in the article by Roger and Jeanne Kasperson. They trace the different phases of social amplification from the time that an event is channeled through individuals and networks, through the communication process with its potential ripple effects, including the creation of stigma. A case study from Goiânia, Brazil, illustrates the impact of the media on tourism in the aftermath of a radiation accident in the region. The media's coverage produced a decline in tourism, resulting in social and economic consequences far greater than one would expect given the limited degree of radiation exposure and risk from the event. The Kaspersons conclude that one needs to create political regimes and institutions for risk containment and risk reduction.

Kip Viscusi and Richard Zeckhauser examine the role of hazard warnings in communicating information on risk. They point out that warnings can facilitate decentralized risk-taking decisions when there are heterogeneous preferences. In issuing warnings, one needs to consider the length, format, and type of warning as well as who receives it. It is particularly important to focus on how individuals process information, so one can determine how likely a particular warning will be understood. The article concludes by posing a set of challenges for communicating information on risks.

The process of risk management

Howard Kunreuther and Paul Slovic contend that risk and its management should be viewed as a game in which the rules must be socially negotiated within the context of a specific problem. This contextualist view provides insight into why technical approaches to risk management often fail. It also highlights the need to understand the values and goals of the interested parties, thus emphasizing the importance of institutional, procedural, and societal processes. The siting of hazardous facilities is used to illustrate this importance of process as well as outcome measures in developing risk management strategies.

Ralph Keeney points out that the role of values in the risk management process requires making trade-offs between costs and reductions in specific risks such as the chances of death. He argues that there are differences in how a person should evaluate a particular strategy if it involves just that person as an individual (for example, "What should I pay for an air bag?") or if it involves society (whether cars should be required to have air bags). In order to determine a person's values, one needs to specify that person's objectives and the attributes that define them. Two case studies illustrate how this methodology can be used for making trade-offs between costs and benefits.

Robin Cantor examines the role that risk management will play in the policymaking process in the coming years. Some people feel that congressional reform of the risk management process will lead to a more rational process, with peer review and scientific consensus. Others feel it will paralyze the federal role in risk management. A key question that needs to be addressed is whether reforms in the risk assessment process will enable one to reach some type of consistency in guidelines and consensus across different groups. Cantor concludes the article by indicating the importance of considering equity in developing risk management strategies and having an open and participatory process rather than relying solely on experts.

Risk management strategies

In their article, Richard Zeckhauser and Kip Viscusi point out that it is necessary for government to supplement market processes due to public misperceptions of risk and the negative externalities resulting from particular activities, such as water and air pollution. They suggest that one appropriate role for government is to reassure the public about certain risk levels in products through testing, as performed by agencies such as the Food and Drug Administration. Another role is for the government to insure certain risks against which the private sector cannot offer protection, such as catastrophic losses from natural disasters. A third role is setting standards for certain risks that the public cannot easily measure or that produce negative externalities, such as the number of asbestos fibers in the air.

Patrick Field, Howard Raiffa, and Lawrence Susskind explore strategies for siting hazardous facilities in poor neighborhoods. Through a hypothetical brainstorming session between community and state representatives, the interested parties conclude that the facility will be acceptable only if it is part of a broader development program jointly created by the citizens in the poor neighborhoods and other interested parties. The community needs to feel it is better off with the facility than without it with respect to its economic well-being as well as its health and safety. The article concludes with a set of principles for effective siting.

Roger Noll suggests that one of the reasons that it is difficult to determine whether risk regulation is too stringent or not stringent enough is the difficulty that the public has in identifying health, safety, and environmental risks and effective responses to them. Due to the uncertain nature of these risks, the regulators are highly dependent on the type of information provided to them. Hence the stringency of each regulation reflects the intensities of political support and opposition in a particular situation that are partially determined by public perception. Noll feels that one needs to recognize that risk regulations are often based on dreaded consequences that are beyond an individual's control. The challenge is how to design better institutional arrangements and public education to construct regulations for coping with these risks.

The final article in this volume, by James Krier, explores how the legal system can utilize information on risk effectively. He points out that the legal system includes both legislative and administrative bodies, both of which often play a more significant role than the courts in dealing with risk issues. He stresses the importance of the legal system in making sure that administrative agencies fulfill their regulatory requirements and in enabling victims to seek compensation from a risk producer through the law of torts. Krier suggests that cost-benefit analysis be used to determine how much risk is acceptable. Today experts feel we overregulate due to irrational fears on the part of the public concerning the dangers of new technologies. It is an open question as to how public perceptions of risk can be incorporated in benefit-cost analyses.

HOWARD KUNREUTHER
PAUL SLOVIC

ACKNOWLEDGMENTS

We would like to express our appreciation to Eugene Lecomte of the Insurance Institute for Property Loss Reduction (IIPLR) for his interest in this issue of *The Annals*. Thanks to the financial support of IIPLR and the Harvard Program on Negotiations, we were able to hold an authors' meeting in June 1995 in Cambridge, Massachusetts, where those preparing articles for this issue were able to share their ideas with each other at an early stage in the preparation of their manuscripts. The lively interchange that took place at this meeting provided all of us with a deeper appreciation of the complexity of the problems associated with estimating and managing environmental, health, and safety risks today. The opinions, findings, conclusions, and recommendations expressed in this volume are those of the authors and do not necessarily reflect the views of IIPLR.

Special thanks to Anne Stamer of the Wharton Risk Management and Decision Processes Center for coordinating the June workshop as well as organizing the drafts of the articles so that they were readable on disk.

HOWARD KUNREUTHER
PAUL SLOVIC

How Risks Are Identified and Assessed

By JOHN D. GRAHAM and LORENZ RHOMBERG

ABSTRACT: Risk analysis can usefully be applied to potential health and safety risks from technology and pollution. We examine historical examples of how knowledge about risk is developed, discussing the capabilities as well as the limitations of analyses to identify potential risks, establish causes, and estimate the probability that harmful effects will occur. One speaks of "risk" because, in any particular instance, an adverse outcome may or may not occur; causative factors skew the probabilities of different outcomes. Accordingly, the detection and measurement of risk must be derived from samples of instances. Real-world observations of risk may be supplemented with controlled experiments, and risks of interest must often be estimated indirectly through extrapolation from analogous circumstances. The ensuing uncertainty affects the clarity of ranking risks against one another and limits the usefulness of risk analysis alone as a means of resolving social conflicts about risk.

John D. Graham is professor of policy and decision sciences at the Harvard School of Public Health and director of the Harvard Injury Control Center and the Harvard Center for Risk Analysis. He is the author of five books and many scientific articles.

Lorenz Rhomberg is an assistant professor at the Harvard School of Public Health. He studies quantitative methods for risk assessment of human health effects from chemical exposure and the use of such methods by regulatory agencies.

EACH day citizens are confronted with new information about potential dangers to their health and safety. The alleged danger may be attributed to industrial sources of pollution near their home, new technologies they use at work, design features of their new car, the prescription drugs they are taking, contaminants in their drinking water, the fat content in the foods they eat, or even exposure to naturally occurring substances such as radon gas in their home. Confronted with these allegations, citizens desire authoritative information about which risks are real, how large or serious these risks might be, and what steps can be taken to reduce or prevent the risks through cost-effective interventions.

The emerging science of risk analysis seeks to answer these questions. Although this analysis can provide useful and critical insights into risks and their causes, it frequently has difficulty in providing answers as definitive as the public, politicians, and stakeholders would like. In this article, we explore the scientific basis of risk assessment, that aspect of risk analysis where risks are identified and quantified. By examining how knowledge about risk is developed, we hope to convey a sense of the capabilities of risk analysis as well as the nature of its limitations. Historical examples are used to illustrate how risk assessments, whether formal or informal, have contributed to success in the implementation of protective interventions. We conclude with some sobering observations about whether risk assessment, useful as it often is, should be considered a universal tool of social conflict resolution.

We speak of the "risk" of an adverse outcome—be it an auto accident, a tumor engendered by exposure to a chemical in the environment, or the structural failure of a key component of a nuclear power plant—because, in any particular instance in which the possibly causative risk factors are present, the adverse outcome may or may not occur as a matter of chance. The factors skew the probabilities of different adverse outcomes, but there is no rigid relationship between cause and effect that manifests itself identically in every observation of the process in question. This means that even careful and precise observation of individual cases or instances can rarely succeed in characterizing risks. Instead, one must examine a sample of observations—the larger the better—and even then, the conclusions will retain some statistical uncertainty. We now turn to an overview of the kinds of observations that serve as the basis for detecting and measuring risks.

INFERENCE FROM REAL-WORLD OBSERVATION

The most rudimentary form of risk assessment is the clinical intuition applied by physicians in interpreting their patients' symptoms through a combination of biomedical knowledge and informed, yet fallible, guesswork based on experience and theory. Consider the Turkish hematologist Muzaffer Aksoy, who was perplexed in the 1960s by the large number of shoe workers who began to develop fatal diseases of the bone marrow such as aplastic anemia and certain forms of leukemia.[1] Aksoy's contention that this pattern of disease was caused by the growing use in shoemaking of commercially prepared, benzene-based adhesives was eventually confirmed by laboratory and epidemiological studies.

Clinical intuition is fallible, however, and even if true, clinically based insights are hard to prove. A current example is the failure of large systematic studies of women to confirm clinical reports of autoimmune problems caused by breast implants.[2] The science of epidemiology can go beyond the insight of the practicing physician because of the information value of large samples and the ability to control—through research design or statistical adjustment—for the potential influence of confounding variables. Even when physicians can identify the existence of a risk, it is epidemiology that is typically used to estimate the magnitude of the risk.

As recently as the early 1960s, not all physicians were convinced that smoking caused lung cancer. Practicing physicians observed that many patients who smoked did not develop lung cancer while many nonsmoking patients did. In order to achieve scientific consensus, a systematic statistical comparison of large numbers of smokers and nonsmokers was required—in other words, an analytic epidemiological study. The issue was

ultimately resolved when epidemiologists demonstrated that the rate of lung cancer among British doctors who smoked was, other things being equal, several times the rate of lung cancer among British doctors who did not smoke.[3]

INFERENCES FROM CONTROLLED EXPERIMENTS

While epidemiology is one of the basic sciences underlying risk assessment, a social strategy of risk management that depends solely on epidemiology is ill-advised. Instead of waiting for adverse health effects to be observed in human populations, techniques are needed that can predict future adverse events with sufficient warning to facilitate implementation of prevention programs. If a new entity is hazardous, it can be withheld or introduced with special safety precautions.

The most definitive experimental data in risk assessment come from the randomized controlled clinical trial (RCCT). The Food and Drug Administration, for example, requires that new drugs be tested in RCCTs for efficacy and safety before they are introduced into the marketplace. In a typical trial, volunteer patients are randomly assigned to a regimen involving either the drug of interest or a placebo, and their treatment outcomes are then compared.

The development of health-based air quality standards is also informed

1. John D. Graham, Laura C. Green, and Marc J. Roberts, *In Search of Safety: Chemicals and Cancer Risk* (Cambridge, MA: Harvard University Press, 1988).

2. Sherine Gabriel et al., "Risk of Connective-Tissue Disease and Other Disorders After Breast Implantation," *New England Journal of Medicine*, 330(24):1697-1702 (1994).

3. Department of Health, Education, and Welfare, *Smoking and Health: Report of the Advisory Committee to the Surgeon General of the Public Health Service* (Princeton, NJ: Princeton University Press; New York: Van Nostrand Reinhold, 1964).

by experimental data. For example, the Environmental Protection Agency currently requires states to develop plans to reduce the concentrations of carbon monoxide in outdoor air to an eight-hour average of 9 parts per million or less. The scientific basis of this standard was historically weak, but the Health Effects Institute of Cambridge, Massachusetts, and the Environmental Protection Agency recently affirmed this standard based on a new experiment. A susceptible group of adult angina patients was recruited to exercise vigorously at several different levels of carbon monoxide in the air. The (self-reported) time to onset of chest pain (angina) was not affected significantly by carbon monoxide levels of less than 9 parts per million.[4] Regulators now have a greater degree of confidence that the prevailing carbon monoxide standard protects sensitive people against the health dangers of carbon monoxide exposure.

When it is not feasible, ethical, or optimal to perform experiments on human subjects, scientists use monkeys, rodents, cadavers, or other nonhuman subjects to develop clues about human risk. In the design of automobile airbag systems, for example, auto manufacturers have developed highly sophisticated dummies that are instrumented and calibrated to behave in crash tests as people do in real-world crashes. Now that airbags are in widespread use, epidemiologists are conducting studies to determine whether the predicted benefits of airbags are being realized in the field.

Even more challenging is the task of predicting the cancer-causing potential of chemicals with respect to humans based on the responses of test animals. Rats and mice are typically used as subjects because rodents have short lifetimes (about two years) and are relatively inexpensive to feed and house. In order to keep the cost of a lifetime animal test under $5 million, a standard test is usually restricted to three dose groups (including controls) with 50 animals in each group. With this limit on the number of animals, it is impossible to detect effects that occur with frequencies of less than about 1 in 100. In order to compensate for the limited number of animals, scientists typically increase the dose levels to far above the levels typically experienced by people. The theory is that a chemical that causes cancer at high doses will probably do so at low doses as well, though with less frequency at lower doses. While early animal testing focused on acute toxicity and cancer, newer tests investigate more subtle effects on immune system function, neurological health, and reproductive and developmental functioning.[5]

In recent years, there has been an explosion in risk assessments based on animal data due to public concerns about the presence of man-made chemicals in the air or surface water near factories, in drinking water, and in soil at hazardous waste sites.[6]

4. Elizabeth N. Allred et al., "Short-Term Effects of Carbon Monoxide Exposure on the Exercise Performance of Subjects with Coronary Artery Disease," *New England Journal of Medicine*, 321(21):1426-31 (1989).

5. A. Wallace Hayes, ed., *Principles and Methods of Toxicology*, 3d ed. (New York: Raven Press, 1994).

6. Center for Risk Analysis, *A Historical Perspective on Risk Assessment in the Federal*

Since chemicals vary enormously in toxicity and degree of human exposure, risk assessment is a critical tool in setting priorities for chemical risk management and devising protective standards and regulations.

Overall, experimentation is a critical source of data for the risk assessor. Experiments are scientifically attractive because it is possible to approximate in them the ideal conditions of the RCCT. The drawback of experimentation is that it is difficult to replicate precisely the conditions that people face in the real world.

COMBINING MULTIPLE SOURCES OF DATA

Those who assess the risk of car crashes—or even moderate earthquakes—have the benefit of historical experience, but many risk questions are about future events or about rarely observed outcomes. In these very difficult cases, one begins by characterizing observable risks that are considered analogous to or informative about the risks of interest—for example, describing risks to mice in order to make inferences about human risks—and then extrapolates the results to the case of direct concern.

All studies provide some information, albeit imperfect, about the nature and magnitude of the true risk. Each study is a view through a blurry window at the truth, and the challenge is to find ways to combine those imperfect views into an overall understanding that transcends the knowledge contained in any single study.

Pooling studies

There are frequently several studies of more or less similar design that appear somewhat inconsistent. For example, the concerns about potential carcinogenic effects of secondhand smoking arose from 15 to 20 studies of the lung cancer rates among nonsmoking spouses of smokers. Several studies show a positive effect—sometimes weak and not statistically significant—while others seem to show no risk elevation or even a slight deficit.[7] In such circumstances, it may be possible to combine the study results into a single overall analysis that can have greater power to detect and characterize effects than any of its components, an approach often referred to as "meta-analysis." Such methods are based on the idea that if there is a true—albeit small—effect, then one can detect an otherwise unexpected tendency for the individual studies all to lean the same way. In the case of lung cancer risk from secondhand smoke, meta-analysis has made it possible to raise the limits of detectability of epidemiological studies and has helped frame a scientific debate in which interpretation of the results remains an area of vigorous discussion.

Real-world and experimental data

When both experimental and real-world data are available, the best risk assessment may entail a creative

---

Government (Boston, MA: Harvard School of Public Health, 1994).

7. Environmental Protection Agency, *Respiratory Health Effects of Passive Smoking: Lung Cancer and Other Disorders* (Washington, DC: Environmental Protection Agency, 1992).

synthesis of both types of information. The key question is determining the degree to which experimental and real-world observational studies support or contradict one another.

For instance, formaldehyde, a gas that irritates nasal and respiratory passages, has been demonstrated to induce nasal tumors in rats at high exposure levels, yet widespread human exposure to this compound has produced only limited evidence of elevated tumor rates. A study by the National Cancer Institute showed a modest increase in larynx and lung cancers.[8] These tumors, although not statistically significant and while different from the nasal tumors seen in rats, are biologically plausible since humans breathe not just through the nose, as rats do, but also through the mouth, exposing deeper parts of the respiratory tract.

Are the human and animal study results contradictory? In the case of formaldehyde, for example, the National Cancer Institute study examined the life histories of over 26,000 exposed workers, more than 3000 of whom had died. Yet among these deaths, only 12 cases of cancer of the larynx were found. From data on the general unexposed population, one can calculate that on average 8 background cases would be expected in a group of this size and age composition.[9] Is the study result evidence

8. Aaron Blair et al., "Mortality Among Industrial Workers Exposed to Formaldehyde," *Journal of the National Cancer Institute*, 76:1071-84 (1986).

9. Background cases are those appearing in the studied population due to causes other than the ones being investigated—in this case, larynx cancer cases that would appear even without exposure to formaldehyde.

that the formaldehyde exposure caused 4 additional laryngeal cancers, or is the finding of 12 total laryngeal cancers simply an expected statistical fluctuation in the number of background cases that happened to be captured in the studied population? No one knows for sure![10]

The formaldehyde case remains controversial owing to questions about the biological mechanisms of carcinogenesis in the rats; rats respond with nasal tumors only at exposure levels causing toxicity to the cells lining the nasal cavity, and response drops sharply—arguably, to zero—at air concentrations not causing such toxicity. Thus there are reasons to doubt whether even rats would get tumors at lower doses, in the range of air concentrations experienced by humans, and therefore the projection of such risks to humans is problematic.

Linking mechanistic theories with the empirical data

Investigations of underlying mechanisms can suggest whether extrapolation is warranted as well as how better to accomplish it. The most common mechanistic question about chemical pollutants is whether they can cause mutations and other genetic changes in cells. Such changes are key to the process of transforming normal cells into lines of cancer cells that lose the ability to control their replication. Many mutagenic compounds, although not all, are also carcinogenic, and this mechanism of carcinogenesis—unlike toxicity to

10. Graham, Green, and Roberts, *In Search of Safety*.

cells—is plausibly assumed to act at some level even at very low doses.[11] Thus the demonstration that a chemical is a mutagen raises concern that there may be no threshold of exposure below which no risk is incurred, although the magnitude of the risk will diminish with decreasing exposure.

Formaldehyde provides a good example of the importance of the mechanistic issue. The high air concentrations at which rat nasal tumors occurred also produced toxicity, cell death, and cell replication in the same region of the nasal cavity. If such toxicity is necessary for tumor formation, lower exposures, which provoke no such reaction, would be essentially safe, at least as far as nasal cancer is concerned. But if the demonstrated weak ability of formaldehyde to cause genetic mutations is sufficient to cause some risk at low doses, then a nearly linear extrapolation of risks to lower doses seems indicated, and even tiny exposures might entail some small but nonetheless elevated cancer risk. The lack of response among rats at the lowest exposures could be a detectability problem similar to the one encountered in the epidemiological studies, or, under a different conclusion about formaldehyde's cancer-causing mechanisms, it could indicate a true lack of risk, owing to a lack of toxicity.

Toxicity to cells is not the only cancer mechanism of interest. For instance, the carcinogenicity of the various related forms of dioxin and dioxinlike compounds (including furans and some polychlorinated biphenyls) may be tied together by their common property of binding to a cellular receptor that in turn controls the expression of genes thought to control the carcinogenic response. An emerging concern is for the ability of some persistent chemical pollutants in the environment to mimic the biological action of estrogen in the body, possibly affecting sexual development in wildlife as well as raising the question of effects on hormonally mediated cancers, such as breast cancer, in humans.[12]

COMPARING RISKS

In noting the challenges in the detection and characterization of risks, we do not want to paint too bleak a picture of the results of risk assessment. While one must recognize its limits, risk assessment can be of enormous help in distinguishing big risks from little ones.

Even when absolute estimates of risk are highly uncertain, confident risk comparisons may still be made if the hazards to be compared share common uncertainties. Thus the lead in soil at abandoned hazardous waste sites is believed to cause less neurological risk to children than the lead in paint that is deteriorating on the walls and windows of older homes, since the opportunity for childhood exposure in the homes is greater.[13]

11. Interagency Staff Group on Carcinogens, "Chemical Carcinogens: A Review of the Science and Its Associated Principles," *Environmental Health Perspectives*, 67:201-82 (1986).

12. Theo Colburn and Coralie Clement, *Chemically-Induced Alterations in Sexual and Functional Development: The Wildlife / Human Connection* (Princeton, NJ: Princeton Scientific, 1992).

13. Karen L. Florini and Ellen K. Silbergeld, "Getting the Lead Out," *Issues in Science and Technology*, 9:33-39 (1993).

For important yet uncertain assessments, risk assessors should accept the task of fully characterizing the array of tenable estimates along with presenting to the users of the assessment guidance on the relative credence that should be placed in the various alternatives. That is, while the risk assessment may not make definitive statements about risk, it can aim to convey which interpretations of the data are most likely to be providing a good guide to risk, which interpretations are possible but judged less likely, and how these judgments hinge on particular scientific interpretations of the data at hand. Devising methods to accomplish this in an objective and operational way, without simply interjecting hopes and fears into data interpretation, is a great challenge, but a necessary one to pursue.[14]

One way to express this uncertainty is to present the various possible outcomes, each with a probability expressing the likelihood that that outcome will come about. For example, Table 1 presents four hypothetical risks, each of which has uncertainty about its true value.

Suppose we were asked to designate which of the risks in Table 1 is the worst based on the best estimate of each risk. Is there a scientifically correct answer?

If the worst risk is the one with the worst possible outcome, then Risk A is the worst, since one faces the possibility of 100 deaths. If, on the other hand, each risk is best characterized by the particular outcome judged to be most plausible, then Risk C is the worst; its most likely value is 40 deaths, higher than the most likely value for any other factor. Risk A, by this criterion, is the least onerous, since its most plausible outcome is zero deaths! If one defines the worst risk as the one most likely to exist at all, then Risk B, with only a 10 percent chance of being zero, is worse than all others. Finally, if one judges the risks by the average number of deaths expected over all possibilities—that is, if one weights each outcome by its probability of occurrence—then Risk D is worst, with an expected value of 39 deaths. The point of Table 1 is not that some definitions of "worst" are right and others wrong but, rather, that, when risk estimates are uncertain, there may be no unambiguous definition of "worst." To resolve this dilemma, more information is needed about the decision to be made about the four risks and the preferences of the decision makers.[15]

CONFLICT RESOLUTION

We wish to conclude with a sobering comment on the role of risk assessment as a tool for resolution of social conflicts. The reason that risk assessment has received such public attention is that risk issues are frequently bound up in questions of conflicting interests between individuals and groups of stakeholders in society. The various parties may differ in who bears the risk and who stands to gain by any particular settlement of the issues.

14. Roger M. Cooke, *Experts in Uncertainty: Opinion and Subjective Probability in Science* (New York: Oxford University Press, 1991).

15. Charles A. Holloway, *Decision Making Under Uncertainty: Models and Choices* (Upper Saddle River, NJ: Prentice Hall, 1979).

TABLE 1
**FOUR HYPOTHETICAL UNCERTAIN RISKS, ILLUSTRATING THAT
WHICH RISK IS WORST IS A MATTER OF DEFINITION**

	Probability	Outcome (Deaths)	Worst Outcome	Most Plausible Outcome	Most Proven Risk	Expected Value
Risk A	.80	0	100	0	0.2	15
	.10	50				
	.10	100				
Risk B	.10	0	50	20	0.9	30
	.50	20				
	.40	50				
Risk C	.20	0	50	40	0.8	33
	.70	40				
	.10	50				
Risk D	.20	0	80	30	0.8	39
	.50	30				
	.30	80				

The problem with trying to settle such conflicts with risk assessment is severalfold. First, although it may be possible for risk assessment to clear up some contentious issues, it is frequently the case that the facts that can be brought to bear are insufficient to provide answers that satisfy the concerns of all the contending parties. Arguments arising from conflicting interests may simply be recast as arguments about conflicting interpretations of data and their proper bearing on risk estimation. It should not be overlooked, however, that when a conflict is fundamentally about uncertainty over a factual matter, then new information—or a more insightful interpretation of existing information—can indeed serve to narrow the scope of uncertainty and reduce the social conflict. For example, pesticide manufacturers have sometimes been able to ease conflict over uncertain predictions of complex mathematical models of exposure by directly monitoring the groundwater supplies to validate model predictions.

Second, risk assessment may clarify who the potential winners and losers are in any particular settlement, thereby exacerbating the social conflict. The risk assessments of smoking certainly increased social conflict by pitting public health professionals against tobacco interests. More recently, the risk assessments of environmental tobacco smoke have added fuel to the social conflicts about smoking.

Third, parties are often in conflict not because of confusion about science or uncertainty about risk but because they hold different values. Parties that agree about the risks posed by nuclear power may legitimately disagree about whether the risks are worth the benefits. Even when the risks are crystal clear (for example, the danger of not wearing a motorcycle helmet), citizens may differ about whether it is appropriate for government to take protective actions, such as requiring motorcyclists to wear helmets. Risk assessment can be useful but it cannot create public consensus about ethical questions.

While we are strongly in favor of using risk analysis to identify and assess risks, and while we endorse the improvement of the scientific basis of risk estimation, we feel that recourse to risk analysis alone is bound to fail at resolving many social conflicts. As we have argued, as much as risk assessment science is able to discover, it is often unable to answer a meaningful question completely, definitively, and without a considerable degree of uncertainty.

ANNALS, *AAPSS*, **545**, May 1996

Government Risk Regulation

By ROBERT A. POLLAK

ABSTRACT: This article argues that risk assessment, supposedly the scientific component of risk regulation (as opposed to risk management, the policy component), cannot be very scientific because too little is known. Without firm scientific knowledge, risk assessment must rely on conventions promulgated by bureaucrats or on the professional judgments of scientific experts; such conventions and judgments reflect not only scientific knowledge but also policy judgments and cultural values. The inadequacy of scientific knowledge, coupled with the lack of public trust in government and in experts, suggests that risk regulators should be concerned not only with creating institutional arrangements likely to foster trust but also with creating mechanisms for providing concerned individuals with credible reassurance. The article concludes by discussing divergences between public perceptions and expert perceptions of risks, and the weights that a democratic society should give to each in assessing and managing risks.

Robert A. Pollak is the Hernreich Distinguished Professor of Economics in the College of Arts and Sciences and the John M. Olin School of Business of Washington University in St. Louis. He was on the faculty of the University of Pennsylvania from 1964 until 1990. He serves on the editorial boards of three journals and is a senior consultant to the Economics Initiative of the John D. and Catherine T. MacArthur Foundation.

NOTE: The author is grateful to Yoram Barzel, Samuel Bowles, Gardner Brown, Robert Halvorsen, Laurie Johnson, Howard Kunreuther, John Pencavel, Edward Pollak, Cass Sunstein, and Kent T. van den Berg for helpful conversations and to Judith Goff for editorial assistance. This article draws heavily on the author's earlier article, "Regulating Risks," *Journal of Economic Literature*, 33(1):179-91 (Mar. 1995).

I begin by discussing risk assessment, which is the scientific component of risk regulation, as opposed to risk management, its policy component. I argue that risk assessment cannot be very scientific because too little is known—for example, how much would reducing the occupational exposure standard for benzene from 10 parts per million (ppm) to 1 ppm reduce the incidence of leukemia 25 years in the future? Without such knowledge, however, risk assessment must rely on conventions promulgated by bureaucrats or on the professional judgments of scientific experts. Such conventions and judgments reflect not only scientific knowledge but also policy judgments and cultural values.

I then discuss the implications for risk regulation of the lack of public trust in government and in experts. I argue that risk regulators should be concerned not only with creating institutional arrangements likely to foster trust but also with creating mechanisms for providing concerned individuals with credible reassurance. I conclude by discussing divergences between public perceptions and expert perceptions, and the weights that a democratic society should give to each in assessing and managing risks.

RISK ASSESSMENT AS SCIENCE

In the United States, risk regulation is separated into two components: risk assessment, the scientific or technical component; and risk management, the policy or political component. I begin with risk assessment, using formaldehyde to illustrate the complexity of the scientific phase of risk regulation. Formaldehyde is an industrial chemical widely used to make insulating materials, protective coatings, drugs, cosmetics, and textiles. The controversy over formaldehyde regulation is well documented because the participants—chemical manufacturers, unions, environmental groups, and government agencies—understood that the criteria used to regulate formaldehyde would set a precedent for the regulatory treatment of other chemicals.

The government divides risk assessment into four officially designated stages: risk identification; dose-response assessment; exposure assessment; and risk characterization. Risk identification is the starting point: a substance such as formaldehyde is suspected of causing adverse health effects, for example, lung cancer, nasal cancer, leukemia, and brain cancer. Dose-response assessment estimates the relationship between the amount, intensity, or duration of exposure and the risk of a particular outcome: for example, the relationship between the airborne concentration of formaldehyde in the workplace and a worker's lifetime probability of contracting leukemia. Exposure assessment might measure airborne concentration or the dose delivered to or absorbed by workers. Risk characterization combines dose-response assessment and exposure assessment to obtain a summary measure of the impact of a substance on human health.

Dose-response assessment and exposure assessment sound like appropriate assignments for "regulatory science." Dose-response assessment, on which I focus, poses the more difficult task. Two types of studies provide evidence on dose-response relationships: bioassays (studies of laboratory animals) and epidemiological studies (studies of human populations). Each has problems. Bioassays investigate the effects of high doses of a substance on laboratory animals—such as rats or mice—and extrapolate to the effects of low doses on humans. Bioassay data were the primary basis for attempts to regulate formaldehyde.

Table 1 illustrates two of the problems that arise in using bioassay data to estimate human dose-response relationships: the choice of an appropriate species on which to base the extrapolation and the choice of an appropriate formula for estimating low-dose effects from observed high-dose effects.

Graham, Green, and Roberts point out that the differences between rats and mice and the differences between the effects of intermediate and high exposure levels make the results in the table difficult to interpret: when exposed to high doses of formaldehyde, rats are far more likely than mice to develop tumors, and the relationship between the number of tumors and the dose appears to be highly nonlinear.

The epidemiological evidence on formaldehyde, like the bioassay data, is confusing. On biological grounds, one might expect formaldehyde to affect the respiratory system, yet epidemiological studies of workers in occupations in which they are likely to have been exposed to formalde-

hyde show no evidence of elevated rates of lung or nasal cancer. Indeed, several studies show that such occupational groups have significantly lower rates of lung cancer. To complicate the epidemiological picture further, three different occupational studies of pathologists, anatomists, and embalmers show that these groups have significantly higher than expected mortality from brain cancer and from leukemia. "For brain cancer and leukemia, it is difficult to construct a biologically plausible mechanism for formaldehyde-induced effects, but epidemiological investigations have repeatedly revealed excesses of these cancers among some occupationally exposed groups."[1]

Breaking the Vicious Circle: Toward Effective Risk Regulation, a recent book by Stephen Breyer, now an associate justice of the Supreme Court, provides an accessible description of risk regulation in the United States and proposals for its reform.[2] Breyer summarizes the difficulties of risk assessment:

Predicting risk is a scientifically related enterprise, but it does not involve scientists doing what they do best, namely developing theories about how x responds to y, other things being equal. . . . Moreover, where prediction involves a weak relationship, such as that between a small dose of a substance and a later cancer death, as well as long lead times,

1. John D. Graham, Laura C. Green, and Marc J. Roberts, *In Search of Safety: Chemicals and Cancer Risk* (Cambridge, MA: Harvard University Press, 1988), p. 68.

2. Stephen Breyer, *Breaking the Vicious Circle: Toward Effective Risk Regulation* (Cambridge, MA: Harvard University Press, 1993).

TABLE 1

ADJUSTED INCIDENCE OF SQUAMOUS CELL CARCINOMA OF THE NASAL CAVITY IN RATS AND MICE AFTER INHALATION OF FORMALDEHYDE FOR 24 MONTHS

| | Number of Tumors per Animal at Risk | |
Formaldehyde Concentration (ppm)*	Rats (percentage)	Mice (percentage)
0	0/208 (0)	0/72 (0)
2	0/210 (0)	0/64 (0)
6	2/210 (1)	0/73 (0)
15	103/206 (50.0)	2/60 (3.3)

SOURCE: John D. Graham, Laura C. Green, and Marc J. Roberts, *In Search of Safety: Chemicals and Cancer Risk* (Cambridge: Harvard University Press, 1988), p. 40, reproduced from James E. Gibson, ed., *Formaldehyde Toxicity*.

* Parts per million.

such as exposure for twenty years or more, it is difficult or impossible for predictors to obtain empirical feedback, which is necessary (for them as for all of us) to confirm or correct their theories.[3]

A little later, he writes:

In respect to many regulated substances, the scientific answer to the question "Which extrapolation model?" is "We do not know." . . . Unfortunately, ignorance about these issues is matched by their importance. The choice of a dose/response extrapolation model can make an enormous difference to how risky small doses of the substance appear to be. Two scientifically plausible models for the risk associated with aflatoxin in peanuts or grain may show risk levels differing by a factor of 40,000.[4]

The privileged status of risk assessment, the scientific component of risk regulation, has been challenged at two levels. The first is epistemological. Some postmodern critics argue that scientific knowledge has no stronger claims to truth or certainty than other kinds of knowledge and, hence, that scientific knowledge should not be privileged. The second

3. Ibid., pp. 42-43.
4. Ibid., p. 45.

level of challenge does not contest the privileged status of scientific knowledge; instead, it denies that regulatory science in general and risk assessment in particular, despite their scientific pretensions, are real Science.

RISK ASSESSMENT
AS POLICY AND CULTURE

In the United States, risk assessment and risk management were separated in the 1980s and responsibility for them assigned to different officials. One of Breyer's proposals for increasing the effectiveness of risk regulation would reintegrate risk assessment and risk management, yet Breyer says little about the history of or the rationale for their separation. Sheila Jasanoff, director of Cornell University's Program on Science, Technology, and Society, describes the background:

In 1983, NAS [National Academy of Sciences] published a report calling upon the federal government to make a clearer separation between the scientific and political phases of risk management. Agencies were asked to distinguish between an objective, quantitative approach to determining risk (assessment) and a subjective, political approach to developing regulatory controls (management).[5]

The difficulty, as the formaldehyde example suggests, is that the leap from the objective, quantitative data obtained from bioassays and epidemiological studies to conclusions about the effects on humans of relatively low levels of exposure is a leap of faith. Jasanoff argues that similar difficulties arise in identifying a substance as a carcinogen because "for the vast majority of potential carcinogens, the scientific basis for determining whether they will increase the incidence of human cancer is highly uncertain."[6]

The mixture of scientific and policy judgments involved in risk assessment is the subject of *Acceptable Evidence: Science and Values in Risk Management*, edited by Deborah G. Mayo and Rachelle D. Hollander.[7] In their introduction, they attempt to position themselves between two views that they characterize as extreme:

The first extreme supposes that issues of evidence of risk can and ought to be separated from the individual and social values that necessarily enter in reaching policies about risk (i.e., risk management). This view assumes that evidence of risk is largely a matter of objective scientific data, which may be captured in standard quantitative measures of risk. The second extreme is found in varying

degrees in much of the interdisciplinary work relating science and values in risk assessment. Here the recognition that values (methodological, political, and others) may enter into every stage of risk management—even at the level of establishing evidence of risk—has often been taken to imply that there is little objective or empirical basis on which to criticize risk assessments.[8]

The anthropologist Mary Douglas is often depicted as advocating the second view. For example, Shrader-Frechette accuses Douglas and Wildavsky of being "cultural relativists" and of assuming that "all risk evaluation is merely a social construct."[9] Douglas, however, is quite clear that the risks are real: "Note that the reality of the dangers is not at issue. The dangers are only too horribly real. . . . This argument is not about the reality of the dangers, but about how they are politicized."[10]

In his introduction to a collection of articles about risk, Burger provides a more accurate characterization of Douglas's views, saying that she discounts the "importance of objective fact in considering risks" in order to emphasize the role of cultural factors.[11] Thus her starting point is that environmental pollution, crime, and economic instability are real risks. Her interest, however, is in what sorts of people (and what sorts of societies)

8. Ibid., p. xi.
9. Kristin Shrader-Frechette, "Reductionist Approaches to Risk," in *Acceptable Evidence: Science and Values in Risk Management*, ed. Deborah G. Mayo and Rachelle D. Hollander (New York: Oxford University Press, 1991), p. 220.
10. Mary Douglas, "Risk as a Forensic Resource," in *Risk*, ed. Edward J. Burger, Jr. (Ann Arbor: University of Michigan Press, 1993), p. 8.
11. Burger, ed., *Risk*, pp. vii-xiii.

5. Sheila Jasanoff, *Risk Management and Political Culture* (New York: Russell Sage Foundation, 1986), p. 26.
6. Ibid., p. 17.
7. Deborah G. Mayo and Rachelle D. Hollander, eds., *Acceptable Evidence: Science and Values in Risk Management* (New York: Oxford University Press, 1991).

focus on the dangers of environmental pollution rather than the dangers of crime or the dangers of economic instability. As Douglas and Wildavsky put it: "The choice of risks and the choice of how to live are taken together. . . . We choose the risks in the same package as we choose our social institutions."[12] Her emphasis, then, is "how particular kinds of danger come to be selected for attention"[13] and "which kinds of risks are acceptable to what sorts of people."[14]

Douglas has been the leading exponent of the view that risk perception is a social phenomenon and that cultural anthropology provides a useful lens through which to view the perceptions and values that underlie risk regulation:

The professional discussion of cognition and choice has no sustained theorizing about the social influences which select particular risks for public attention. Yet it is hard to maintain seriously that perception of risk is private. . . . With no link between cultural analysis and cognitive science, clashes inevitably occur between theory and evidence. Since the theory is not being radically adjusted, irrationality tends to be invoked to protect the too narrow definition of rationality. So instead of a sociological, cultural, and ethical theory of human judgment, there is an unintended emphasis on perceptual pathology.[15]

From a political science perspective, a key issue is whether the authority to decide what inferences to draw from inconclusive epidemiological and bioassay evidence rests with scientifically trained experts or with lawyers, administrators, and politicians. To reduce or eliminate the discretion of experts, the Environmental Protection Agency (EPA) has attempted to develop "generic guidelines" (that is, guidelines that apply to all substances, not just a single substance) that "resolve most questions of judgment, interpretation, and extrapolation" required to infer the effect of low doses of a substance on human health.[16] The following laundry list of assumptions embodied in one set of EPA-proposed generic guidelines indicates the range of issues that any set of generic guidelines must resolve:

no thresholds in dose-response functions; linearity in the dose-response function at low doses; cumulative lifetime exposure as the measure of dose; a presumed proportional relationship between administered and delivered doses, even at low levels; inclusion of benign tumors in dose-response estimation, unless there is compelling information to the contrary, and use of the most sensitive animal species as the basis for extrapolation of cancer risk to humans.[17]

Science resolves none of these issues.

To "bring a degree of uniformity and rationality" to risk regulation, Breyer proposes a bureaucratic solution: for example, establishing a new career path for civil servants and a small, centralized administrative group responsible for rationalizing risk regulation across fields.[18] Uni-

12. Mary Douglas and Aaron Wildavsky, *Risk and Culture: An Essay on the Selection of Technological and Environmental Dangers* (Berkeley: University of California Press, 1982), pp. 8-9.

13. Ibid., p. 8.

14. Ibid., p. 4.

15. Mary Douglas, *Risk Acceptability According to the Social Sciences* (New York: Russell Sage Foundation, 1985), p. 31.

16. Graham, Green, and Roberts, *In Search of Safety*, p. 177.

17. Ibid., pp. 176-77.

18. Breyer, *Breaking the Vicious Circle*, p. 61.

formity is attainable; whether rationality is attainable depends on how we interpret it. If rationality means uniformity (that is, consistency with other decisions), then it is clearly attainable. If rationality means scientifically determined, then it is not. Breyer, unfortunately, does not pursue these issues or discuss how we should interpret rationality when decisions—such as whether to base rat-to-man extrapolations on comparative body weight or on comparative surface area—cannot be fully warranted by scientific evidence. In risk assessment, there is a certain discomfort in acknowledging that rat-to-man extrapolations will be determined by generic guidelines or administratively established conventions rather than by science. Indeed, the legitimacy of risk assessment may depend on maintaining the illusion that such issues are determined scientifically.

This brings us to the uneasy issue of quantification. Since 1980, when the Supreme Court rejected the Occupational Safety and Health Administration's regulations lowering the workplace standard for benzene from 10 ppm to 1 ppm, the imposition of risk regulations in the United States has been accompanied by numerical estimates of the number of lives that a proposed regulation would save. Epidemiological data provided the basis for attempting to regulate exposures to benzene. But for exposures as low as those covered by the proposed benzene regulations, epidemiological data cast no light on the effects on human health.

In the benzene case, a plurality—although not a majority—of the Supreme Court insisted on numerical estimates to justify the imposition of more stringent regulation. Many observers have suggested that although quantitative risk analysis serves to legitimate risk regulation in the American legal and political system, it does not lead to better decisions. From a practical standpoint, however, there is probably no turning back.

Quantification may not lead to better decisions, but it does lead to decisions that are less personal and less dependent on the whims and prejudices (as well as the judgments) of the individuals who happen to be responsible for making them. Theodore M. Porter interprets quantification in public administration as a strategy for limiting the role of subjective factors in decision making and achieving what Allan Megill calls "procedural objectivity."[19] Porter argues that quantification removes or greatly reduces the discretion of unelected bureaucrats and experts who, in a democratic polity, have no mandate for exercising discretion.

In the long run, quantification may lead to better decisions because it creates pressure and provides resources for systematic data collection and analysis, even if, in the short run,

19. Theodore M. Porter, *Trust in Numbers: The Pursuit of Objectivity in Science and Public Life* (Princeton, NJ: Princeton University Press, 1995); idem, "Objectivity as Standardization: The Rhetoric of Impersonality in Measurement, Statistics, and Cost-Benefit Analysis," in *Rethinking Objectivity*, ed. Allan Megill (Durham, NC: Duke University Press, 1994), pp. 197-237.

it fails to improve policy. Long-run benefits require only that quantification increase the knowledge base on which policy depends and that the regulatory system eventually incorporate new scientific knowledge. Yet generic guidelines may severely limit the ability of the regulatory system to incorporate new scientific information promptly, delaying its incorporation until it can meet the burden of proof required by regulators and courts.

Quantification is one of several features that sets the U.S. regulatory style apart from that of other advanced, industrial societies. Jasanoff, who has written extensively about national differences in approaches to risk regulation, identifies several others:

The U.S. process for making risk decisions impressed all observers as costly, confrontational, litigious, formal, and unusually open to participation. European decision making, despite important differences within and among countries, seemed by comparison almost uniformly cooperative and consensual; informal, cost conscious, and for the most part closed to the public. . . . The special status of the United States was particularly apparent in the forms of evidence deemed suitable as a basis for policy. A noteworthy trend in the public justification of American regulatory decisions was the growing resort to quantitative representations of risk.[20]

Jasanoff argues that the intensity of political competition in the environmental policy arena in the United States—for example, "among interest groups, between Washington and the states, and among the branches of the federal government"[21]—is much greater than in Europe. The intensity of political competition is heightened by the willingness of the federal courts to intervene in environmental policymaking and by what Jasanoff calls "scientific pluralism,"[22] that is, the presence of scientists in regulatory agencies and public interest groups as well as in industry and academia. The final and perhaps most fundamental difference that underlies many of the specific differences between U.S. and European risk regulation is in the level of public trust in experts and in government.

TRUST

Trust, or the absence of trust, in government and in experts, is a recurrent lament in discussions of risk regulation. For example, Breyer writes that "public perceptions, Congressional actions and reactions, and technical regulatory methods reinforce each other" and "tend to create a vicious circle, diminishing public trust in regulatory institutions and thereby inhibiting more rational regulation." Three pages later, discussing aspects of risk perception, under the heading "Trust in experts," he writes, "People cannot easily judge between experts when these experts disagree with each other. The public, since the mid-1960s, has shown increasing distrust of experts and the institutions, private, academic, or governmental that employ them."[23]

20. Sheila Jasanoff, "American Exceptionalism and the Political Acknowledgment of Risk," in *Risk*, ed. Burger, pp. 63-64.

21. Ibid., p. 65.
22. Ibid., p. 67.
23. Breyer, *Breaking the Vicious Circle*, pp. 33, 36.

One difficulty is that in most cases neither the public, the press, nor Congress can determine whether risk regulators are doing their jobs well. Risk assessments do not make unconditional predictions about the immediate future and, hence, unlike the daily weather forecast, are not readily susceptible to ex post verification. Instead, risk assessments construct complex counterfactuals about the distant future. For example, instead of predicting the prevalence of leukemia tomorrow, a risk assessment must estimate the reduction in the prevalence of leukemia 25 or 30 years in the future that would be caused by reducing the occupational exposure standard for benzene from 10 ppm to 1 ppm. Investigative reporting and congressional oversight are likely to focus on stories about workers with leukemia and charges that regulators have accepted money or favors from those they are supposed to regulate, topics that are more easily understood and more dramatic than bioassays and epidemiology. Yet human interest stories about workers with leukemia cannot establish that health regulators are failing to do their jobs well, and even if oversight hearings could establish the total absence of corruption, they could not establish that risk regulators were doing a competent job of dealing with the technical problems of risk regulation.

Hence proposals for bureaucratic reform such as those put forward by Justice Breyer are unlikely to satisfy those who do not trust regulators and are concerned that they are vulnerable to capture by the industries they are supposed to regulate. Indeed,

Breyer's reform proposals seem designed to protect regulators from capture by Congress and the public. Yet, by insulating regulators from scrutiny by Congress and the public, the bureaucratic reforms Breyer proposes may make regulators more vulnerable to capture by the industries they are supposed to regulate.

Economists ignore some of the crucial issues in the design of regulatory and political institutions, including the extent to which concerns about capture can be met by creating agencies with the trappings of independence from the political process such as the Federal Reserve System and the National Academy of Sciences. From an economist's perspective, much of the risk regulation literature's hand wringing about the absence of trust seems a bit naive. Instead of lamenting the public's lack of trust in experts, bureaucrats, and politicians, it may be more fruitful to think about mechanisms for providing credible reassurance. Economists, after all, do not lament prospective customers' lack of trust in used-car dealers; instead, they talk about guarantees and other ways of providing credible reassurance.

CONCLUSION

A fundamental issue in risk regulation is the treatment of public perceptions and beliefs when they diverge from those of experts. Suppose, for example, that people living near hazardous waste sites worry that they or their children will get leukemia 25 years in the future, even though experts "know" that these fears are unwarranted. Most public policy analysts would probably follow Breyer in assuming that disparities between the public's rankings of hazards—such as indoor air pollution or toxic waste sites—and those of the experts "reflect not different values but different understandings about the underlying risk-related facts."[24] They would probably also follow Breyer in assuming that government policy ought to be based on these "risk-related facts" and not on the public's (mis)perceptions.

Divergence between public perceptions and expert perceptions poses four distinct but related issues. The first belongs to the philosophy of science and is epistemological: how can scientists infer "risk-related facts"—such as the amount by which reducing the occupational exposure standard for benzene from 10 ppm to 1 ppm would reduce the incidence of leukemia 25 years in the future—given the difficulties of drawing such inferences from bioassay and epidemiological data?

The second belongs to social psychology and the sociology of science: how are public perceptions and expert perceptions actually formed?

24. Ibid., p. 35.

The third belongs to political philosophy: how should governments regulate risks when public perceptions diverge from expert perceptions? What weight, if any, should be accorded public (mis)perceptions?

The fourth belongs to political science: how do governments regulate risks when public perceptions and expert perceptions diverge?

Even if the notion of "risk-related facts" were not problematic on epistemological grounds, it would not be obvious that a democratic government should ignore public (mis)perceptions. Public fears and (mis)perception, after all, are also "risk-related facts." Such fears clearly do play a role in the formulation of government policies regulating risks, and it is not obvious that such fear should not play a role. If the public cannot be "educated" to give up its misperceptions and accept the beliefs of the experts, then a utilitarian—and welfare economics and policy analysis are essentially utilitarian—ought to have doubts about whether expected benefits and costs should be calculated on the basis of the expert's perceptions and beliefs rather than the public's.

Scientific Uncertainty and the Political Process

By DALE JAMIESON

ABSTRACT: In this article, a notion of scientific uncertainty is sketched that is in many ways different from the prevailing view. Scientific uncertainty is not simply an objective value that can be reduced by science alone. Rather, scientific uncertainty is constructed both by science and by society in order to serve certain purposes. Recognizing the social role of scientific uncertainty will help us to see how many of our problems about risk are deeply cultural and cannot be overcome simply by the application of more and better science.

Dale Jamieson is professor of philosophy at the University of Colorado, Boulder, and adjunct scientist in the Environmental and Societal Impacts Group at the National Center for Atmospheric Research. He received his Ph.D. from the University of North Carolina at Chapel Hill and previously taught at North Carolina State University and the State University of New York. He has also held visiting positions at Cornell, Oxford, and Monash University in Australia. He is the editor of five books and has published many articles on ethics, science policy, and environmental philosophy.

SOME of the most controversial public policy decisions in American society involve risks that are primarily understood through scientific processes and institutions. The evidence for climate change, for example, comes mainly from experiments run on highly complex climate models rather than from our everyday experience. Other issues with important scientific dimensions include ozone depletion, biodiversity loss, acid rain, and exposure to radon and various toxic chemicals. Without science and scientists, there would be little public concern about a wide range of important issues.

Although science has been very effective in bringing these issues into the public arena, it has been quite ineffective at providing solutions. There are a number of views about why this is the case. Over lunch and at professional meetings, scientists often complain about the lack of understanding or downright perversity on the part of political leaders who ignore scientific information. On the other hand, many policy analysts fault scientists for talking to each other rather than producing "policy-relevant" science.[1] My own view, which cannot be fully developed here, is that the very characteristics of science that enable it to have its unique cultural authority as a knowledge producer disable it from bringing public decisions to closure.[2]

The conventional wisdom about why science is often so ineffective in providing solutions to problems with important scientific dimensions focuses on the role of uncertainty. In this view, problems such as climate change are characterized by high levels of scientific uncertainty about the likelihood and effects of key events, and so partisans of various policies can use—or misuse—scientific information and authority for their own purposes. For example, although the weight of scientific evidence suggests that large-scale emissions of greenhouse gases are likely to change climate, there are so many uncertainties about the roles of clouds, carbon sinks, and various possible feedbacks that both greenhouse "hawks" and "doves" can reasonably enlist science as an ally while accusing their opponents of misusing science.[3] The only way out of this situation, some argue, is for uncertainties to be reduced to the point at which science can determine a rational policy. What is needed is a new generation of supercomputers, greater remote sensing capability, and a larger and more active research community.

In the conventional view, uncertainty is seen as an objective quantity whose value can be reduced by investing in more science. While this may usefully be thought of as one of several understandings of uncertainty, it is at best simplistic and mis-

1. See, for example, E. S. Rubin, L. B. Lave, and M. G. Morgan, "Keeping Climate Research Relevant," *Issues in Science and Technology*, 8(2):47-55 (1991-92).

2. I have developed this view more fully in a number of papers. See, for example, "Ethics, Public Policy and Global Warming," *Science, Technology and Human Values*, 17(2):139-53 (1992).

3. The typology of greenhouse "hawks," "doves," and "owls" is developed in Michael H. Glantz, "Politics and the Air Around Us: International Policy Action on Atmospheric Pollution by Trace Gases," in *Societal Responses to Regional Climate Change: Forecasting by Analogy*, ed. M. Glantz (Boulder, CO: Westview Press, 1988), pp. 41-42.

leading to think of it as the only or most important one. Rather than being a cause of controversy, scientific uncertainty is often a consequence of controversy.[4] This suggests that the social world is active in the construction and characterization of uncertainty, and if we want to understand uncertainty, we need to understand the social factors that help to produce it.

FALLIBILITY, UNCERTAINTY, AND INDETERMINISM

The first step in understanding uncertainty involves distinguishing it from some related notions with which it is often confused.[5]

Uncertainty is often conflated with fallibility. Fallibility relates to the fact that we could be wrong about virtually any proposition to which we give our assent, from the most homely (for example, "I know how old I am") to the most exotic (for example, "I know how old the universe is"). Fallibility lurks in the background of scientific claims and moves to the foreground when new evidence comes flooding in that suggests that our previous views about some matter were not just wrong, but deeply and profoundly wrong. The discovery of the ozone hole, which was not predicted by any of the atmospheric models, is one example of this, as is

4. This point is argued forcefully in Brian L. Campbell, "Uncertainty as Symbolic Action in Disputes Among Experts," *Social Studies of Science*, 15:429-53 (1985).

5. Although I draw the distinctions in a somewhat different way, my discussion in this section is indebted to Brian Wynne, "Uncertainty and Environmental Learning: Reconceiving Science and Policy in the Preventive Paradigm," *Global Environmental Change*, 2:111-27 (1992).

the recognition of the chronic toxicity of DDT.[6]

Fallibility looms large with respect to many health and environmental risks. In some cases, we may know that various exposures are associated with harms, but we may have little idea of what causal mechanisms are at work. Although the statistical evidence may be strong enough for some to attribute causality, even in these cases we may worry about the fallibility of such claims. Our view of the matter may simply be wrong—not in details, but thoroughly so. We may not even be in a position to assess the probability of our being wrong. The fact of our fallibility is usually—indeed, often must be—ignored, but it constantly presents the possibility of bringing down an entire edifice of knowledge.

Uncertainty arises from ignoring fallibility. We take various features of a problem as given and focus on other dimensions. For example, it is widely agreed that the case for climate change is weakened by the fact that we are uncertain about the effects of clouds on the climate system. The solution is more intensive study of cloud formation and effects. But to identify clouds as an area of uncertainty is to presuppose that our general knowledge of the climate system is not uncertain, that the climate models are basically correct, and so on. This background knowledge is "black boxed"—it is taken as a set of assumptions from which we proceed to try to reduce uncertainty. This ap-

6. For discussion of these cases, see D. Budansky, "Scientific Uncertainty and the Precautionary Principle," *Environment*, 33(7):4-5, 43-44 (Sept. 1991).

proach of taking some propositions as fixed while interrogating others is a fundamental part of scientific practice. Scientific progress would be impossible if every proposition were problematized in every investigation.

The general point can be seen from an everyday example: I discuss selling my bike to a friend. In this context, there is no uncertainty about whether I own the bike. We both take it as given that this is the case. Of course, it may be that due to fraud or forgetfulness I do not own the bike. But in our discussion, these possibilities are not on the table, and so there is no uncertainty about whether I own the bike even though it could turn out that I do not. Now imagine a situation in which we are highly suspicious of each other: it is well known that I was once convicted of running a bike theft ring, or that I suffer from amnesia. When the context is changed in one of these ways, the problem of uncertainty may arise. My friend may demand proof that I really own the bike before she will continue the discussion with me. What this homely example shows is that while we can always be wrong about (most) things, uncertainty requires particular contexts and social conditions.

Indeed, this very example has implications for uncertainty about risk. Uncertainty disappears or is minimized when we have complete trust in the institution, person, or data set that is being interrogated. It is magnified or accentuated when there is mistrust, whether founded on fraud

or other failings.[7]

Uncertainty should also be distinguished from indeterminacy. Often what appears to be uncertainty cannot be reduced because there is no reliable fact of the matter to be learned that directly bears on improving our beliefs. At least three sources of indeterminism can be identified: agency, underdetermination, and categorical relativity.[8]

Many of the most serious environmental and health problems we face involve agency. Part of why we do not know what will happen to global climate in the twenty-first century is because we do not know how people will behave in the future. Will they continue to increase their use of fossil fuels? Or will other energy sources be substituted? Will governments undertake policies to geoengineer climate? Will there be other responses to early signs of global warming? These are just a few of the questions whose answers matter in determining what will happen to future climate. Similar questions could be raised about the effects of tobacco smoke, the prevalence of HIV, and so on.

The indeterminism that results from agency is made worse by the fact that predictions about human behavior can themselves change the behavior that is being predicted. Consider a simple case. At 8 a.m. on a warm summer day, the local radio station predicts that there will be massive traffic jams as thousands of people flock to the beach. The traffic jam

7. For further discussion, see Paul Slovic, "Perceived Risk, Trust, and Democracy," *Risk Analysis*, 13(6):675-82 (1993).

8. In addition, some have argued that indeterminism is a fundamental property of nature. See, for example, John Dupré, *The Disorder of Things: The Metaphysical Foundations of the Disunity of Science* (Cambridge, MA: Harvard University Press, 1993).

fails to materialize. Many people heard the radio broadcast and decided to stay home.

A second source of indeterminism flows from the underdetermination of theory by data.[9] Any particular observation is consistent with an indefinite number of logically distinct theories. For example, the observation that there are a variety of life forms is consistent both with evolutionary theory and creationism. Often we try to distinguish theories by designing a crucial experiment, one in which distinct theories support different predictions. But there are distinct theories that cannot be distinguished in this way. In such cases, people often appeal to conceptual concerns in order to justify the choice of one theory over another—one theory is simpler, coheres better with other beliefs, and so on. While there may be grounds for preferring one of two empirically equivalent theories, in such cases there is no empirical fact of the matter about which theory is true; rather, the matter is indeterminate, for there are no empirical discoveries that would support one theory at the expense of the other.

The third source of indeterminism is even more basic than the other two. Knowledge claims presuppose categories, but categories are relative. For example, some people point to increases in global mean temperatures and extreme climatic events as evidence of global warming. But why is global mean temperature a significant category? Why not instead focus on, say, average temperatures? And why bring together in the single class of extreme events such diverse phenomena as hailstorms, droughts, hurricanes, heat waves, cold snaps, and so on? What are the baselines from which the claims of increasing frequency or increasing temperature are projected? What may appear to be an increase from a baseline of 50 years ago may appear to be a decrease from a baseline of 500 or 5000 years ago. Of course, stories can be told about why one form of categorization is better than another; the point is that empirical investigation presupposes categories, without being able to justify them empirically in advance.

Rather than being epistemological problems, fallibility and indeterminism are metaphysical conditions. We have no idea how to overcome our fallibility or how to tame those regions of the world that are indeterminate. Uncertainty, on the other hand, is an epistemological problem. Uncertainty arises from ignoring our fallibility and winking at indeterminacies. What allows us to do this is a substratum of conventions, shared purposes, common contexts, and collective knowledge. Uncertainty is produced not just by narrow scientific mechanisms but also by broad cultural processes. Assertions of uncertainty are not just expressions of our ignorance but part of what brings order to our world. Uncertainty implies both the existence of certainty and the existence of a path from one to the other. Claims of uncertainty reflect and establish epistemological order and imply a research program and a way of moving toward closure.

9. The classic argument for underdetermination can be found in W.V.O. Quine, *Word and Object* (Cambridge: MIT Press, 1960).

THE USES OF UNCERTAINTY

Sometimes, uncertainty claims are used directly in attempts to bring policy debates to closure. For example, the precautionary principle, which has been endorsed by various nations and international bodies, states (roughly) that if an action or policy potentially has catastrophic effects, then we should refrain from undertaking it even if the probabilities are uncertain.[10] On the other hand, some argue that unless it is certain that an action or policy will have harmful consequences, then it should be permitted. Both views figure in the climate change debate. Greens argue that since there is a significant chance that climate change will occur and have catastrophic consequences, we should "purchase some insurance" by capping greenhouse gas emissions. "Browns" argue that unless it is certain that greenhouse gas emissions will cause catastrophic climate change, we should not impose the costs on the economy that capping emissions would entail.

Direct appeals to uncertainty are rarely effective in bringing policy debates to closure. Instead they often open the door to the spectacle of dueling experts—scientists of equal training and stature who have diametrically opposed views about what is the case and what ought to be done. If the experts cannot agree about, for example, climate change, what is an ordinary person to think? Rather than providing a rational means for resolving epistemological differences, uncertainty reduces science to

10. For further discussion, see Budansky, "Scientific Uncertainty."

just another playground for competing ideologies.

While it is true that scientific uncertainty and the debates that it engenders can be corrosive to scientific authority, those who see scientific uncertainty as destructive and delegitimating overlook the fact that virtually all parties to various conflicts have an interest in maintaining scientific authority. The interest of scientists in maintaining scientific authority is obvious. But scientists also benefit from the right amount of uncertainty. If there is too much uncertainty, an area of research looks hopeless; if there is too little, research appears not to be needed. The right amount of uncertainty supports a call for further research.

Political actors of whatever ideological outlook have an interest in preserving scientific authority because science can provide a rationalization for decisions that are made on other grounds. When a policy decision can be presented as dictated by science, it is a way for a decision maker to evade responsibility for his or her choice. A decision backed by science can be viewed as implied by the nature of things, not as a decision for which a leader should be held accountable. Although political actors have an interest in preserving scientific authority, they also have an interest in keeping it in its place. The optimal role of scientific information for decision makers is to enable and structure decisions, not to determine them.

What I have suggested is that scientific uncertainty mediates between the closed world of scientific knowledge and the open world of public policy formation. If what I have said is correct, the cultural imperative with respect to scientific uncertainty is not simply to reduce it but more generally to manage it. In a recent article, Shackley and Wynne have identified some of these management strategies.[11]

Quantifying uncertainty is one way of managing it. In 1990, the Intergovernmental Panel on Climate Change (IPCC) estimated that a carbon dioxide doubling will produce an increase of global mean temperatures of 1.5-4.0 degrees centigrade. This estimate summarizes the results of some experiments run on what are regarded to be the best climate models. The IPCC estimate does not represent a probability estimate nor any kind of normal distribution. Yet specifying this range as the likely result of a carbon dioxide doubling sets limits on the uncertainties, thus making them more manageable.

Locating uncertainty is another way of managing it. When a climate model fails to successfully retrodict a past climatic condition, this could be regarded as evidence against the model. Typically, however, the uncertainties are located not in the model but in the data that the model manipulates. We are directed not toward a fundamental rethinking of the model but toward improving our data collection. When the uncertainties are located in the data rather than in the models, they do not threaten the general project of predicting future climate on the basis of computer models.

Scheduling reductions in uncertainty is a third way in which uncertainty is managed. The 1990 IPCC report speaks confidently of reductions in uncertainty that will occur as a result of better data sets and more powerful computers. In 1988, the British Department of the Environment laid out a 25-year plan for eliminating all of the uncertainties with respect to future climate.[12] Of course, no one knows exactly how these uncertainties will be eliminated. Nonetheless, simply attaching a date to their elimination appears to make the problems more tractable.

IMPROVING DECISION MAKING

Despite the fact that scientific uncertainty plays a functional role in our public decision-making processes, many people are unhappy about how we make decisions that have important scientific dimensions. The core of the unhappiness, I believe, is that the gap between science and policy seems unnecessarily wide. As a society, we have a large investment in science, yet science seems to influence policy only indirectly. Science and policy can be brought into closer contact, but there is a price that must be paid. Here are some positive suggestions for how science can be brought into closer contact with policy questions.

First, greater attention can be paid to problem definition at the beginning of a decision-making process. When policy problems are not clearly defined and characterized, it is quite

11. Simon Shackley and Brian Wynne, "Representing Uncertainty in Global Climate Change Science and Policy: Boundary-Ordering Devices and Authority," *Science, Technology and Human Values* (in press).

12. Ibid., p. 25 (in manuscript).

unclear what scientific information is relevant to bringing them to closure. Better problem definition involves being clear not only about what questions are being asked but also about the context in which they are asked and the purposes that answers to these questions are supposed to serve. The debate over climate change policy is an example of how things can go wrong when there is little agreement about what question is being asked. Some people claim that it is uncertain whether emitting greenhouse gases will change climate; others seem to deny this. In some cases, they are not really disagreeing. Both parties to the dispute may agree that, for the purposes of counting as scientific knowledge, the proposition is uncertain. More research needs to be done, data collected, and so forth. But those who seem to deny that there is significant uncertainty are often claiming not that there is no scientific uncertainty but that there is no uncertainty for the purposes of public decision making. In their view, the risk of climate change is known to be great enough, and the costs of mitigation and prevention are low enough, that some "no regrets" strategies ought to be pursued. This is an example of a case in which it is clear that the scientific data may rightfully be regarded as uncertain for some purposes but not for others.[13]

Second, various reforms in the practice of science would help in bringing scientific information into closer contact with public decision making.[14] Science, as it is practiced in American society, is an elite institution, to a great extent self-governing, with primary allegiance to its own internal values. While many people have access to the deliverances of science, very few people are involved in the production of science, and scientists themselves are overwhelmingly white, male, and upper middle class.

Finally, there are various reforms in our public decision-making processes that would also help to bring science into greater contact with policy. As things now stand, science and science policy are scattered throughout the federal government. We are one of the few industrialized nations that does not have a cabinet-level department of science and technology. Moreover, the adversarial way in which policy debate is conducted in this country may also have the effect of marginalizing or needlessly problematizing scientific information. Scientific institutions are in many ways authoritarian and directed toward the creation of consensus and thus are often at odds with the prevailing values of policy debate.

Broad changes in the areas I have identified would bring scientific information into closer contact with policy, but as a result, science would become less autonomous, and public decision making might become more technocratic. Even if it were thought that this price was not too high to pay, the effect that science would have on

13. These suggestions are more fully developed in Charles Herrick and Dale Jamieson, "The Social Construction of Acid Rain," *Global Environmental Change*, 5(2):105-12 (May 1995).

14. I have discussed some of these reforms in "What Society Will Expect from the Future Research Community," *Science and Engineering Ethics*, 1(1):73-80 (1995).

policy decisions would still remain limited.

One reason the role of science would remain limited is that our most important public policy decisions involve questions of value that cannot be addressed by science. A second reason why science would continue to have a limited role relates to the prevailing cultural attitudes that frame our decision-making practices. We are living in a time in which citizens are deeply insecure about their own futures and those of their children and have very little trust in institutions of any sort. In such an atmosphere, the bonds of community are strained and the willingness to make trade-offs is limited. Against such a background, science, however certain, is of limited effectiveness in shaping people's view of the world.

CONCLUDING REMARKS

In this article, I have sketched a notion of scientific uncertainty that is in many ways different from the prevailing view. Scientific uncertainty is not simply an objective value that can be reduced by science alone. Rather, scientific uncertainty is constructed by both science and society in order to serve certain purposes. Recognizing the social role of scientific uncertainty will help us to see how many of our problems about risk are deeply cultural and cannot be overcome simply by the application of more and better science.

Risky Thinking: Irrational
Fears About Risk and Society

By WILLIAM R. FREUDENBURG

ABSTRACT: Scientists have made remarkable progress in dealing with technical challenges but not in dealing with society. Given that public concerns have grown, in the face of declining "real" risks, the common if simplistic tendency has been to blame public ignorance or irrationality and to argue that policy decisions should be based on quantitative risk estimates, effectively ignoring public concerns. Such assertions are superficially plausible, but they reflect fundamental misunderstandings of the nature of technological societies, as well as of the reasons behind declining scientific credibility and of actual strengths and weaknesses of risk assessment. Scientific credibility has been undermined not so much by shadowy enemies as by actions of self-proclaimed friends, and there are inherent limitations to the practical usefulness of risk assessment in policy disputes. If proposals for risk-based decision making were actually implemented, they could well lead not to increased credibility for specific technologies but to self-reinforcing losses of credibility for science and technology as a whole.

William R. Freudenburg is professor of rural sociology and environmental studies at the University of Wisconsin–Madison. His articles on technological controversies and risk assessment have been published in Science; Risk; *and* Risk Analysis, *among other journals. His latest book—*Oil in Troubled Waters *(1994)—analyzes conflicting reactions to offshore oil development in Louisiana and California. A life member of the American Association for the Advancement of Science, he chairs the association's Section on Social, Economic and Political Sciences.*

I N 1933, the guidebook to the Chicago "Century of Progress" exhibition contained the motto, "Science Finds—Industry Applies—Man Conforms." After another half Century of Progress, however, the relationships no longer seemed quite so straightforward. In an influential book, a well-known political scientist and well-known anthropologist would ask, "What are Americans afraid of? Nothing much, really, except the food they eat, the water they drink, the air they breathe, the land they live on, and the energy they use."[1]

By many measures, science and industry have indeed made great progress over the course of the twentieth century, but today neither men nor women show much interest in "conforming." Instead, whether scientists and industry are searching for oil offshore or attempting to dispose of nuclear or other wastes onshore, their efforts now seem less likely to be welcomed with open arms than to open the public policy equivalent of armed warfare. While science and technology have achieved many remarkable successes, it would be difficult to argue that dealing well with the public should be counted among them.

At least to date, however, perhaps the most common response has been for representatives of science and industry to blame someone else—most often the purportedly "irresponsible" media or "irrational" public. Serious academic books as well as a stream of editorials in otherwise cautious scientific journals now describe the public in terms that seem strikingly out of place with the kinds of staid, judicious terminology normally preferred in such well-respected publications. One after another, scientists argue that the public is unreasonable, irrational, even hysterical, decrying everything from "phantom risk," to "higher superstition," to "eco-hysterics and the technophobes."[2]

Political leaders who claim themselves to be friends of science have responded in kind. By December of 1994, there would be no fewer than four bills moving through Congress to require "risk-based" decision making—decreeing, for example, that the Environmental Protection Agency should ignore public concerns in deciding what to regulate, allocating its budget instead based on scientific assessments of the levels of risk involved. As this article will spell out, however, there are at least three significant problems with these proposals. The first is that they are based on erroneous assumptions rather than on facts about the nature of public reactions, perhaps in part because they grow out of a fundamental misunderstanding of the nature of an advanced, technological society. The second is that the proposals are based more on the aspirations than on the actual attributes of risk analysis, which in fact is still a relatively young, un-

1. Mary A. Douglas and Aaron Wildavsky, *Risk and Culture: An Essay on the Selection of Technological and Environmental Dangers* (Berkeley: University of California Press, 1982).

2. Kenneth R. Foster, David E. Bernstein, and Peter W. Huber, eds., *Phantom Risk: Scientific Inference and the Law* (Cambridge: MIT Press, 1993); Paul R. Gross and Norman Levitt, *Higher Superstition: The Academic Left and Its Quarrels with Science* (Baltimore, MD: Johns Hopkins University Press, 1994); Peter Beckmann, *Eco-Hysterics and the Technophobes* (Boulder, CO: Golem Press, 1973).

derdeveloped specialty. The third is that, if the proposals were actually to be implemented in a serious way, they could well provide scientists with at least as much reason to fear as to cheer, contributing not so much to the potential rationality of decision making as to the potential death spiral of scientific credibility.

UNDERSTANDING PUBLIC REACTIONS TO TECHNOLOGICAL RISKS

Part of what makes the declining public deference toward science and technology so puzzling to many observers is the fact that, by many indicators, the past century and a half have brought unprecedented progress. As illustrated by one of the two lines in Figure 1, the risks that have been the traditional focus of science and technology—the risks of death, as measured by life expectancies—have indeed gone down substantially since the start of the nineteenth century, declining by nearly 50 percent.

Does this mean that public concerns about science and technology should automatically be assumed to be based on ignorance or irrationality? That may be one possibility, of course, but another is that the tendency to lash out at critics reflects a kind of ignorance as well—specifically including a basic misconception about what it means to say we live in an "advanced, technological" society. Collectively, of course, those of us who live today do know more than did our great-great-grandparents. Individually, however—to note a point by the eminent analyst of "intellectualized rationality," Max Weber, roughly

three-quarters of a century ago[3]—we actually know far less today than did our great-great-grandparents about the tools and technologies on which we depend.

In the early 1800s, roughly 80 percent of the American population lived on farms, and those farm residents were often capable of repairing, or even of building from scratch, the tools and technologies upon which they depended. By contrast, today's world is so specialized that even a Nobel laureate is likely to have little more than a rudimentary understanding of the tools and technologies that surround us all, from airliners to ignition systems and from computers to corporate structures.

Far more than was the case for our great-great-grandparents, in other words, we tend to be not so much in control of as dependent on our technology—and hence on whole armies of specialists, most of whom we will never meet, let alone be able to control. As indicated by the second line in Figure 1, the result of this increased interdependence has been a technological risk crossover.

Most of the time, of course, we find that we can indeed depend on the technologies and on the people who are responsible for them—yet the exceptions can be genuinely troubling. One of the reasons is that increases in technical control have come about, in part, at the cost of decreases in social control. In this sense, too, we are very much unlike our great-

3. Max Weber, "Science as a Vocation," in *From Max Weber: Essays in Sociology*, trans. and ed. H. H. Gerth and C. W. Mills (1918; New York: Oxford University Press, 1946), pp. 129-56.

great-grandparents: in the relatively few cases where they needed to buy an item of technology from someone else, it was often from a person whom they knew quite well or whom they would know how to find if something went wrong. Today's citizens often discover that when something goes wrong—be it a car or a computer or a chemical—the "responsible" person or organization can prove almost impossible to find.

The problem, to use the term from the technical literature, involves *recreancy*—in essence, the failure of an expert, or for that matter a specialized organization, to do the job that is required. The word comes from the Latin roots *re-* (back) and *credere* (to entrust), and the technical meaning is analogous to one of the dictionary meanings, involving a retrogression or failure to follow through on a duty or a trust. The term is unfamiliar to most, but there is a simple reason for its use: we need a specialized word if we are to refer to behaviors of institutions or organizations as well as of individuals and, importantly, if the focus of attention is to be on actual behaviors. One indication of the societal importance of trustworthiness, in fact, is that virtually all of the common words having comparable meanings have come, over time, to take on a heavily negative set of connotations. To say that a technical specialist is responsible, competent, or trustworthy, for example, is to offer at least a mild compliment, but to accuse that same person of being *ir*responsible, *in*competent, or of having shown a betrayal of trust, is to make a very serious charge indeed. While "recreancy" may not be an everyday term,

the need for it grows quite directly out of the necessity of avoiding the emotional and/or legal connotations of the available alternatives.

How important is recreancy? Empirically, far more important than the factors that have been stressed in the many editorials about the mass media and the public. Unlike media coverage and public knowledge levels, in other words, trustworthiness and recreancy have been shown by systematic research to be key factors behind the increasingly toxic interpersonal chemistry that has been associated with an ever increasing range of technologies. An analysis of attitudes toward a proposed low-level nuclear waste facility, for example, found that recreancy variables more than tripled the amount of variance that could be explained by the sociodemographic and the ideological variables combined.[4] The growth in interdependence, and in the risks of recreancy, appear to be among the reasons why trust and trustworthiness have been found to be key variables in a growing range of other studies as well.[5]

THE RISKINESS OF RELYING ON THE RISK NUMBERS

The importance of trustworthiness might be of little concern if the field of risk assessment were capable

4. The data on the waste facility, as well as much of the basic argument, have been drawn from William R. Freudenburg, "Risk and Recreancy: Weber, the Division of Labor, and the Rationality of Risk Perceptions," *Social Forces*, 71:909-32 (1993).

5. One forthcoming review finds that, of 15 studies that empirically test the hypothesis that environmental risk concerns will be predicted by a lack of technical information, only

FIGURE 1
THE TECHNOLOGICAL RISK CROSSOVER

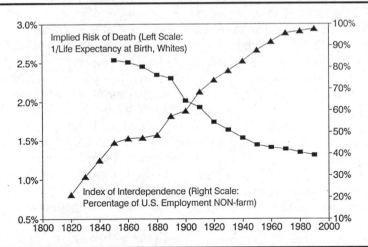

SOURCE: Adapted from William R. Freudenburg, "Risk and Recreancy: Weber, the Division of Labor, and the Rationality of Risk Perceptions," *Social Forces*, 71:909-32 (1993). Data are drawn from *Historical Statistics of the United States: Colonial Times to 1970* (Washington, DC: Department of Commerce, Bureau of the Census, 1975) and from issues of *Statistical Abstract of the United States* (Washington, DC: Department of Commerce, Bureau of the Census).

NOTE: National figures are available only as far back as 1900. Data from 1850 to 1900 are drawn from Massachusetts, where 99 percent of the enumerated population at the time was white. The 1870 figure for risk of death is an interpolation.

of extremely high levels of reliability. To ask for such a capacity, however,

5 support it, while 7 encounter significant findings in the opposite direction. See Debra Davidson and W. R. Freudenburg, "Gender and Environmental Risk Concerns: An Empirical Reexamination," *Environment and Behavior* (in press). Actual media studies provide similarly little support for common beliefs. See K. L. Salomone and Peter M. Sandman, "Newspaper Coverage of the Diamond Shamrock Dioxin Controversy: How Much Content Is Alarming, Reassuring, or Intermediate?" (Report, Environmental Communication Research Program, Rutgers University, New Brunswick, 1991); A. C. Gunther, "Biased Press or Biased Public: Attitudes Toward Media Coverage of Social Groups," *Public Opinion Quarterly*, 56:147-67 (1992); William R. Freudenburg et al., "Media Coverage of Hazard Events: Analyzing the Assumptions," *Risk Analysis* (in press).

would be to misunderstand the nature of the decisions that need to be made as well as to place a far greater burden on the still-young field of risk analysis than it is able to support.

In simple terms, the best that can be hoped in almost any case of technological controversy is to boil the matter down to three questions. The first, which can at least in principle be answered scientifically, is, "How safe is the technology?" The second question is one that, by its nature, cannot be answered scientifically: "Is that safe enough?" The third question, which often contributes in unseen ways to the difficulty of answering both of the first two, is, "Are we overlooking something?" Technological controversies, in other words, almost invariably combine three very different types of questions: questions about facts, about values, and about blind spots. Risk analysts' answers to all three sets of questions have often proved to be problematic, but given space limitations, plus the reviews of these findings that are already available from other sources,[6] this article will simply offer a brief note on the third and least-often recognized set of challenges, involving blind spots.

The difficulties start with the fact that blind spots include not just unknowns but "unknown unknowns." All of us, it turns out, have a signifi-

cant risk of failing to understand how powerfully our view of the world can be shaped by the spot from which we do our viewing—the risk of being prisoners of our own perspectives. Sometimes the limitations on our vision do come from our values, which lead us to focus more intently on some parts of the picture than on others, but often the problem is a matter of blind spots—of parts of the picture that are obscured from our view or that we simply fail to see. What makes the blind-spot problem so vexing is that, not only do we often fail to see something, but we fail to see that we fail to see.

That problem, in turn, can create difficulties even for the assessing of facts, as illustrated by what has been called "the statistical power of the hidden flaw,"[7] a problem that is particularly significant in the case of low-probability estimates. Consider two technologies, one of which has been calculated to have a one-in-a-million chance of failing, and the other of which is expected to fail several times a year. If risk assessors have overlooked just one minor problem in each case—say, a problem so obscure that it will occur only once in 12 years, as when the newest, largest, and best-equipped tanker owned by the largest oil company in the history of humanity ran straight into a reef that had been shown on navigational charts for over 200 years and that was marked by a flashing red light, as was the case for the *Exxon Valdez*—that obscure risk would dis-

6. On problems of assessing facts, see, for example, Baruch Fischoff, Paul Slovic, and Sarah Lichtenstein, "Lay Foibles and Expert Fables in Judgments about Risks," in *Progress in Resource Management and Environmental Planning*, vol. 3, ed. Timothy O'Riordan and R. Kerry Turner (New York: John Wiley, 1981), pp. 161-202; Kristen Shrader-Frechette, *Risk Analysis and the Scientific Method* (Dordrecht: D. Reidel, 1985); William R. Freudenburg, "Nothing Recedes Like Success? Risk Analysis and the Organizational Amplification of Risks," *Risk*, 3:1-35 (1992). For studies of the additional difficulties introduced by values, see, for example, Steve Rayner and Robin Cantor, "How Fair Is Safe Enough? The Cultural Approach to Technology Choice," *Risk Analysis*, 7:3-9 (1987); F. Lynn, "The Interplay of Science and Values in Assessing and Regulating Environmental Risks," *Science, Technology and Human Values*, 11:40-50 (1986); James Flynn, Paul Slovic, and C. K. Mertz, "Gender, Race, and Perception of Environmental Health Risks," *Risk Analysis*, 14(6): 1101-8 (1994). On blind spots, see William R. Freudenburg, "Strange Chemistry: Environmental Risk Conflicts in a World of Science, Values, and Blind Spots," in *Handbook of Environmental Risk Decision Making*, ed C. R. Cothern (Boca Raton, FL: CRC Press, forthcoming); J. F. Short, Jr. and Lee Clarke, eds, *Organizations, Uncertainties, and Risk* (Boulder, CO: Westview Press, 1993).

7. William R. Freudenburg, "Perceived Risk, Real Risk: Social Science and the Art of Probabilistic Risk Assessment," *Science*, 7 Oct. 1988, pp. 44-49.

appear as rounding error for the technology that is expected to fail several times a year, while it would be more important than the combined total of all the factors considered in the one-in-a-million estimate.[8]

Contrary to the common assumption, moreover, a hidden flaw in one portion of a probabilistic analysis is often not offset by conservatism in another—not even in the case of what many risk assessors see as a problem of exaggerated conservatism. A simple example can be provided by a technology that is calculated to have a one-in-a-million chance of failing, where risk assessors managed to identify all potential risk factors but two—one of them making the technology a thousand times safer than the official estimate during 10 percent of its operational life, and the other making it a thousand times less safe, also 10 percent of the time. The result would be that the technology would still have a one-in-a-million level of risk during 80 percent of its operational life, but that 10 percent of the time, the real risk would be one in a thousand, and 10 percent of the time, the risk would be one in a billion. The true risk of the technology would thus be $(.1 \times 10^{-9} + .8 \times 10^{-6} + .1 \times 10^{-3})$, that is, 10 percent times 10^{-9} (one in a billion), plus 80 percent times one in a million, plus 10 percent times one in a thousand, respectively. This overall probability comes to .0001008001, or slightly more than one in ten thousand. Rather than being offset by the presence of the unexpected safety factor, in other words, the unexpected problem dominates the ultimate probability. Indeed, such is the statistical power of the hidden flaw that, even if the risk assessment were to have been so conservative in other respects that the real risks were to be no higher than one in a trillion except for the 10 percent of the operating experience where the one-in-a-thousand estimate would hold, the overall probability would still be higher than one in ten thousand.

BE CAREFUL WHAT YOU ASK FOR

All in all, while it can make a great deal of sense for narrow, technical questions to be delegated to narrow, technical experts, many of the most important questions about risk and technology are neither narrow nor technical. The strength of the expert, however, is in the technical details, not the broader philosophy; the job of the technical specialist is to implement societal choices about values, not to make them. It may not be without reason that a popular definition describes an expert as someone who knows more and more about less and less. Charles Perrow offers a slightly more formal definition: an expert is "a person who can solve a problem better or faster than others, but who runs a higher risk than others of posing the wrong problem."[9]

By asking for risk assessment to provide answers to what are often actually questions about values and

8. For details, plus a broader discussion, see Lee Clarke, "The Disqualification Heuristic: When Do Organizations Misperceive Risk?" *Research in Social Problems and Public Policy*, 5:289-312 (1993).

9. Charles Perrow, *Normal Accidents: Living with High-Risk Technologies* (New York: Basic Books, 1984).

blind spots, policymakers may well be making matters worse. Note that this is not an argument for the abandonment of risk assessment; it is an argument that this misuse of risk assessment could do a disservice to society, as well as inflicting substantial damage on the credibility of risk analysis and, potentially, on science as a whole. Note also that this is not an argument about science and technology having lost all credibility; in fact, the problem is nearly the opposite. Studies show that, while science has indeed lost some of the credibility it once enjoyed, it has suffered less erosion in public confidence than have most institutions of society.[10] The reasons for concern, instead, are created by the very fact that scientific credibility, while somewhat shakier than in earlier years, still remains reasonably strong, at least in relative terms. The remaining credibility, unfortunately, can prove almost irresistibly tempting for societal institutions that do not enjoy the high credibility of science and technology—government and industry, to name two—and that wind up looking to science and technology to provide cover.

When a proposal or technology runs into strong opposition, the typical approach has been to commission another study—the results of which are used to "demonstrate" that the benefits of the proposal or technology are great and the risks are small—and then to forge ahead more or less

as originally planned. Particularly in politicized contexts, such studies are often less useful for the results they provide than for the technique they permit—a technique that politicians have long known and used but that studies of technological controversy have only begun to note, under the label of "diversionary reframing."[11] The essence of the technique is that, when a group of citizens opposes a specific facility or technology, then even if their opposition is based on legitimate concerns about the particular technology in question, they can be accused of being opposed to "science" in general. This accusation diverts attention away from their actual concerns and, importantly, reframes the debate in such a way that politicians can take sides not so much on a technology or facility that has been called into question but for or against "science and rationality"— with or without the apple pie.

What makes matters worse is that science has often been called upon not just in addressing questions of fact, but also in legitimating what are actually value decisions and in glossing over what often remain blind spots. Even in matters of fact, however, there have been any number of cases where subsequent events wound up sending a "signal"[12] that things were not actually so well understood or controlled, as illustrated by fatal accidents such as the *Chal-*

10. Cora B. Marrett, "Public Concerns About Nuclear Power and Science," in *Public Reactions to Nuclear Power: Are There Critical Masses?* ed. E. A. Rosa and W. R. Freudenburg (Boulder, CO: American Association for the Advancement of Science, Westview Press, 1984), pp. 307-28.

11. For a broader discussion of the concept and an analysis of its use in a specific controversy, see William R. Freudenburg and Robert Gramling, *Oil in Troubled Waters: Perceptions, Politics, and the Battle over Offshore Drilling* (Albany: SUNY Press, 1994).

12. Paul Slovic, "Perceived Risk, Trust, and Democracy," *Risk Analysis*, 13(6):675-82 (1993).

lenger disaster, by near misses such as Three Mile Island, and by any number of more prosaic but still disturbing difficulties, such as supposedly leakproof landfills that proved to be something else entirely. The net result is that, while articles, books, and editorials may continue to warn that science is being done in by shadowy enemies, the ironic reality is that, increasingly, science is being done in by those who profess to be its friends.

Over two decades ago, a now-classic article in *Science* warned that the public was becoming "wary" of the uses to which science was being applied,[13] and, given the growing number of cases in which the public is no longer buying the old sales pitches, matters may have continued to worsen since then. Diversionary reframing does sometimes still seem to succeed today, in cases of individual facilities or disputes, but it often does so at the cost of greatly increased public distrust toward the institutions of science and technology. That distrust often explodes when the next proposal comes along. As a result, in an ever increasing number of cases, the net effect of the technique has been not to increase the credibility of specific proposals but to decrease the credibility of the social institutions involved. In short, in what Robert Merton once called "a self-fulfilling prophecy,"[14] the technique seems to be creating people who genuinely do come to mistrust science and technology as a whole.

13. Todd R. LaPorte and Daniel Metlay, "Technology Observed: Attitudes of a Wary Public," *Science*, 18 Apr. 1975, pp. 121-27.

14. Robert K. Merton, *On Theoretical Sociology: Five Essays, Old and New* (New York: Free Press, 1967).

CONCLUSION

What is wrong, then, with what seem to be motherhood-and-apple-pie calls for public decisions to be made in a way that is more rational and scientific, based on the best estimates of risk now available? Nothing much, really—just a failure to understand the weaknesses of the risk estimates, combined with a fundamental misunderstanding of what it means to say that we live in an advanced, technological society, all brought together in a way that could well do lasting damage to the public credibility of science and technology.

It is tempting to assume that scientists can identify "real" risks, while public concerns are due simply to misinformation or irrationality. Such assumptions may cause few problems where the stakes are low, consensus is high, experience is vast, and decisions do not impose burdens on one group for the benefit of another. The assumptions are clearly problematic, however, for controversies that involve high stakes, low consensus, new technologies, and unequal distributions of burdens and benefits. These are precisely the kinds of technological controversies, unfortunately, where the perceived-versus-real argument is often propounded with greatest passion.

The problem can be made even worse in cases where proponents take the common yet dangerous next step of accusing their opponents of being opposed to science in general. Given that members of the broader public often obtain their most vivid evidence about the credibility of science from contact with specific, individual scientists, this step can be particularly dangerous if it is taken by scientists who are expected by the public to play a more neutral role. Given that the world is full of people who fail to live up to their responsibilities—of stereotypical used-car salesmen, fast-buck operators, con artists, and others who have something to gain from promising more than they can deliver—it is not at all unreasonable for citizens to become suspicious when they see evidence suggesting that yet another specialist, or even another specialty, might prove a little less than responsible.

What probably is unreasonable is when any member of the scientific community provides evidence, even unintentionally, that scientists should be tarred with the same stereotypes that afflict hucksters and hired guns—or that science, as an institution, is more interested in profit than in truth and the broader public good. Scientists have suffered far less than have most groups in society from the erosion of public confidence, at least to date, but past experience gives us no reason to conclude that scientists are immune to the broader malaise. Instead, the credibility appears to have been earned, slowly and painfully, by the fact that, in the vast majority of cases, scientists have shown by actual behaviors that we can, in fact, be trusted.

That credibility is far too precious to be put up for sale—not even for the institutions that employ us and support us, and perhaps especially not for them. As Paul Slovic has noted, following up on an earlier observation by Abraham Lincoln, any examination of trust needs to take note of a powerful "asymmetry principle": the fact that trust is hard to gain but easy to lose. As Slovic so aptly illustrates the point, if a specialist such as an accountant takes even one opportunity to steal, that single act creates a level of distrust that is not counterbalanced if the accountant decides not to take the next opportunity to steal—or even the next several dozen such opportunities.[15]

It would probably be melodramatic, although it might nevertheless be true, to argue that as scientists, all of us are in effect trustees for something more important than money. We are trustees for the credibility of science and technology. Unlike the accountant, moreover, we need to be alert not just for outright embezzlement but also for far more subtle kinds of blind spots. In areas of science that are often probabilistic, as in the case of environmental risks, the consequences of a willingness to fudge a technical judgment—or a political one, as in characterizing an opponent to a given facility as being opposed to science in general—may not become obvious for years. Ultimately, however, it may prove to be no less serious. The public trust is valuable, but it is also fragile, and it is highly susceptible to the corrosive effects of scientific behaviors that fall short of the highest standards of responsibility. In short, at least for those of us who care about the continued viability of the scientific enterprise, the risks of recreancy may ultimately prove to be the greatest risks of all.

15. Paul Slovic, "Perception of Risk," *Science*, 17 Apr. 1987, pp. 280-85.

Valuing Risks to the Environment

By ROBIN GREGORY, THOMAS C. BROWN, and JACK L. KNETSCH

ABSTRACT: Increasing awareness of exposure to environmental risks has focused attention on measures that would give greater assurance that such risks are effectively managed and that the adverse consequences of risky activities are mitigated. Implementing such actions is made more difficult by the uncertainties of environmental changes, their often delayed impacts, the great importance attached to extremely small risks, and the lack of clear measures of the values of environmental losses. Findings from recent behavioral studies of people's time preferences, valuations of losses relative to gains, and risk perceptions are providing information that should lead to more effective risk management strategies.

Robin Gregory (Ph.D., interdisciplinary studies, 1982, University of British Columbia) is a senior researcher with Decision Research in Eugene, Oregon. Thomas Brown (Ph.D., resource management and economics, 1983, University of Arizona) is a research scientist with the U.S. Forest Service in Ft. Collins, Colorado. Jack Knetsch (Ph.D., economics, 1963, Harvard University) is professor of resource management and professor of economics at Simon Fraser University, Burnaby, British Columbia, Canada. All three have extensive research and project experience on topics related to the valuation of natural resources and the management of environmental risks.

NOTE: Research reported here was, in part, supported by the U.S. Environmental Protection Agency and the National Science Foundation (SBR95-25582) and by the Social Sciences and Humanities Research Council of Canada. The views expressed in this article do not necessarily represent those of these funding agencies.

REPORTS of potentially catastrophic environmental losses such as those accompanying the Chernobyl nuclear accident in Russia, the *Exxon Valdez* oil spill in the United States, and the cutting of tropical forests have focused increasing attention on environmental risks. These risks range from local concerns to global changes; they result from natural processes as well as human activities; and they include risks to the environment as well as risks to human welfare.

The growing awareness of environmental risks and the cost of mitigating their impacts has brought greater attention to matters of responsibility, fairness, and how incentives encourage people to pursue activities that increase risks or motivate people to undertake precautionary measures. Yet setting limitations on risky actions and choosing levels of protection invariably pose difficult trade-offs between commercial and noncommercial interests, between geographic areas, and often between current and future generations. Valuing exposures to environmental losses is made more demanding by their uncertain impacts, by the lack of market prices, and by the rarity and delayed consequences of many potential effects. These issues also can erode trust in the managers and institutions charged with the responsibility to look after the interests of the wider community.

OBJECTIVES OF ENVIRONMENTAL RISK VALUATION

The general objective of valuing environmental risks is to improve the ways in which we make choices that allow or discourage risky activities and the means of mitigating adverse consequences of such actions when they occur. A world of zero environmental risks is clearly impossible. Some risks are more worrisome than others, however, and the public interest would be better served by regulations and policies that control the more serious risks and by expenditures that are cost-effective in reducing risks and mitigating losses that are more important to the environment and to people. Greater awareness of relative values would improve our ability to recover appropriate damages from individuals responsible for environmental harms and encourage people to choose alternative activities and precautionary efforts that are consistent with the full monetary and nonmonetary losses imposed by risky activities.

Valuations of environmental losses are often contentious, however. Individuals differ widely in their valuations and willingness to make sacrifices to deal with possible adverse impacts on the environment. Understanding of the probabilistic exposure to potential sources of loss is often lacking, and the great importance imputed to extremely small, or de minimis, risks effectively blunts many people's acceptance of any compromises or trade-offs. Rationalization of risk management efforts, reflecting the relative importance of environmental losses, would not only result in more efficient use of resources but could also lead to easier resolution of disputes and make restrictions far more acceptable to affected parties.

KEY ISSUES IN VALUING ENVIRONMENTAL RISKS

Some of the reasons why environmental risk assessments are often difficult are well known, such as the lack of actuarial experience with many such risks, the limited knowledge of ecological relationships, and the prominence often given to particular episodes or events by media attention that can heavily influence people's perceptions of their relative importance. There are, however, other less well appreciated reasons of particular concern for the valuation of environmental risks. In some cases these have become apparent only as the result of recent experience and research.

Risk and characteristics

A major issue in dealing with environmental risks is that risks have multiple characteristics and people weigh these attributes differently. The results of a 1990 U.S. study demonstrated the significance of this issue by revealing striking differences between U.S. Environmental Protection Agency scientists and members of the public when asked to rate the seriousness of a list of environmental problems. Not only were the relative weights very different, but many items high on the list of one group were not even included in the concerns of the other group. This difference between public and expert perceptions of the seriousness of various risks is a common finding.[1] The problem raised for valuations is deciding

1. Paul Slovic, "Perceptions of Risks," *Science*, 236:280-85 (1987).

whose weighings will be taken into account when identifying and setting priorities to deal with risks that have differing characteristics and therefore are considered to be more serious by some people than others.

Such differences in perspective are common and important when valuing environmental risks. The disparities may result from different information or different interpretations of facts; from different subjective calculations, particularly concerning the reluctance of many people to disregard even extremely low probability events; and from different levels of trust that cleanup activities will be as thorough or as speedy as suggested. In some cases, individuals may be confused or base their preferences on erroneous facts or interpretations; but they may also value risks differently because particular characteristics of potential events are important to them in addition to the narrower calculations of probabilities and expected losses on which expert rankings are largely based.

The differing views of the public and technical experts from industry or government laboratories toward cleanup of government-owned hazardous waste sites in the United States illustrate the nature of the problem. After many years of study, the experts have quite clear ideas of the major contaminants, their principal pathways, and the environmental costs and benefits of alternative cleanup strategies. People in local communities and throughout the country, however, maintain that values such as uses of the areas by migratory animals, the extent of public involvement in decision making, or the religious importance of some sites to local Indian nations have been ignored. They are also concerned about the perceived catastrophic effects of several extremely low probability sources of emissions considered to be irrelevant by experts. The ensuing lack of agreement on which risk characteristics should be valued, and how, has resulted in a costly paralysis of the country's cleanup efforts and an alarming loss of confidence in the capabilities of government risk managers.

The case-by-case nature of risk reduction efforts in itself can pose a problem because it has the effect of legitimizing only particular types of actions. Thus an individual may be concerned about a broad class of environmental risks, but the only opportunity for expressing these preferences may be through referenda or regulations focused on specific actions that are only distantly related to the more fundamental concern. Because the resources for risk reduction activities are scarce, highly valued risk management initiatives may be neglected due to the lack of a suitable forum for their expression.

The principle seems clear that risk management decisions should be more sensitive to what really matters to people by taking account of their informed valuations of the differing characteristics of environmental risks.[2] Sorting out confusion from legitimate values may well be a problem in specific applications, however.

2. Richard H. Pildes and Cass R. Sunstein, "Reinventing the Regulatory State," *University of Chicago Law Review*, 62:1-129 (1995).

Economic measures of loss

Environmental resources, like other goods or assets, have economic value to the extent that people are willing to make sacrifices of other things in order to acquire them or to prevent their loss. If a person is willing to pay, for example, $10 to enjoy a day of fishing, we can say that this individual is willing to sacrifice the $10—or really the things that $10 could buy—in order to acquire a day of angling and this is therefore its economic value. It does not matter whether or not the $10 is actually paid, so long as we are sure that this person would really be willing to pay it if necessary. Similarly, if a person would take no less than $20 to accept the loss of access to a park, we can say that he or she would be willing to give up what $20 would buy and so this is the person's economic valuation of the loss of the park. Thus the economic value of gains is measured by how much people are willing to pay (WTP) to acquire them, and the value of losses is measured by how much people demand to accept them (their willingness to accept [WTA]).

Until recently there was little disagreement with a conventional assumption that these two measures of economic value, WTP and WTA, would be, for all practical purposes, equivalent. That is, except for limitations of wealth on the amount that individuals could pay, and similar income effects, estimates of both measures would yield the same value. Consequently, despite wide agreement that WTA is appropriate for assessing the value of losses, the equivalence assumption has been used to justify the nearly universal practice of using the WTP measure to assess both gains and losses.

The empirical evidence strongly shows, however, that people commonly value losses more highly than otherwise commensurate gains. Results of tests demonstrating large disparities in valuations of environmental losses were first reported two decades ago, based on responses to hypothetical questions indicating that duck hunters would demand four times as much money to give up habitat than they were willing to pay to maintain the same resource.[3] Other studies based on real exchanges of money and goods showed similar differences. Further tests, using a variety of methods and controlling for such factors as strategic behavior, repeated bids and offers, and income constraints, have provided numerous replications of this basic finding,[4] with the WTA measure typically found to be from two to five or more times larger than the WTP measure.

Given the large difference between the two measures, using the amount of money that people are willing to pay to prevent a loss to assess its value is, on present evidence, almost

certain to seriously bias environmental decisions and environmental risk assessments. Too few restrictions will be placed on activities posing environmental risks, as the losses will be systematically underestimated; compensation and damage awards will be too small to provide proper levels of deterrence; and too few efforts will be made to avoid environmental harms, as the value of their prevention will be inadequately assessed.[5]

Mitigation and compensation remedies

An important risk valuation issue concerns the development of appropriate remedies for harms to environmental resources attributable to human activities and actions. Whether before or after the fact, changes and remedies typically take one of two broad forms, mitigation or compensation. Mitigation refers to measures designed to either reduce the statistical risk of injury or decrease the adverse impact of a past harm. These might include, for example, redesign by installing double liners around a waste site, changes in operations by including local participation on a facility's operating board, or restoration of a damaged coastline through habitat enhancement. Compensation generally takes the forms of monetary payments or in-kind transfers to affected individuals and groups. These may include, for example, tax reductions, property value guaran-

3. Judd Hammack and Gardner Brown, *Waterfowl and Wetlands: Toward Bioeconomic Analysis* (Baltimore, MD: Johns Hopkins University Press, 1974).

4. Daniel Kahneman, Jack L. Knetsch, and Richard H. Thaler, "Experimental Tests of the Endowment Effect and the Coase Theorem," *Journal of Political Economy*, 98:1325-48 (1990). An extensive review of many of these studies is provided in Elizabeth Hoffman and Matthew L. Spitzer, "Willingness to Pay vs. Willingness to Accept: Legal and Economic Implications," *Washington University Law Quarterly*, 71:59-114 (1993).

5. Jack L. Knetsch, "Environmental Policy Implications of Disparities Between Willingness-to-Pay and Compensation-Demanded Measures of Values," *Journal of Environmental Economics and Management*, 18:227-37 (1990).

tees, or the construction of new recreation or health facilities in an affected locality.[6]

While risk management strategies commonly involve both mitigation to reduce harmful impacts and compensation to offset the consequences of environmental losses, conventional risk analysis is subject to a bias that unduly favors compensation remedies. The source of the bias is an assumption that compensation is likely to be more efficient than mitigation remedies because compensation allows injured parties to use an award for whatever they value most, whereas mitigation restricts the remedy to reducing a specific injury, which may not be the thing of highest value. However, the assumed superiority of compensation over mitigation ignores people's greater valuations of losses relative to gains. This pervasive asymmetry suggests that compensation may be a less, rather than more, efficient remedy for environmental losses; mitigation provides a highly valued reduction of a loss whereas compensation leaves people with the loss and provides a less valued gain of money or whatever in-kind change is on offer.

Time

Risk management commonly involves decisions about whether or not to initiate precautionary efforts to reduce the possibility of environmental losses that might take place decades, or even centuries, in the future. An important valuation issue is, there-

6. Robin Gregory et al., "Incentive Policies to Site Hazardous Waste Facilities," *Risk Analysis*, 11:667-75 (1991).

fore, how costs and benefits occurring at different times should be compared.

Current practice calls for weighing the importance of future gains and losses by discounting with a particular interest, or discount, rate. The procedure is analogous to compounding a present sum into the future: $100 compounded every year at a 6 percent rate would be worth $1842 at the end of fifty years, and a benefit or cost estimated to be worth $1842 fifty years in the future would, at a discount rate of 6 percent, be worth the equivalent of having $100 today. Normal procedures and analyses suggest that it is worth taking precautions today to prevent a loss worth $1842 accruing in fifty years only if the current cost is less than $100; if greater, then it would not be worth doing because the future loss counts for less than the prevention costs incurred today.

Most of the debate in the past has concerned the choice of a specific discount rate; there has been little questioning of the standard procedure of using whatever rate is selected to discount all future gains and losses by a constant rate. The results of recent research indicates, however, that a constant and unvarying discount rate may provide a poor reflection of people's actual time preference and choices.

Both anecdotal evidence and the results of controlled tests suggest that people have widely varying rates of time preference, depending on the particular circumstances or characteristics of a potential future event or outcome. For example, many individuals simultaneously borrow and save at differing rates, particularly in connection with purchases of consumer durables; they frequently choose wage time patterns that may not be in their best financial interest; and they choose sequences of pleasurable and onerous events that are inconsistent with positive discount rates. Further, people appear to have much lower discount rates for long periods in the future than for short times, to discount future gains at a higher rate than future losses, and to use lower rates in discounting more important future outcomes.[7] Thus there is little evidence that individuals use a constant and unvarying rate to discount all future outcomes.

To the extent that the results of recent studies accurately depict people's true time preferences, they hold substantial implications for environmental risk valuations. Incurring present costs to avert potentially catastrophic losses far in the future, which would not appear to be worth undertaking using the constant discount rates of standard analyses, may well be economically worthwhile when account is taken of the lower time preference rates for losses, for longer time horizons, and for more important outcomes. For similar reasons, there may be less economic justification for actions that provide short-term benefits at the expense of costs accruing over future decades. Thus valuations of the benefits and costs of proposed climate-change actions, risk management proposals for dealing with hazardous wastes, and strategies for maintaining the productivity of natural systems might well differ substantially depending on whether the standard invariant discount rate is used or whether the choice of rates reflects the empirical evidence of people's actual time preferences.

VALUATION TECHNIQUES AND STRATEGIES

There are no active and competitive markets for many environmental resources or amenities. People clearly value cleaner air and reductions in risks from groundwater contamination, but they do not purchase these in market exchanges as they do other valued goods such as food or most consumer products.[8] This is also the case with values that are not derived from direct use of the environment but instead are based on nonuse, or passive, values such as knowing that a species exists, having the option of being able to see it in the future, or being free of the guilt or feeling of responsibility of being even an indirect party to diminishing or degrading the quality of the environment.

This nonmarket, or nonpecuniary, nature of many environmental values in no way makes them less economically important. Nonpriced values still represent economic worth; people are willing to sacrifice other goods and services in order to preserve or obtain access to them.

The absence of prices, however, does make the assessment of envi-

7. Richard H. Thaler, "Some Empirical Evidence on Dynamic Inconsistency," *Economic Letters*, 8:201-7 (1981); George Loewenstein and Drazen Prelec, "Anomalies in Intertemporal Choice: Evidence and an Interpretation," *Quarterly Journal of Economics*, 107:573-97 (1992).

8. Thomas C. Brown, "The Concept of Value in Resource Allocation," *Land Economics*, 60:231-46 (1984).

ronmental values much more difficult. Instead of direct observations of
prices, which measure the added
costs of supplying more of a product
and the added benefits of consuming
it, assessments of environmental values frequently must depend in large
part on indirect measures of value.
Consequently, while a narrow range
of such impacts can be estimated
with useful precision, there is as yet
no generally applicable method that
is agreed upon as yielding appropriate assessments of environmental
values, and particularly none for
measuring the costs of increased exposure to environmental losses.

In some instances, an action may
lead to an environmental disruption
that can be remedied by replacement
or restoration, and implementation
costs then may serve as a useful indication of the value of the loss.[9] However, the costs serve as a measure of
loss only when the harm lends itself
to full replacement or restoration, in
the sense that the restored asset is
taken as a complete substitute for the
original endowment. The number of
cases of such convergence are likely
to be limited in practice.

Another instance in which market
prices can be indirectly used is the
so-called hedonic price method of
valuation. There is usually no market for scenic views, for example, but
the value of such an amenity may be
captured in the price of land or
houses. The value of the view is then
measured by the difference in prices
of houses with and without a view.

9. Raymond J. Kopp and V. Kerry Smith,
eds., *Valuing Natural Assets: The Economics of
Natural Resource Damage Assessments* (Washington, DC: Resources for the Future, 1993).

While this method provides a means
for estimating environmental values,
the number of cases relevant to risk
management in which it could be
used is limited.

A somewhat related, and widely
discussed, method of valuing environmental assets such as parks or
other areas that prompt direct use is
the travel cost method. Using the relationship between the number of
people who visit a site and the travel
costs they incur, this technique derives an estimate of how much visi-
tors would pay over and above their
cost of travel to gain access to the site.
This provides a valid estimate of the
value of the site. The value, however,
is in terms of how much current users
are willing to pay to use the site and
not how much they would need to be
compensated to forgo this use due to
loss or degradation of the resource.
Further, the method is limited to
valuations of particular sites that are
visited by people and has little appli-
cability to more general environmental values that may be at risk.

By far the most widely used means
of estimating environmental values
is the contingent valuation method,
in which respondents are asked to
state the maximum amount of money
they would be willing to pay to obtain
more of a desired good or to reduce
their exposure to an environmental
disruption or loss. Several question
formats are used and, with varying
success, they produce estimates for a
nearly limitless range of applications. Contingent valuation techniques, however, are ill suited to establishing loss valuations in terms of
people's willingness to accept compensation to agree to give up an envi-

ronmental asset. Further, recent research has shown that the method is very susceptible to hypothetical effects, as actual payment levels tend to be much smaller than those indicated by respondents; to anchoring effects, whereby people are influenced by initial sums or suggested payment levels; and to factors such as embedding, in which the value of an asset can vary widely depending on how it might be combined with other goods.[10] There is also evidence that survey respondents will pay close attention to contextual cues and construct their expressed environmental values during the elicitation process rather than simply reveal them.[11] As a result, responses to contingent valuation questions may tell little about people's economic measures of value.

Recognition of these serious limitations of current valuation methods has motivated a wider search for alternative approaches that can provide useful guidance for policy design and management choices. At least three general strategies offer promise of yielding information that may well be superior, at least for some purposes, to the valuation numbers provided by more traditional methods.

The first approach focuses on the concerns of a small group of individuals who are selected to be representative of the key interests potentially affected by a proposed action. Elicitation procedures drawn from decision analysis are used to define and clarify their objectives, to determine how alternative actions would contribute to these objectives, and to structure and integrate value tradeoffs as a means for rating the worth of policy alternatives. These value integration procedures are often lengthy, but they have been used with success in several complex environmental risk cases.[12]

A second alternative approach relies on a small group of people who together form a values jury.[13] Members of an environmental values jury would act as direct representatives of the larger society, including future citizens who might be affected by an action or decision, in much the same way that jurors frequently are asked to address other tough social problems, such as guilt, responsibility, and compensation awards.

Both the values integration and jury approaches could be used to assess specific environmental risks or to select a preferred course of action from a set of alternatives that imply different environmental risks. This latter use of the approaches, which relies on a comparative judgment, can be helpful because it permits concerned parties to participate directly in the creation of alternatives and because it avoids the often difficult estimation of explicit values.

10. Daniel Kahneman and Jack L. Knetsch, "Valuing Public Goods: The Purchase of Moral Satisfaction," *Journal of Environmental Economics and Management*, 22:57-70 (1992).

11. Robin Gregory, Sarah Lichtenstein, and Paul Slovic, "Valuing Environmental Resources: A Constructive Approach," *Journal of Risk and Uncertainty*, 7:177-97 (1993).

12. Robin Gregory and Ralph Keeney, "Creating Policy Alternatives Using Stakeholder Values," *Management Science*, 40:1035-1048 (1994).

13. Thomas C. Brown, George L. Peterson, and Bruce E. Tonn, "The Values Jury to Aid Natural Resource Decisions," *Land Economics*, 71:250-60 (1995).

A third strategy centers on the derivation of a "damage schedule" that would provide scaled rankings of the relative importance of various environmental harms. The rankings reflect relative values, of which people are more certain, rather than absolute values, of which people are far more uncertain.[14] These rankings would form the basis for the design of various forms of regulatory or other controls and for the setting of damage awards, much in the way that schedules now are used to settle worker's compensation claims and establish workplace safety regulations.

CONCLUSION

The desire for improved risk assessments has led to new demands for environmental valuations to resolve disputes, to set damage awards, and to determine preferred allocations of environmentally sensitive resources. Such valuations would allow comparisons of the consequences of environmentally risky activities across a range of alternative actions.

Substantial progress has been made in recent years, leading to greater understanding of key valuation issues and of the strengths and limitations of current methods. Research studies continue to uncover new behavioral considerations, revealing the multidimensionality of people's perceptions of risks, the disparities in their valuations of losses relative to gains, and how their time preferences vary depending on characteristics of the future outcomes at issue. Such findings have a great potential to improve environmental risk valuations and risk management.

The current strong demands for valuation numbers may divert such efforts, however, and could compromise the continued rapid progress being made in understanding risk valuation issues. The recent rapid advances in this area have come far less from massive evaluation exercises geared to some specific episode—and real or threatened litigation—than from careful research. There is little reason to expect this pattern to differ greatly in the future.

14. Murray B. Rutherford, Jack L. Knetsch, and Thomas C. Brown, "Assessing Non-Pecuniary Environmental Losses: Rankings and Interim Damage Schedules" (Working paper, Simon Fraser University, 1995).

Risk and the Human Environment

By ROY A. RAPPAPORT

ABSTRACT: This article is concerned with the nature of what federal legislation calls "the human environment" as a preliminary to understanding impacts upon it and risks to it. After discussing the features that distinguish human systems from others, emphasizing nonmetrical aspects of their sociocultural characteristics, eighteen points concerning risks and impacts are made. The article concludes with a discussion of the possible place in the human environment of what Stephen Toulmin calls "post-modern science and risk analysis."

Roy A. Rappaport is Walgreen Professor for the Study of Human Understanding at the University of Michigan, where he has been a member of the Anthropology Department since 1965. He is currently director of the Program on Studies and Religion. A past president of the American Anthropological Association, he has conducted ethnographic fieldwork in Papua New Guinea and has worked on energy issues in the United States. He is author of three books, coauthor of one, and has published many articles.

S TUDIES of risk, under the guise of environmental impact studies, have, by legislative mandate, been part of environmental and resource planning for several decades now, and the complex nature of that which is at risk—the environment—has increasingly been recognized. Thus, for instance, the Outer Continental Shelf Lands Act as Amended,[1] in accordance with which the Department of the Interior leases rights to extract hydrocarbons from the Outer Continental Shelf (OSC), requires studies of risks to what it calls "the human environment." This term subsumes not only features of ecosystems related to human populations but those populations themselves and their social, cultural, and economic systems as well. Because this simple characterization masks enormous complexity, it is necessary to enlarge on the distinctive nature of human environments before considering possible risks to them.

Human systems are complex not only because they include innumerable elements in continuous interaction but also because some of their components are qualitatively different from others. Some, including humans themselves, are natural products of genetic, geological, and ecological processes. Others—the sociocultural elements of such systems—are symbolically conceived and socially constructed. The latter include their more or less distinctive political, legal, economic, social, religious, recreational, and aesthetic conventions: rules, practices, ways of doing

1. Outer Continental Shelf Lands Act Amendments, Pub. L. 95-372, 43 U.S.C. §§ 1801-66 (1978).

things standardized by law, custom, or habitual usage as well as the conceptions, perceptions, and understandings on which these rules and practices are founded. Several points follow.

First, all human systems can, of course, be characterized in terms of a range of fundamental demographic, economic, physical, and social properties and activities. Such obvious and quantifiable variables are those most often considered in assessments of the impacts of resource extraction or other forms of economic development on human systems.

But, second, any adequate description of such systems must also consider their social, symbolic, and conceptual elements. Indeed, economic systems are subsets of social systems, and inasmuch as they are conventionally established and not "naturally" constituted, they are themselves social and symbolic in nature, and the value of money is purely conventional.

The understandings on which conventional rules and practices are founded are not all narrowly focused on specific instrumental aspects of human affairs. They also include more general and, from the point of view of the actors, more fundamental conceptions of morality, equity, justice, and honor; religious doctrine; ideas concerning sovereignty, property, and rights and duties; and aesthetic values and what constitutes quality of life. There are also distinctive understandings concerning the nature of nature, of the place of humans in it, of proper behavior with respect to it, and of equitable distribution of its fruits, its costs, and its dangers. At levels yet deeper lie assumptions about the nature of reality: what is given, what requires demonstration, what constitutes evidence, how knowledge is gained. Such loosely structured bodies of understandings and the conventions and practices they inform are what anthropologists call "cultures" and what laypeople probably mean by such phrases as "way of life" or "tradition."

Demographic and economic aspects of human systems are relatively amenable to numerical representation, but other aspects of society and culture, including most of those just listed, are not. They are no less real for that, however, nor are they less compelling as factors in human affairs for, as vaguely articulated as they often are, they command great loyalty. It is through such conceptions that risks are not only perceived but defined as such: such conceptions specify what those who are at risk understand to be at risk. Risk analysis risks resistance or rejection if it ignores such conceptions.

Third, although it is proper to speak of a generalized American society and culture, regional, ethnic, class, and other differences play variations on that common theme. In some instances—for example, Native American groups—the local version diverges widely from the generalized. In all instances, the divergence is significant. It follows that the features of local sociocultural systems cannot be taken for granted but must be explored.

Fourth, it follows that impacts are always in part relative to the particulars of the affected sociocultural sys-

tem. It would be one thing for an oil spill to decimate marine life in an area exploited only by white commercial fishermen and quite another to decimate an equivalent fauna in Bristol Bay, Alaska, which is fished and hunted by Yupik-speaking Native Americans. For white fishermen the loss of their fishery is economic. For Yupik it is not simply economic. Because subsistence activities are central to their cultural reproduction, Yupik maintain that the destruction of their fishery would constitute genocide. It would be more accurate to call it ethnicide.

Given this complexity, the conception of the human environment on which many impact studies have been based seems impoverished. To the extent that the concept has been formulated at all, it seems to have been operationalized only in terms of economics, demographics, and government services. But adequate consideration of ultracomplex human systems, conventionally constituted as they are, must also rely on social, cultural (anthropological), and even psychological analyses. An integrated approach is required if information is to be adequate to the gravity of such actions as OCS development. This framework needs to be sufficiently comprehensive to allow the full range of phenomena constituting human systems to enter into analyses, and it must be inclusive enough to take into consideration the concerns of all interested parties—especially those who are likely to experience impacts directly. It should, furthermore, be sufficiently consistent to make for reasonably commensurate studies, thus

facilitating extrapolation, comparison, and generalization—in short, to
encourage learning from experience.

EIGHTEEN THESES ON THE HUMAN ENVIRONMENT

More specific observations concerning both the nature of what the
Outer Continental Shelf Lands Act as
Amended awkwardly terms "human
environments" and how they are to be
characterized are now possible.

1. Because human systems are ultracomplex and always unique in
some particulars, the range of possible social, cultural, and economic effects of human activities on them
cannot be specified, even in principle,
in advance of studies based upon empirical research. It is not legitimate
to stipulate a priori what qualifies as
a social, cultural, or economic impact.
The establishment of such specifications constitutes an attempt to legis-
late reality, but the degree to which
reality is amenable to such legislation is slight. Any limitation on the
nature of what counts as a real impact—for example, that it is physical
or quantifiable or translated into
monetary terms—can only misrepresent actual conditions. Given the responsiveness of human systems,
such misrepresentations are likely to
have political, legal, and social repercussions, themselves properly regarded as impacts.

2. Humans respond not only to
events but also to information concerning events. Indeed, in this age of
rapid communication, the preponder-
ance of response is not to direct observation of events but to news of them.

When news of events, rather than
events, provides stimuli, the events
need not have yet occurred for them
to have significant effects. Thus apprehensions about undesirable developments, and not simply developments themselves, are real and
immediate effects of announcements
of possible developments. For example, uncertainty concerning the future of a coastal region ineluctably
increases from the moment a tract
appears on a Department of Interior
five-year hydrocarbon leasing plan
until a lease sale fails or until exploration ends in either abandonment or
drilling. Uncertainty itself constitutes a real impact. Both apprehension and uncertainty about future activities and their consequences are
properly construed as impacts in the
present because they may alter the
current psychic, social, and perhaps
economic well-being of a community
and because they influence subsequent attitudes and behavior.

3. It follows that in ultracomplex
human systems, some effects are not
simply linear outcomes of earlier actions. Between causes and effects—
that is, between perturbing factors
and responses to them—lie conceptions and evaluations of not only how
the world is constructed and how it
works but also how it should be constructed and how it should work. It is
in terms of the latter (values) that the
former (perceptions of actual conditions) are understood. Such values
are, of course, culturally or even sub-
culturally variant.

4. The relationship between the
news of an event and the physical
characteristics of the event is not

simple. News is not simply radiated from an event, as light from a bulb, but is subject to amplification, dampening, editing, and distortion in transmission, and it requires interpretation by receivers.

Interpretation takes into account the reliability and credibility of transmitters and channels. Credibility can be a serious problem for both transmitters and channels, and its loss can be a consequence of their responses to events. For instance, OCS environmental impact statements that an affected public takes to be inadequate or misleading can discredit their sources. There are, moreover, grounds for believing that risks are perceived to be higher when information sources are distrusted. Such perceptions can lead people to oppose even projects that could benefit them.

5. If impacts include responses of systems to perturbations, then the legal, political, and organizational responses of states, municipalities, tribes, and interest groups to announcements of development plans are themselves impacts, as are their opportunity costs. Antagonisms developing between affected groups as conflicts between their interests become apparent, and conflicts between such parties and the federal government are also impacts.

6. The previous points suggest an order in which impacts of different natures become dominant. Earliest effects—for example, those following soon after the listing of a region on a five-year OCS oil leasing plan—are likely to include increased apprehension and uncertainty about the effects of future OCS development. Apprehension is always unevenly distributed in populations, and immediate subsequent effects are likely to include attempts by their more interested elements to raise concern among the less sensitive. Activity of state and local agencies and already existing environmental groups and trade associations soon increases, and special state and local bureaucracies and special-purpose grassroots organizations often spring into being. Conflict between those taking various positions comes next. All of this happens before any lease sale takes place. Subsequent exploration and production have their own effects, including disaster and its possibility, and so, finally, does termination, subsequent to which there may be as yet unexplored residual effects.[2]

7. That certain important consequences of development in general and of gas- and oil-related OCS activity in particular can be strongly felt well in advance of any actual physical activity on the part of oil companies may contradict some recent court decisions. The general failure to recognize prelease sale effects of OCS activities may be related to their typical resistance to plausible quantitative representation. More easily quantifiable impacts generally come later in

2. See W. R. Freudenburg and R. Gramling, "Community Impacts of Technological Change: Toward a Longitudinal Perspective," *Social Forces*, 70:937-57 (1992); R. A. Rappaport, "The Human Environment: Appendix B," in *Assessment of the U.S. Outer Continental Shelf Environmental Studies Program*, vol. 3, *Social and Economic Studies*, by Committee to Review the Outer Continental Shelf Environmental Studies Program, Socioeconomics Panel (Washington, DC: National Academy Press, 1992).

the sequence. It may be because early effects resist representation in terms—such as monetary—familiar to many or most administrators that public awareness of them has been slight.

8. Although some aspects of events and their consequences are metrical in nature, or easily represented in numerical terms, other aspects of the same or other events cannot be so represented. It should be clear that a good many significant effects of OCS and other developments—the psychic and social tensions that attend uncertainty, or anger at and alienation from the government—cannot be represented adequately, or even at all, in quantitative terms of any sort, let alone monetary terms.

The prevalence of opinions should, of course, be sampled. It is one thing, however, to quantify the prevalence of particular opinions on particular issues as they may be indicated by responses to the limited range of choices offered by particular questions asked at particular moments in an ever changing history, and it is another to grasp the underlying cognitive structures out of which these relatively evanescent opinions emerge in response to unfolding events. Attempts to force the representation of such structures into inappropriately quantitative terms or, alternatively, to dismiss them because they cannot be quantified is to misrepresent reality. The aesthetic considerations of affected populations, for instance, or violations of their religious beliefs or of their conceptions of equity or even of their vague conceptions of the good life cannot be ruled inadmissible because they resist quantitative representation, for they are likely to be those aspects of their lives that these populations take to be most seriously at risk. Such considerations cannot be disqualified as mere preferences or prejudices of uninformed laypeople. They are embedded in views of the world no more and no less arbitrary than other views of the world, and as such have valid claims on reality. More decisively, they are social facts and as such serve as grounds for action.

In sum, metrical representation—including the results of opinion surveys—should be pushed to the limits of plausibility but no further, and it is necessary to recognize that some considerations, often decisive ones, lie beyond the reach of plausible numerical representation. Attempts to reduce radically unmeasurable components of the world to common metrics preliminary to bottom-line calculations are not to be justified as aids to clear thinking—the clarity and certainty so claimed are false.

9. The term "significant" in point 8 is meant in both its major senses: both "consequential" and "meaningful." To say that a phenomenon is meaningful is to say that it enters into the motivational processes of actors. This implies that values are of crucial importance in risk analysis and that their consideration cannot be avoided. Risk assessment cannot be value free because values define what is at risk, and what is at risk may be values themselves.

In some contexts, the conception of value, particularly when accompanied by a modifier—for example, "food value"—seems intrinsically metrical.

But the term also refers to such conceptions as truth, honor, honesty, integrity, life, liberty, and happiness. Two subsidiary points follow.

First, there is a radical incompatibility between most such values and metrics of any sort, and an absolute contradiction between some of them and monetary valorization, a contradiction indicated by such questions as "How much money is your integrity (or honesty or vote) worth?" Any assignment of monetary metrics to such values renders them false. It follows that attempts to mitigate the violation of strongly held values through cash awards may be taken by those to whom they are offered as insults heaped on previous injuries. The Shoshone, for instance, have refused to accept a cash award of tens of millions of dollars as compensation for what they construe to be seizure of their lands by the federal government in violation of the Ruby Valley Treaty of 1863. Similarly, many people in Nevada characterized as attempted bribery the suggestion that they receive large cash payments in return for accepting a national nuclear waste repository.

Second, fundamental or basic values tend to be low in specificity. What, after all, constitutes liberty or happiness or, for that matter, life? To say, however, that values are not specific or even vague does not say that they are not cogent, or even decisive, in the formation of positions on which social actors stand and from which they understand the world and act in it. Furthermore, it may even be that the vagueness of a value and the strength of the motivations it engenders are

directly correlated. People will sacrifice themselves to protect whatever they mean by "liberty" or "democracy" but not to balance the budget of the federal government.

10. A general value of sufficient significance to warrant special mention is fairness. Americans are likely to take such actions as OCS oil and gas development leasing to be in their nature unfair. First, affected populations are quick to perceive that the most substantial benefits of development are likely to flow to parties other than those most directly exposed to attendant risks. Second, and even deeper, it seems that the attitude of local publics to local land is that it is in some sense theirs. That a private or alien interest can curtail or endanger their use of what they see as their own—whether private property or public amenity—violates not only a deep sense of right but possibly also a deep sense of connection to place: "Who are *they* to endanger *our* wetlands (or fish or beach)?" Such sense of violation and its attendant feelings of outrage and alienation are properly regarded as possible impacts of such development, as are any political reactions that ensue.

11. The next point is related. Communities may take projected developments to endanger something that may seem even vaguer and more general than fundamental values. They may refer to whatever it is as their "way of life," or they might use the slightly more esoteric term, "culture." At the heart of a culture or way of life are symbolically mediated and socially constructed conceptions that are realized, maintained, and restruc-

tured through customary action. We have already noted that among certain Native Americans, such customary actions involve subsistence activities. Hunting and fishing are, thus, among the main means by which Intuit, Aleut, and other indigenous cultures are kept alive, and perceived threats to them will therefore be bitterly resented and resisted. It need hardly be said that there is no valid way to assign a monetary value to a culture. Its destruction, Yupik insist, would be unmitigable.

Violations of a community's values, or threats to its way of life, must be understood to constitute, in and of themselves, serious impacts on that community. To elaborate an earlier suggestion, the less amenable to metrical representation and the vaguer the threatened value, the stronger the response to its violation, for in such instances the defenders understand themselves to be acting on general principle rather than out of personal interest.

12. It follows that threats to a community's conceptions of its rights, to its conceptions of justice and equity, to its general way of life, or to its basic canons of reality often take precedence over material considerations in the formulation of action. Furthermore, actions so undertaken are likely to be more highly charged emotionally, more physical, and more aggressive than those undertaken in the service of economic or material advantage. The higher principles invoked in response to perceived threats to a way of life or its highly valued constituents seem to license, or even to sanctify, forms of action

that the actors themselves would in other circumstances condemn. We may recall here civil disobedience campaigns in the American south, and otherwise law-abiding citizens breaking laws in pro-choice versus pro-life confrontations. Even when, or especially when, such actions are by law criminal, they may be viewed by their partisans as legitimate or even heroic.

13. This account proposes that when a community's concerns are ignored by analysts and decision makers, the matters at issue change. The dominant issues become matters of high principle. When conflicts are escalated to the level of high principle, they are no longer objective disagreements resolvable by fact, logic, or even self-interest. Rather, in the principled mode an economic form of rationality is replaced by claims to virtue vouchsafed by self-sacrifice. Escalation into the principled mode is a risk of development activity.

14. An implication of the discussion so far is that whether a community's understanding of the world's nature, or whether its values concerning it, is "realistic" in terms of "objective" criteria established by putatively disinterested analysts, or whether the community's fears are, in the view of analysts or officials, fanciful is, in some degree, beside the point. Impacts and risks are, in considerable degree, to be understood relative to the affected community's definitions of reality. The concerns of local people must therefore be given full and respectful treatment because it is the environment as these people conceive it that, as far as they are

concerned, will be affected, and it is in terms of these understandings that the community responds to intrusions. Failure to treat local understandings seriously risks widespread citizen alienation and anger, political and legal action, and even threats of violence.

15. Note, however, the qualifications "in some degree" and "in considerable degree." It would be a serious error to suppose that risks and impacts are to be defined only in relation to the community's understandings, for many serious consequences may be unforeseen by those who will be exposed to them. It is the responsibility of those who prepare environmental impact statements not only to grant reality to the concerns of affected communities but also to bring to those communities' attention risks that they might not perceive.

16. It follows that impact studies themselves are not free of possible impacts. For an impact statement to ignore, dismiss, disqualify, underestimate, or, in the view of affected parties, misrepresent or represent inadequately their concerns is for the statement itself to provide evidence to those affected parties that they are being unjustly treated. It is both plausible and prudent to assume that the community will respond to perceptions of injustice in whatever ways are available and that they deem appropriate. Active responses can include emigrating (likely when strong opposition combines with the sense of powerlessness and failure of trust in the institutions responsible); voting those viewed as responsible out of office; or, even more aggressive, forming ad hoc organizations, demonstrating, or even committing sabotage.

That such overt actions fail to materialize should not be taken to indicate unambiguously that projected developments or environmental impact statements have elicited no responses, for responses can include cognitive and attitudinal effects expressing themselves in such stress-related phenomena as substance abuse, domestic violence, racial antagonism, and other forms of social pathology.

17. Among the most significant components of environmental impact statements, as far as affected communities are concerned, may well be estimates concerning the probability and magnitude of disasters. If, for example, the probability of oil spills is represented—rightly or wrongly—to be much lower than the common sense of a coastal community projects, or if their effects are, in the community's view, significantly underestimated, and if these projections cannot be plausibly justified, the trustworthiness of the institutions preparing the impact statement may be at risk. Distrust may be contagious, spreading from the specific agency preparing the statement—for example, the Minerals Management Service—to the department of which it is a part—in this case, Interior—or even to the federal government generally. Impact statements that do not win the credence of affected communities may thus put trust in government as a whole at risk. Undermining confidence in government and even questioning the legitimacy of government itself are thus possible risks of impact studies themselves.

18. The last point alluded to "affected communities," but full analytical isolation of "affected communities" is impossible if the term is understood to include all of those that take themselves to be in some way threatened and all who respond in some way. Communities in Alaska were most affected by the *Exxon Valdez* oil spill, but there were, and will continue to be, responses to the Alaskan events in communities distant from Alaska. Such nonlocal responses must be included in any serious and comprehensive account of impacts.

The responses of those distant from Prince William Sound have varied in ways that can be fully grasped only through empirical research, but it can be suggested that they have combined to produce a cognitive, social, political, cultural, and perhaps even economic environment increasingly hostile to OCS activity. To use a medical metaphor, the *Exxon Valdez* may have inoculated the society against OCS development, stimulating organizational, cultural, cognitive, and political antibodies against it. Subsequent spills could be regarded as booster shots. The antibody effect must be included among the possible impacts of OCS activity.

CONCLUSION

If modern science is based upon the objectivity of disinterested observers radically detached from the systems concerning which they seek to develop dispassionate theoretical understanding through replicable empirical procedures, then risk and impact analysis cannot qualify as modern science. Analysts are never radically separated from the systems they observe and, furthermore, those systems are composed of human subjects with cognitive capacities equal to, and local knowledge usually greater than, those of the analysts. As such, they are likely to respond to analyses in highly engaged ways. In sum, risk and impact analyses are themselves interventions in the systems they seek to understand. This does not necessarily impeach their validity, unless it impeaches the validity of virtually all sciences this side of extragalactic astronomy. (Particle physics, after all, has its Heisenberg principle.) Nor does it destroy the usefulness of such analyses, although their nature counsels humility and caution and requires openness to local understandings.

If risk and impact analysis does not qualify as a modern science, it does qualify for inclusion in what Stephen Toulmin has called "postmodern science,"[3] which, he argues, differs from modern science in returning observers to the systems from which modern science exiled them, and which is as concerned with praxis as theory. As such, it is legitimately interventionist, but as such it also eschews claims of value neutrality, for intervention, unless it is mere clumsy intrusion, is directed toward the achievement of some sort of state, condition, or goal. All of this further entails openness to the inside knowledge and understandings of subjects

3. Stephen Toulmin, *The Return to Cosmology: Post-Modern Science and Natural Theology* (Berkeley: University of California Press, 1982).

as well as to the objective outside knowledge of analysts.

The practice of postmodern science will not be easy, but it may be liberating. It may also be that the very characteristics of risk and impact analysis that make it dubious as modern science suit it admirably for leadership among postmodern sciences.

Public Values in Risk Research

By BARUCH FISCHHOFF

ABSTRACT: Risk research is a complex social enterprise, reflecting the beliefs and values of those closest to its creation. For public values to be expressed in risk research, the public needs the same access as those who conduct and directly sponsor that research. Providing that access requires more open research management and more responsive research methods.

Baruch Fischhoff is professor of social and decision sciences and of engineering and public policy at Carnegie Mellon University. He is a member of the Institute of Medicine of the National Academy of Sciences, past president of the Society for Judgment and Decision Making, and a fellow of the Society for Risk Analysis and of the American Psychological Association.

NOTE: The research summarized in this article was supported in part by the National Science Foundation and the Environmental Protection Agency. They are gratefully acknowledged. The opinions expressed are those of the author.

SCIENCE is often justified by its contribution to the common good. At times, that contribution is presented as a matter of faith. Society is said to be a better place for having this kind of activity in its midst, much as it benefits from having clerics say prayers on its behalf. For example, science may be valued for providing a haven for free inquiry, regardless of the topics it pursues and the results it produces. Science may also be valued for fostering a sense of wonder and a connection with issues beyond our mundane existence. In this view, science's contribution to society may be greatest when it addresses impractical and slowly resolved topics, like the origins of the universe and of our species within it.

Most science, though, is justified on more practical grounds. Scientists argue that their work helps other people improve their lot in life. These claims have been effective enough that most industrialized countries devote a significant portion of their gross domestic product to research, with most of these funds being tied to solving specific problems. In the United States, the federal research budget is some $70-80 billion, predominantly distributed by mission-oriented agencies.[1] Even more government support comes indirectly, through laws encouraging research, such as tax credits for industrial research, nonprofit status for universities, and patent and copyright protection for inventors.

Risk research is justified overwhelmingly by its practicality. The

1. National Research Council, *Criteria for Federal Research and Development* (Washington, DC: National Academy Press, 1995).

present volume shows that pure intellectual satisfaction can be derived from pondering mortality through this unusual lens. This taste is not widely shared, however. Moreover, pure risk science would be hard to support financially. Established disciplines often have dedicated funding streams—such as named National Science Foundation programs—allowing some freedom for curiosity-driven research. Newer disciplines typically secure funds by claiming to be useful. In their fund-raising, risk researchers promise to improve the estimation, evaluation, communication, and management of risks.

This article considers how values are expressed in the conduct and communication of risk research. It ends with a set of conditions that risk researchers should satisfy in order to secure public trust; these conditions are modeled on the conditions that researchers typically provide for their colleagues and sponsors. Achieving them will require both good research and good intentions.

VALUES IN RISK RESEARCH

Inevitably, a field is shaped by those who pay its bills. Researchers learn to focus on topics that interest their sponsors. Doing so need not threaten the integrity of research conducted within these constraints. Indeed, the sanctions of science make the outright manipulation of results rare. Nonetheless, sensitivity to sponsors may create more subtle pressures. For example, researchers might double-check uncomfortable results more rigorously than desired ones. They might be unwittingly influenced in the assumptions that they make about variables that are not examined in detail. They may learn to explain their work in terms that sponsors can understand, and to create work that sponsors care about hearing. Over time, any imbalance can be corrected, as the research is exposed to varied critiques. But that may take a while, especially when research is expensive. Risk researchers may be entirely impartial. However, producing balanced research requires a balanced set of pressures.

Direct consumers of research also have the power to judge its usefulness and then reward or punish researchers accordingly. Thus firms may reduce their support for university labs that fail to affect their bottom line. Government agencies may abandon research and development projects with particularly large cost or time overruns. Funders can issue requests for proposals and then solicit bids on favored topics. They can set reporting requirements, demand private briefings, and delay publication (for proprietary or procedural reasons). In all these ways, their values are deeply embedded in the research process.

Risk research bears some obvious stamps of its direct consumers. It was invented, somewhat independently, by various industries—for example, space, chemical, and nuclear—in order to manage their internal affairs by revealing the relative riskiness of alternative designs.[2] It acquired a public face when the need arose to demonstrate the safety of chosen de-

signs.[3] Naturally enough, the risk analysis seen by the public looked much as it always had, addressing the problems and speaking the language of industry. The needs and dispositions of those shaping its creation can be seen in such technical details as how risk analyses treat structural uncertainty and how they define "risk."[4]

Similar shaping processes affect calculations on the benefits side of the ledger. Many of these procedures were devised to guide resource allocations in institutions, such as the U.S. Army Corps of Engineers, for its water management projects. Analysts and theoreticians gradually identified and addressed limits to benefits assessment, such as the thorny problems of assigning market prices to unmarketed goods. At times, there have been imaginative breakthroughs. At other times, analysts have reconciled themselves to shaky conventions, allowing them to get on with the work but without a strong theoretical or empirical basis, as in the selection of discount rates or the treatment of equity issues.[5]

Not surprisingly, these techniques have often evoked skepticism, especially among audiences that were not involved in their creation. The cur-

2. Norman McCormick, *Risk Assessment* (New York: John Wiley, 1981).

3. Nuclear Regulatory Commission, *Reactor Safety Study* (Washington, DC: Nuclear Regulatory Commission, 1975).

4. Baruch Fischhoff et al., *Acceptable Risk* (New York: Cambridge University Press, 1981); Silvio Funtowicz and Jeremy Ravetz, *Uncertainty and Quality in Science* (Dordrecht: Kluwer, 1990).

5. Judith Bentkover, Vincent Covello, and Jeryl Mumpower, eds., *Benefits Assessment: The State of the Art* (Dordrecht: Reidel, 1985); John Campen, *Benefit, Cost and Beyond* (Boston: South End Press, 1988).

rent U.S. debate over risk analysis, risk ranking, and risk comparison is the latest expression of the deep controversy surrounding this enterprise.[6] Opponents are offended, to varying degrees, by risk research's producers, promoters, obscurity, and rhetoric. Some distrust the very idea of analyzing risk.[7]

Much of this opposition reflects a superficial understanding of risk science—as would be expected with procedures that are seldom explained in any detail.[8] Indeed, even the supporters of risk research often seem ill informed, as reflected in the clumsy formulation of recent bills promoting risk assessment.[9] Some opposition, however, is very well informed. Indi-

viduals (and institutions) who are deeply affected by the outcomes of risk research often probe it deeply. Often, they do not like what they find—perhaps because they have sought problems that would justify rejecting analyses that produced troublesome outcomes. Often, the analysts themselves will become targets of suspicion: what kind of people could produce such untrustworthy results? Such personal enmity can be much harder to take than an assault on the work alone.

VALUES IN RISK COMMUNICATIONS

How we speak reflects what we think of ourselves and the targets of our words. Insensitivity to public values can be found in attempts to communicate with the public about risks.

Communication to the public

Most risk messages are just some experts' ad hoc determination of what people ought to know. As a result, communications waste recipients' time and trust, by saying things that are already known or are not worth knowing.[10] Very few messages are evaluated empirically prior to dissemination, again wasting recipients' time and communicators' credibility.

6. Stephen Breyer, *Breaking the Vicious Circle: Toward Effective Regulation* (Cambridge, MA: Harvard University Press, 1993); Adam M. Finkel, "A Second Opinion on Environmental Misdiagnosis," *New York University Environmental Law Journal*, 3:295-381 (1994); Donald T. Hornstein, "Reclaiming Environmental Law," *Columbia Law Review*, 92:562-98 (1992).

7. Maya Fischhoff, *Ordinary Housewives: Women Activists in the Grassroots Toxics Movement* (Cambridge, MA: Harvard University, Department of Social Studies, 1993); *Journal of Pesticide Reform*, 4(2) (1994); William Leiss and Christina Chociolko, *Risk and Responsibility* (Montreal and Kingston: McGill and Queen's University Press, 1994); Mary O'Brien, *A Proposal to Address, Rather than Rank, Environmental Problems* (Missoula: University of Montana, Institute for Environmental Studies, 1993).

8. K. Jenni, M. Merkhofer, and C. Williams, "The Rise and Fall of a Risk-Based Priority System," *Risk Analysis*, 15:397-410 (1995); National Research Council, *Improving Risk Communication* (Washington, DC: National Academy Press, 1989).

9. Some cynics claim that incoherence is the goal of these bills, whose proponents hope to gum up the works, slowing the pace of government action.

10. Ann Bostrom, Baruch Fischhoff, and M. Granger Morgan, "Characterizing Mental Models of Hazardous Processes," *Journal of Social Issues*, 48:85-100 (1992); Caren Chess, Karen Salomone, and B. J. Hance, "Managing Risk Communication Agency," *Risk Analysis*, 15:128-36 (1995); Baruch Fischhoff, "Giving Advice: Decision Theory Perspectives on Sexual Assault," *American Psychologist*, 47:577-88 (1992).

There are benign explanations for this sloppiness: time was short; no one on staff knew how to do it better; a committee approved the communication, undermining its coherence. These excuses imply that the task was not important enough to summon the resources needed to do it right.

A less benign explanation is that only experts' opinions matter. Who has not purchased a heavily marketed product, only to find its instructions incomprehensible? How much more objectionable it becomes when the garbled messages deal with matters of life and death. Insult is added to confusion when laypeople are blamed for these communication failures. Injury is added to insult when misunderstanding keeps workers or consumers or patients from coping with the risks in their lives. Failing to ensure that people can protect themselves would express another value of risk science.[11]

Communication from the public

For public values to inform risk management, policymakers and scientists need to know what those values are. Unfortunately, the procedures for gathering information from citizens often are as flawed as the procedures for providing them information.[12] One conventional approach is the public opinion poll. Unfortunately, polls cannot convey the detailed information that citizens need in order to formulate stable, thoughtful, informed opinions. Polls might obtain snapshots of current beliefs; however, those beliefs should have little value for policymakers who are contemplating long-term policies or anticipating the outcome of an intensive public debate. The typical poll (or polling firm) is ill suited to measuring or creating understanding. As a matter of principle and economics, pollsters typically refrain from providing information, correcting misconceptions, or allowing time to think. They prefer structured questions, which are easily administered and readily analyzed. As a result, they elicit public views on restricted topics with few nuances. Doing so clearly saves money, relative to more labor-intensive procedures. Some pollsters argue that more detailed explication and probing would be unethical, violating the norm of nonreactive measurement—by changing respondents as a result of the elicitation procedure.

Being satisfied with a narrow communication channel reflects a value about the public's role in risk management. Namely, the public should speak when spoken to, by responding quickly to the specific topics on policymakers' minds. Thus the public has a role in choosing policies but not in designing their content—and no right to reflect before answering.

A second conventional approach is the focus group, in which a moderator guides some citizens in discussing an issue. Although these discussions

11. James Reason, *Human Error* (New York: Cambridge University Press, 1990).

12. Robin Gregory, Thomas C. Brown, and Jack L. Knetsch, "Valuing Risks to the Environment," this issue of *The Annals* of the American Academy of Political and Social Science; J. Burgess and C. M. Harrison, "People, Parks, and the Urban Green," *Urban Studies*, 25:455-73 (1988); Baruch Fischhoff, "Value Elicitation: Is There Anything in There?" *American Psychologist*, 46:835-47 (1991).

might allow participants to ask clarifying questions, most moderators are generalists, without the substantive expertise needed to provide answers. These moderators might even be proud of their ignorance, because it keeps them from influencing the discussion. Focus group interactions are typically summarized impressionistically. Indeed, the vendors of focus groups may have an incentive to mystify their synthetic abilities, contrary to the scientific norm of valuing results that different scientists could and would interpret similarly.[13]

Every measurement procedure has its limits. Often a set of complementary flawed methods is needed. Opinion polls, where respondents shoot from the hip, might predict whether a proposed policy will even get a hearing. More intensive interactions, patterned after a citizens' jury, might capture what people really think, when they are given time (and help) to think—thereby putting them on more equal footing with the experts and their immediate clients.[14] The choice of elicitation method expresses a value regarding citizens' role in the political process. That happens even if risk managers know little about the choices that they are making. Not investing enough to know about these methods expresses a low value regarding the public and its views.[15] Placing undue faith in clumsy communications incurs the direct costs of offending and confusing the public, as well as the opportunity costs of not doing something better.

CONDITIONS FOR RECOGNIZING
PUBLIC VALUES

The public lacks the direct access to risk science that is available to the institutions that fund it. Even complaining about incomprehensible messages requires a struggle. These gaps often become apparent first in rapidly escalating confrontations: a risk unexpectedly attracts attention, forcing technical experts to explain their work to a suspicious public.[16] These specialists may be ill prepared not only for explaining the specific risk but for communicating at all. Leiss describes three stages in the development of risk communication as a field, as it gradually recognized complications like those discussed here.[17] A similar developmental sequence often occurs in individuals and institutions, as they come to grips with having a risk problem to explain. Table 1 offers an eight-stage version of this process, expressed in terms of the signal beliefs at each stage.

The challenge to risk managers is to hasten this learning process, especially when trial and error can inflict lasting scars—on the public, the risk specialists, and the relations between them. It is hard to accelerate

13. Robert K. Merton, "The Focussed Interview and Focus Groups," *Public Opinion Quarterly*, 51:541-57 (1987).

14. John Dryzek, *Rational Ecology* (Boston: Basil Blackwell, 1987).

15. Timothy Earle and George Cvetkovich, *Social Trust: Toward a Cosmopolitan Society* (Westport, CT: Praeger, 1995).

16. Roger E. Kasperson and Jeanne X. Kasperson, "The Social Amplification and Attenuation of Risk," this issue of *The Annals* of the American Academy of Political and Social Science.

17. William Leiss, "Three Phases in the Evolution of Risk Communication Practice," this issue of *The Annals* of the American Academy of Political and Social Science.

TABLE 1
DEVELOPMENTAL STAGES IN RISK MANAGEMENT

- All we have to do is get the numbers right.
- All we have to do is tell them the numbers.
- All we have to do is explain what we mean by the numbers.
- All we have to do is show them that they've accepted similar risks in the past.
- All we have to do is show them that it's a good deal for them.
- All we have to do is treat them nice.
- All we have to do is make them partners.
- All of the above.

SOURCE: Baruch Fischhoff, "Risk Perception and Communication Unplugged: Twenty Years of Process," *Risk Analysis*, 15:137-45 (1995).

developmental processes simply by exhorting people to grow up. Lest time just take its course, the norms of grown-up behavior must be explicated. That detail is especially needed when the prescribed behavior is counterintuitive, for those hoping to short-circuit the learning process.

Table 2 offers one specification of the conditions that risk specialists must meet in order to secure public trust. It is patterned after the conditions that experts must meet in order to secure one another's trust. It includes both scientific and social conditions, concerning, respectively, the content and the conduct of science. In each domain, there are conditions associated with both each specific case and the general process of analyzing risk issues.

Thus, in order to trust a specific risk (or benefit) analysis, a specialist would want to understand the models being used, review the parameter estimates, request appropriate sensitivity analyses, and double-check results. Professionals can exercise such due diligence because they know the historical process that led to the selection of currently favored methods, the basic science underlying the analysis, the (often unwritten) auxiliary assumptions that the analysis incorporates, and the philosophy of using models to manage risks.

To be fully comfortable with an analysis, experts typically need more than just its written artifacts. Science is a social institution. It helps to know the analysts, especially when one has a continuing relationship with them, encouraging their candor. It helps to have one's concerns explicitly recognized in the analysis, to be rewarded for participation, and to be treated respectfully. More generally, it helps to feel like part of the enterprise, to know the players, to influence the regulatory process that specifies the terms of analysis, and to have a long-term interest in the process. Finally, it helps to feel part of the analytical community, comfortable with its accommodation to the inevitable limit of analysis.

Why should the public expect less from the experts than the experts do from one another?

ACHIEVING THE CONDITIONS
FOR PUBLIC TRUST

These conditions are achieved routinely in any healthy, functioning sci-

TABLE 2
CONDITIONS FOR PUBLIC TRUST IN RISK ANALYSES

Scientific Conditions
Immediate
- Familiarity with specific models
- Familiarity with specific inputs
- Access to sensitivity analyses
- Ability to double-check

Ambient
- Familiarity with historical development
- Familiarity with underlying science
- Familiarity with auxiliary assumptions
- Familiarity with analytical perspectives

Social Conditions
Immediate
- Familiarity with analysts
- Recognition by analysis
- Reward for participation
- Respectful treatment

Ambient
- Familiarity with analytical community
- Influence on regulatory process
- Long-term involvement
- Accommodation with process

entific or technical community. Members have relatively similar training and outlooks. Their behavior holds few surprises. They extend one another professional courtesy. Their actions show how they value one another, as individuals, even as they fiercely dispute specific results and compete for particular contracts. The institutions that fund risk research typically have technical staffs to monitor fulfillment of the scientific conditions for trust; their financial leverage assures fulfillment of the social conditions.

Enterprising members of the general public can—and often do—learn enough to see whether risk research meets the scientific conditions for trust. Alternatively, they may hire consultants to provide that assurance. The very fact of the struggle, however, will undermine the social conditions for trust. Outsiders seldom have the resources or the access needed to conduct fully satisfactory reviews or independent studies. What they cannot verify they may distrust. Thus lacking the social conditions for trust may magnify the importance of gaps in the science. What should one think when the evidence is buried in mountainous computer codes or laboratory protocols?

Risk research conducted for or by government agencies, or in response to government edicts, is ostensibly done in the public's name. Nonetheless, its connection with the public's values is usually tenuous. As noted, the communication channels between government and public are ill suited to sharing complex messages about risk issues. As a result, government actions are only vaguely related to public concerns. For example, the United States has institutes bearing the names of most major diseases. Inquiring citizens can, therefore, be told that "we are working on it," for a great many "its." Yet those institutes historically paid little attention to women's health risks. Can one claim that this is what the public wanted? Pundits today revel in blaming the public for misplaced risk priorities. Yet those priorities primarily reflect the machinations of politicians, bureaucrats, interest groups, and pundits, speaking for the public. Indeed, the public might be aghast at much of what is done in its name.

Providing sustained public access to risk research will require changes in how research is conducted, how public input is solicited, and how results are reported.

How risk research
is conducted

Research driven by public values would focus on the most important aspects of those problems that most concern the public: problems where scientific progress is a possibility. Identifying those topics requires explicitly characterizing the public's problems and analyzing the opportunities for scientific progress.[18] Letting public values direct research might change which topics are studied, how projects are formulated, and how results are summarized. There would be less place for vague claims of usefulness and greater demand for candid expressions of uncertainty.

How public
input is solicited

In order to address public concerns, risk scientists need to know what those concerns are. That requires systematic measurement of public values, in a way that provides citizens with a balanced overview of the issues, and time to think about them. In order to express their views in a rich and nuanced fashion, citizens need a broad communication channel. Something like these conditions is created by the Environmental Protection Agency in the citizens' commissions that it has convened for states and regions, in order to rank the risks that these communities face.[19] Indeed, citizens' commissions might be a better guiding metaphor for assessing public values than the opinion poll, which creates nothing like these conditions.[20]

How research
results are reported

Once the research has been completed, it must be summarized appropriately. Citizens need to know what the results mean, not only in the aggregate but also for them personally.[21] They need to understand the quality of the science underlying the analyses and not just receive best guesses at expected risks and benefits. The presentation of results must be evaluated empirically in order to ensure that it is understood as intended. The chances of that happening are increased by research identifying the mental models that recipients bring with them to interpreting the messages.

18. National Research Council, *Priority Mechanisms for Toxic Chemicals* (Washington, DC: National Research Council, 1983).

19. Environmental Protection Agency, *Comparing Risks and Setting Environmental Priorities* (Washington, DC: Environmental Protection Agency, 1993).

20. B. Fischhoff, "What Do Psychologists Want?" in *Determining the Value of Non-Marketed Goods*, ed. N. Schwarz and R. Kopp (New York: Plenum, forthcoming).

21. B. Fischhoff, "Acceptable Risk: A Conceptual Proposal," *Risk*, 5:1-18 (1994), which argues that a policy is acceptable if it produces acceptable risk-benefit trade-offs for everyone affected by it. See Jon Merz et al., "Decision-Analytic Approach to Developing Standards of Disclosure for Medical Informed Consent," *Journal of Toxics and Liability*, 15:191-215 (1993).

The task ahead

Addressing these challenges requires political work, legitimating concern for the public's values, and scientific work, creating credible procedures for incorporating those values. Even if we would like to give risk research away, it is not clear that we know quite how.

Three Phases in the Evolution of Risk Communication Practice

By WILLIAM LEISS

ABSTRACT: Effective communication between interested parties is widely held to be a vital element in health and environmental risk management decision making. There have been three phases in the evolution of risk communication during the last twenty years. Phase I emphasized risk: in a modern industrial economy, we must have the capacity to manage risks at a very exacting level of detail. Phase II stresses communication: statements about risk situations are best regarded as acts of persuasive communication, that is, as messages intended to persuade a listener of the correctness of a point of view. Now, in Phase III, public and private sector institutions increasingly are recognizing their responsibility to deal adequately with both dimensions and to carry out sound risk communication as a matter of good business practice.

William Leiss is a fellow of the Royal Society of Canada and holds the Eco-Research Chair in Environmental Policy at Queen's University, Kingston, Ontario. He chairs the Research Policy Committee of the Canadian Global Change Program. He has held academic appointments in political science, sociology, environmental studies, and communication. He is author, collaborator, or editor for nine books and numerous articles. He works extensively with industry and government in the area of risk communication, risk management, public consultation, and consensus building.

RISK communication may be defined as the flow of information and risk evaluations back and forth between academic experts, regulatory practitioners, interest groups, and the general public. The sharp disagreements that can occur between members of these constituencies over the best ways to assess or manage risks sometimes are based on disagreements over principles or approaches, sometimes on differences in the information base available to various parties, and sometimes on a failure to consider carefully each other's position.

In such situations, the risk communication process itself often becomes an explicit focus of controversy. Charges of media bias or sensationalism, of distorted or selective use of information by advocates, of hidden agendas or irrational standpoints, and of the inability or unwillingness of regulatory agencies to communicate vital information in a language the public can understand are common. Such charges are traded frequently at public hearings, judicial proceedings, and conferences, expressing the general and pervasive sense of mistrust felt by many participants toward others. Of course, there are also genuine differences in principle, outlook, and values in the citizenry; disagreements will persist even with the most complete and dispassionate knowledge of others' views. Perhaps the most contentious area of all is that of risk-benefit trade-offs, especially where different types (or distributions) of risk are at stake, or where there is no consensus on acceptable risk (thus preventing trade-offs).

Risk communication research, which seeks to clarify our understanding of the processes just described briefly, is the newest of the four risk subfields; the phrase itself appears to have been coined during 1984.[1] It arose out of the problems being investigated in the risk perception area, which since its inception had concentrated on the disparities between risks as assessed by experts, on the one hand, and as understood by the general public, on the other. Risk perception studies have been concerned with explaining those disparities. The interest in risk communication, however, has from the beginning had a practical intent: given that these disparities exist, are deeply entrenched in human awareness, and form the basis of strongly held attitudes and behavior, how can we improve the quality of the dialogue about risk across the gap that separates experts from the general public? Second, how can we apply this improved dialogue to achieving a higher degree of social consensus on the inherently controversial aspects of managing environmental and health risks?

In seeking to answer these questions, risk communication researchers have married their knowledge about risk assessment and management issues with the approaches used in the field of modern communication the-

1. This is the year of the earliest uses of the phrase "risk communication," according to the references listed in Bernd Rohrmann, Peter M. Wiedemann, and Helmut U. Stegelmann, eds., *Risk Communication: An Interdisciplinary Bibliography*, 4th ed. (Jülich, Germany: Research Center Jülich GmbH, 1990), pp. 26, 56, 111.

ory and practice. Statements about risk by various parties are treated as messages intended to persuade others to believe or do something; like all such messages circulating among persons, their effectiveness as acts of persuasive communication can be evaluated according to well-established criteria: whether they gain attention, are understood, are believed, are acted on, and so forth. This paradigm of communication research has become very well established since 1945 and has an enormous published literature to support it.[2] Risk communication research has been able to draw on this resource and adapt its findings to the particular concerns of the risk studies area, and as a result it has made substantial progress in a relatively short time.

THE THREE PHASES

There are three phases in the evolution of risk communication, occurring over the past 15 years, and each of the later stages has emerged in response to the earlier ones. The earlier ones do not become irrelevant; rather, they are incorporated into the later phases, for each has contributed something of lasting value to the present. Phase I (about 1975-84) stressed the quantitative expressions of risk estimates and argued that priorities for regulatory actions and public concerns should be established on the basis of comparative risk estimates.[3] Phase II (about 1985-

94) stressed the characteristics of successful communications: source credibility, message clarity, effective use of channels, and, above all, a focus on the needs and perceived reality of the audiences.[4] Around 1995, we entered a new phase, which will be described briefly later.

One of the leading authorities in the risk studies field, Baruch Fischhoff of Carnegie-Mellon University, recently presented a somewhat different account of the developmental stages in risk communication. He used colloquial expressions to identify seven such stages:

1. "All we have to do is get the numbers right."
2. "All we have to do is tell them the numbers."
3. "All we have to do is explain what we mean by the numbers."
4. "All we have to do is show them that they've accepted similar risks in the past."
5. "All we have to do is to show them that it's a good deal for them."
6. "All we have to do is treat them nice."
7. "All we have to do is make them partners."[5]

---

cluding W. W. Lowrance, *Of Acceptable Risk* (Los Altos, CA: Wm. Kaufmann, 1976); William D. Rowe, *An Anatomy of Risk* (New York: John Wiley, 1977). Any such separation of a dynamic process into phases and dates is somewhat arbitrary; the activities in each phase overlap.

4. The seminal work is Vincent T. Covello, Detlof von Winterfeldt, and Paul Slovic, *Risk Communication: Background Report for the National Conference on Risk Communication* (Washington, DC: Conservation Foundation, 1986).

5. Baruch Fischhoff, "Risk Perception and Communication Unplugged: Twenty Years of Process," *Risk Analysis*, 15:137-45 (1995).

2. William Leiss, "On the Vitality of Our Discipline: New Applications of Communications Theory," *Canadian Journal of Communication*, 16:291-305 (1991).

3. The wide purview now enjoyed by the risk approach stems from a few sources, in-

The first two correspond roughly to my Phase I, the next four to my Phase II, and the last one to the current phase. Any such typology is arbitrary. The one I have devised highlights the radical nature of the transition from Phase I to Phase II, and in my view, the field of risk communication as we know it today was formed by this wrenching transition.

Phase I (1975-84)

The enduring strength of what was accomplished in Phase I is captured in the following statement: in order to function sensibly in a world of expanding opportunity, we must have the capacity to assess and manage risks at a very exacting level of detail; the scientific approach to risk management offers us an imperfect but indispensable tool for doing so. Although risk is conventionally understood as "exposure to the chance of loss," we derive enormous benefits from judicious risk-taking behavior, so long as we are clever enough to know where to draw the line. For example, industrial chemicals are the basis of most consumer goods today, but all of them are also dangerous in certain doses; we have to know what the doses are that are likely to produce adverse effects on human health and the environment, and we must have institutional mechanisms in place to ensure that we do not exceed those doses.

Some serious weaknesses emerged in this phase, the worst of which could be labeled the "arrogance of technical expertise." Faced with public opposition to the results of risk-based decision making, many experts responded with open contempt toward the public perception of risk.[6] For them, perceived risk is correlated with false understanding and is further contrasted with real risk, which is allegedly an objective—that is, "true"—account of reality. Fortunately, one encounters this invidious distinction less and less now, since there is a greater appreciation of the errors in judgment that experts are prone to making.[7] Partly as a result of the arrogance of expertise, there exists on the part of the public a profound distrust of experts and the institutions they represent, which weakens the force of the quite sensible contributions that technical experts can make to the public discourse on risk taking. Another weakness is that critical data gaps and ever changing scientific research results are common in all significant risk management areas; the uncertainties introduced thereby produce legitimate concerns when yes/no decisions must be made.

The underlying message of permanent value in Phase I is that, for individuals as well as societies, managing opportunities and dangers on the basis of comparative risk information is an inescapable duty of intelligent life. However, this message could not be communicated effec-

6. See, for example, Ernest Siddall and Carl R. Bennett, "A People-Centered Concept of Society-Wide Risk Management," in *Environmental Health Risks: Assessment and Management*, ed. R. Stephen McColl (Waterloo, ON: University of Waterloo Press, 1987), p. 272.

7. A good summary of the errors in judgment to which experts are prone is National Research Council, *Improving Risk Communication* (Washington, DC: National Academy Press, 1989), pp. 44-47.

tively to a wide range of public audiences, partly because its authors were often so openly contemptuous of the fundamental beliefs about risk taking that were held by the very audiences whom they were addressing.

Phase II (1985-94)

The radical break that defines the transition from Phase I to Phase II was the realization that statements about risk situations ought to be regarded as acts of persuasive communication, that is, as messages intended to persuade a listener of the correctness of a point of view.[8] Guidance for this new approach was found in the history of twentieth-century marketing communications, which had demonstrated—first in commercial advertising, then more broadly— the effectiveness of a strategy that takes into account two key factors: the characteristics of the audience itself, and the intrinsic legitimacy of the audience's perception of the situation. The coinage of good communication is trust in the message source ("Will you believe me when I tell you something?"), and this is the underpinning for credibility, which is a perception of the intrinsic honesty of the whole process.

The great strength of this new approach was that the formulae of good communication practices adapted

from modern marketing had been tested and refined in minute detail over a long period and, for some purposes at least, were known to be highly successful. But there proved to be severe difficulties in adapting this marketing communication paradigm to risk issues. Slovic and MacGregor have diagnosed the main problem well:

Although attention to communication can prevent blunders that exacerbate conflict, there is rather little evidence that risk communication has made any significant contribution to reducing the gap between technical risk assessments and public perceptions or to facilitating decisions about nuclear waste or any other major sources of risk conflict. The limited effectiveness of risk communication efforts can be attributed to the lack of trust.[9]

The paradigm of persuasion in the marketing communication approach had identified a broad range of techniques for enhancing trust and credibility for messages. The early studies on propaganda already had recognized, however, that too strong a focus on the persuasive techniques themselves—especially those that seek to manipulate audiences' emotions—is potentially dangerous, for it could result in any rational content in the message being subordinated or even dissolved by those excessively clever techniques. In the more prosaic world of risk issues, therefore, emotive techniques of effective persuasive communication—that is, techniques for convincing that audience that a particular person is a

8. Another way of putting this point is to say that "risk is a construct," that is, an understanding of a risk-type situation that is related to the situation of each participant. See Bayerische Rück, ed., *Risk Is a Construct* (Munich: Knesebeck, 1993). This transition represents a complete change of emphasis within the components of the phrase "risk communication": in Phase I, the emphasis is on the adjective; in Phase II, on the noun.

9. Paul Slovic and Donald J. MacGregor, "The Social Context of Risk Communication" (Paper, Decision Research, Eugene, OR, 5 May 1994), p. 17.

credible spokesperson on risk issues—could take precedence over the informational content of the risk message itself.[10]

The underlying message of permanent value in Phase II may be stated as follows: there is an obligation on the part of major institutional actors in society to communicate effectively about risks, not by simply touting the superiority of their own technical risk assessments but, rather, by making an honest effort to understand the bases of public risk perceptions and by experimenting with ways of constructing a reasoned dialogue around different stakeholder assessments of risk situations.[11] The residual weakness here is that trust is often far too low for these experiments to succeed.

Phase III (current)

Phase III starts with the recognition that that lack of trust is pervasive in risk issues and that, because of this, risk communication practice must move away from a focus on purely instrumental techniques of persuasive communication. Phase III is characterized by an emphasis on social context, that is, on the social interrelations between the players in the game of risk management.[12] It is

10. In this period, institutional risk managers (government and industry) were often told that up to 75 percent of message content—as received by audiences—was based on the nonverbal dimensions of the message delivery format itself: body posture, hand gestures, style of dress, facial expression, and so forth.

11. See William Leiss, " 'Down and Dirty': The Use and Abuse of Public Trust in Risk Communication," Risk Analysis 15:685-92 (1995).

12. The best guide is Slovic and MacGregor, "Social Context of Risk Communication."

based on the presumption that, despite the controversial nature of many risk management issues, there are forces at work also that favor consensus building, meaningful stakeholder interaction, and acceptance of reasonable government regulatory frameworks. Should those forces turn out to be relatively weak, both public sector fiscal constraint and the current delegitimization of government may leave the field of risk management exposed to wide-open confrontation between stakeholder interests.

As noted earlier, Phase II remained incomplete because the key ingredient of successful persuasive communication—trust—cannot be manufactured by the use of techniques alone, no matter how artful the practitioners are. A working hypothesis is that trust in institutional risk actors (governments and industry) can accumulate, slowly, through the commitments by those institutions—as demonstrated by deeds, not words—to carry out responsible risk communication and, furthermore, to do so consistently, as a matter of daily practice over the long term, not just in response to crisis events. At the moment, there is no code of good practice in this area that might provide some benchmarks for determining what is and what is not responsible risk communication, although I suspect that events during Phase III will lead in that direction. For now, we will have to make do with case study examples, two of which follow in the concluding section.

Thus the underlying message of permanent value in Phase III may be stated as follows: a demonstrated commitment to responsible risk communication by major organizational actors can put pressure on all players in risk management to act responsibly.

PHASE III CASE STUDIES

A typical Phase III case involves a company that has a sensitive issue, as well as one or more documents in highly technical language, that must be discussed with nonexpert stakeholders (employees, community associations).[13] The two cases that will be identified here occurred in Canada during 1995. Responsible risk communication practice suggests that it is unacceptable to simply distribute the relevant document or documents to the public with a cover note saying, "Here it is; you figure out what it's supposed to mean to you." The risk communication challenge takes this form: the documents provide the information, but what is the message?

Case study 1: Dow Chemical Canada Inc., report on dioxin emissions from vinyl plant stacks

Dow Chemical Canada voluntarily took responsibility to develop, in cooperation with government agencies, a protocol to measure dioxin emissions from the stacks at its vinyl plant in Fort Saskatchewan, Alberta. Then the company commissioned an independent, university-based expert group to do an exposure assessment for areas within a certain radius of the plant. The expert group's report contains various figures for "incremental" additions to "background" dioxin levels, with the estimated human intakes expressed as picograms per kilogram of body weight per day (the relevant Canadian guideline is 10 pg/kg/d).[14]

Prior to communicating publicly about this exposure assessment, the company undertook a series of internal meetings to discuss the most effective way of communicating this information to the community. All of the following statements, as well as many variants that were considered, had to pass a "threshold criterion," namely, each one had to be believed to be a factually truthful statement by everyone who participated in these exercises. With this criterion in place, and recognizing the considerable challenge in the technical description of exposure assessment contained in the report, the objective of the company's "key messages" was to convey its own understanding of the "bottom-line" conclusions that it contained. The first two statements in the following list were selected as the bases for framing the communication message.

"The [Institute for Risk Research] Report results show that

— "dioxin emissions from our vinyl plant do not add significantly to the existing 'background exposure' level for dioxins";

13. The only published case study of this type of which I am aware is Caron Chess et al., "The Organizational Links Between Risk Communication and Risk Management: The Case of Sybron Chemicals, Inc.," *Risk Analysis*, 12:431-38 (1992).

14. John Hicks and Stephen McColl, "Final Report: Exposure Assessment of Airborne Dioxins and Furans Emitted from the EDC/VCM Facility at the Dow Chemical Canada Fort Saskatchewan Site" (Report, Institute for Risk Research, University of Waterloo, ON, 31 Mar. 1995).

— "all together, dioxin levels at and nearby the plant site are well within the current Health Canada guidelines";

— "the incremental contribution to background levels from the vinyl plant is exceedingly small";

— "the incremental contribution . . . is insignificant";

— "the incremental contribution . . . is very small, that is, less than ___% of background levels and ___% of the Health Canada guideline";[15]

— "in assessing total human exposure to dioxins, an insignificant portion is attributable to the emissions from Dow sources";

— "current background levels of dioxins in Fort Saskatchewan, and virtually everywhere in North America, are known to be about 3.2 pg/kg/day. The vinyl plant stacks at the Dow site add about ___% additional exposure to the background level. All together, these numbers are still well below the current Health Canada guideline of 10 pg/kg/day."

It is important to note as well that the formulation of these key messages, considered as an exercise in responsible risk communication, occurred in the context of a broader risk communication strategy. This broader strategy included, first and foremost, the decision to commission an independent group to undertake the study, which, of course, also entailed making it public in exactly the

form in which it was written. Second, the company undertook to bring the study's principal author to a meeting of its Citizen Advisory Panel in Fort Saskatchewan, where a face-to-face discussion of the report's findings could take place.

Case study 2: CXY Chemicals (North Vancouver plant), worst-case scenario at a chlorine plant located in an urban area

A quantitative risk assessment (QRA) of the public safety risk associated with the plant was undertaken by an independent consulting firm. The QRA report concluded that the worst case was a possible breach of all of the plant's pressurized storage tanks, containing a maximum total of 1500 tonnes of chlorine, as a result of a severe earthquake (a 1-in-475-year event); a second scenario assumed the possibility of a much reduced chlorine inventory. Air movement (wind speed and direction) at the site was a prime factor in the "risk contours" that were developed in the QRA; the contours are expressed as elongated circles showing varying probabilities of fatalities as a result of the hypothesized event.[16] The results showed that, under conditions of operation prevailing at the time of the study, the plant would not meet criteria established by the Major Industrial Accidents Council of Canada (MIACC)

---

15. The actual percentages depend on which section of the Institute for Risk Research report is being referred to.

16. Ertugrul Alp et al., "CanadianOxy North Vancouver Plant: Quantitative Assessment of Safety Risks" (Report, Bovar–Concord Environmental, Downsview, Ontario, Aug. 1994). CanadianOxy changed its name to CXY Chemicals in 1995.

for acceptable risk for land uses in urban areas.[17]

Prior to communicating publicly about the QRA report, the company undertook a series of internal meetings, evaluating a variety of options, in order to choose how to respond to its findings and to formulate the company's "key messages" at the time when the QRA report would be publicly released. A particularly difficult challenge was in choosing a method for the communication process about the QRA methodology itself, with the need to explain how such a scenario is constructed, including the use of worst-case assumptions for every relevant risk parameter, without regard to probability of occurrence.[18] However successful this communication effort might hope to be, though, the bottom line was that the current plant inventory, as a result of the study findings, would be perceived to be beyond a reasonable contemporary standard for acceptable risk. The company could only respond to this challenge by first making a series of management decisions to reduce the risks associated with plant operations.

The QRA report contained a number of recommendations for immediate risk reduction, in areas peripheral to the main plant operation itself; these were all implemented. The most significant recommenda-

17. MIACC criteria suggest a buffer zone around a risk source and various types of restricted land uses up to the point where the annual fatality risk is no greater than one in a million.

18. Cf. Wil Leplowski, "Chemical Companies Make Public Worst Case Accident Scenarios," *Chemical & Engineering News*, 20 June 1994, pp. 22-26.

tion, also implemented, was to change the plant's inventory management, so that no more than 300 tonnes of chlorine—one-fifth of the level assumed for the worst-case scenario—would be stored at any time. When the risk contours were recalculated using this operational directive, the plant operations fell within the MIACC criteria for acceptable risk.

The risk communication process associated with the QRA study then came to be viewed as an integral part of the risk management decision making that had led to significant risk reduction. The company had always been committed to commissioning an independent group to undertake the study, which, of course, also entailed making the study public. Second, the company has undertaken to hold face-to-face discussions on the original QRA report's findings with any individuals or local groups who request such a meeting. The company's key messages focus on what it regards as that part of the entire story that is of immediate and practical relevance to its employees and to residents of surrounding communities, namely, the company's ongoing commitment to risk management, which had resulted in significant risk reduction. Those key messages are that

— "CXY Chemicals has safely manufactured, stored and transported chlorine and related products from the North Vancouver plant for 37 years."
— "CXY Chemicals, as an industrial chemical manufacturer, is proud of its safety record and continues to take steps to reduce exposure to risk."

CONCLUSION AND EXPECTED FURTHER DEVELOPMENTS

The perspective taken in this article is that the specific features of each phase in the evolution of risk communication strategies set the challenges for the period to follow. The weaknesses in each phase drive this evolution further, and in this process we strive to preserve the strengths of each. The three-phase evolutionary development is summarized in Figure 1.

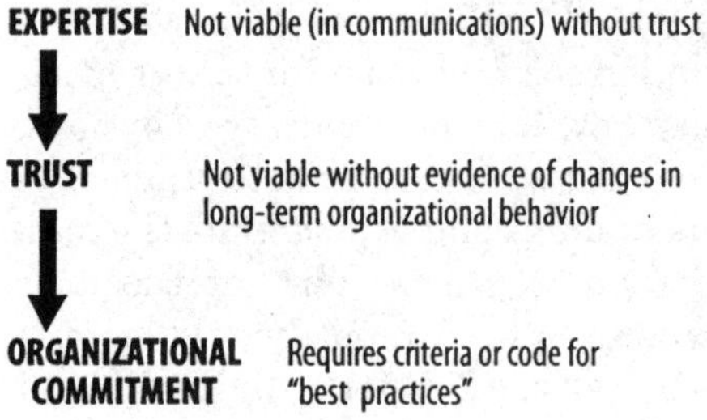

A good theoretical framework for Phase III may be found by extending the "strategic environmental audit" and "environmental responsibility" approach.[19] This could be operation-

19. Grant Ledgerwood et al., *Implementing an Environmental Audit: How to Gain Competitive Advantage Using Quality and Environmental Responsibility* (Homewood, IL: Irwin, 1994).

FIGURE 1
OVERVIEW OF THE THREE PHASES

EXPERTISE Not viable (in communications) without trust

↓

TRUST Not viable without evidence of changes in long-term organizational behavior

↓

ORGANIZATIONAL COMMITMENT Requires criteria or code for "best practices"

alized by the formulation of a "code of good risk communication practice," and compliance with the code could be verified through a "risk communication audit" designed to meet the test of public credibility. Some of the much-needed foundations of trust might be laid in this manner.

ANNALS, *AAPSS*, **545**, May 1996

The Social Amplification
and Attenuation of Risk

By ROGER E. KASPERSON and JEANNE X. KASPERSON

ABSTRACT: Risk is a complex phenomenon that involves both biophysical attributes and social dimensions. Existing assessment and management approaches often fail to consider risk in its full complexity and its social context. The concept of the social amplification and attenuation of risk provides an approach that recognizes that how social institutions and structures process a risk will shape greatly its effects upon society and the responses of management institutions and people. Examples of both amplification and attenuation are provided from recent risk experience.

Roger E. Kasperson is professor of government and geography and senior researcher at the George Perkins Marsh Institute at Clark University.

Jeanne X. Kasperson is research associate professor and research librarian at the George Perkins Marsh Institute at Clark University and senior research associate at the World Hunger Program at Brown University.

THE generation and disposition of risk are surely emblematic of modern society. The familiar scourges of famine, disease, and pestilence no longer dominate the risk experience, which, instead, now involves negotiating a new and perplexing array of global threats associated with modern armaments, chemicals and radiation often invisible to the senses, contaminants whose effects surface only after decades or generations, hazards created by peoples and technologies in distant parts of the globe, and harms arising from the flow and control of information. In what the German social theorist Ulrich Beck has termed the "risk society,"[1] the elimination of risk has stolen center stage from the elimination of scarcity, which preoccupied industrial and preindustrial society.

The risk dilemmas and debates of the past several decades have arisen primarily from the poor fit between, on the one hand, assessment and management approaches fashioned by societal experiences with the risk problems of an earlier time and, on the other hand, the ongoing complexification of risk. Assessment procedures derived from the public health, toxicity, and engineering studies that have dominated the management programs of governments and corporations illuminate one portion of the risk complex while concealing others. Methodologies capable of addressing risk in its full modern complexity, it is clear, await creation and adoption. The concept of the social amplification and attenuation of risk seeks to advance this search for more comprehensive and integrative approaches.

THE SOCIAL AMPLIFICATION AND ATTENUATION OF RISK

In 1988, researchers at Clark University and Decision Research collaborated on a new framework for risk analysis, which they termed the "social amplification of risk."[2] This framework takes as its starting point that risks are interactive phenomena that involve both the biophysical and social worlds. Risk involves threats of harm to people and nature but also to other things or ends that people value, such as community or political freedom. As the joint product of impacts on human health and nature and perturbations in social systems and value structures, the human experience of risk is simultaneously an experience of potential harm and the ways by which institutions and people process and interpret these threats. These interpretations generate rules by which society and its subgroups should select, order, and explain signals concerning the threats emanating from human activities. Risk analysis, then, requires an approach that is capable of illuminating risk in its full complexity, is sensitive to the social settings in which risk occurs, and also recognizes that social interactions may either amplify or attenuate the signals to society about the risk.

1. Ulrich Beck, *Risk Society: Toward a New Modernity* (Thousand Oaks, CA: Sage, 1992); idem, *Ecological Enlightenment: Essays on the Politics of the Risk Society* (Atlantic Highlands, NJ: Humanities Press, 1995).

2. Roger E. Kasperson et al., "The Social Amplification of Risk: A Conceptual Framework," *Risk Analysis*, 8(2):177-91 (June 1988).

FIGURE 1
SOCIAL AMPLIFICATION AND ATTENUATION OF RISK

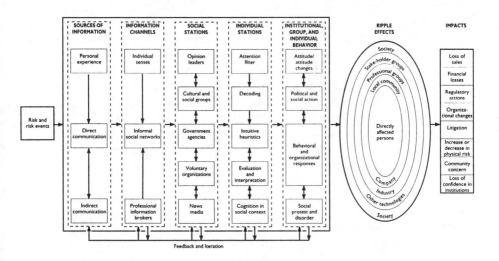

As conceived in this framework (see Figure 1), social amplification or attenuation may occur in several ways. It may begin with a risk event, such as an industrial accident or a chemical release. It may emerge from the release of a government report that provides new information on the causes of airplane crashes. Alternatively, a public interest group that continually monitors the experiential world for hazard information relevant to its political agenda may issue a press release on a new health threat associated with a consumer product. Since most of society learns about the parade of risks and risk events through information systems rather than through direct personal experience, risk communicators, and especially the mass media, are major agents, or what we term social stations, of risk amplification and attenuation. Particularly important in

shaping group and individual views of risk are the extent of media coverage; the volume of information provided; the ways in which the risk is framed; interpretations of messages concerning the risk; and the symbols, metaphors, and discourse enlisted in depicting and characterizing the risk.

The channels of communication are also important. Information about risk flows through multiple communication networks—the mass media represented by television and newsprint, the more specialized media of particular professions and interests (including, increasingly, Internet or the information superhighway), and, finally, the more informal personal networks of friends and neighbors on whom individuals continually rely as reference points for validating perceptions and contextualizing risk. Of these, most is known about the mass media, and particularly their multiple and often conflicting roles as entertainers, risk watchdogs, gatekeepers, and agenda setters. It is also apparent that the mass media cover risks selectively, according those that are rare or dramatic—that is, that have "story value"—disproportionate coverage while downplaying, or attenuating, more commonplace but often more serious risks, such as smoking or aspects of lifestyle. Viewed somewhat differently, risk and risk events compete for scarce space in the media's coverage, and the outcome of this competition is a major determinant of whether a risk will be socially amplified or attenuated in society's processing and disposition of the risk.

Social institutions and organizations also occupy a primary role in society's handling of risk for it is in these contexts that most risks are conceptualized, identified, measured, and managed.[3] In postindustrial democracies, large organizations—multinational corporations, business associations, and government agencies—largely set the contexts and terms of society's debate about risks. These organizations vary greatly in their goals for and commitments to risk management. The President's Commission on the Accident at Three Mile Island, for example, concluded that the "mind set" that permeated the institutions charged with managing nuclear safety represented the primary problem in ensuring the safety of the nuclear

technology used to produce electricity.[4] Freudenburg has implicated breakdowns in internal organizational communications as a contributor to the bureaucratic attenuation of risk, as occurred in the space shuttle *Challenger* accident, when the risk concerns of technical experts failed to reach top decision makers within the National Aeronautics and Space Administration.[5] Yet other studies[6] reveal that large corporations develop markedly different kinds of organizational cultures that shape powerfully their ability to identify and assess the risks of their activities and products and to determine if and how these risks will be communicated to other social institutions and publics. The behavior and interactions of institutions and organizations are major nodes of risk amplification and attenuation and require detailed attention in gauging how different societies respond to risk.

Risk issues are also important elements in the agenda of various social and political groups, such as nongovernmental organizations, with environmental and health concerns. The nature of these groups figures in the

3. James F. Short, Jr., "Defining, Explaining and Managing Risks," in *Organizations, Uncertainties, and Risk*, ed. James F. Short, Jr. and Lee Clarke (Boulder, CO: Westview Press, 1992), p. 4.

4. President's Commission on the Accident at Three Mile Island, *The Need for Change: The Legacy of TMI* (Washington, DC: Government Printing Office, 1979), pp. 8, 10.

5. William R. Freudenburg, "Nothing Recedes Like Success? Risk Analysis and the Organizational Amplification of Risk," *Risk: Issues in Health and Safety*, 3(1):13-14 (Winter 1992).

6. For example, Roger E. Kasperson and Jeanne X. Kasperson, "Hidden Hazards," in *Acceptable Evidence: Science and Values in Risk Management*, ed. Deborah G. Mayo and Rachelle D. Hollander (New York: Oxford University Press, 1991), pp. 9-28.

definition of risk problems, the type of rationality that attends interpretation, and the selection of management strategies. To the extent that risk becomes a central issue in a political campaign or a source of contention between social groups, it will be vigorously brought to greater public attention, often imbued with value-based interpretations. Polarization of views and escalation of rhetoric by partisans typically occur, and new recruits are drawn into the conflict. These social alignments about risk disputes often outlive a single controversy and become anchors for subsequent risk episodes. Indeed, they frequently remain steadfast even in the face of conflicting information.

The information system surrounding risk questions and the processing of risk by the various stations of amplification and attenuation transmit signals to society about the seriousness of the risk and the performance of risk management institutions. The degree of amplification or attenuation will affect the extent to which risk ripple effects accompany the risk or risk event. Where social concern and debate are intense, secondary and tertiary impacts on society beyond the people who are directly affected may occur, including such effects as

— enduring mental perceptions, images, and attitudes (for example, antitechnology attitudes, social apathy, or increased distrust of risk management institutions);
— impacts on the local or regional economy (for example, reduced business sales, declines in residential property values, and falling tourism);

— political and social pressures (for example, political demands and changes in political climate and culture);
— social and community conflict;
— changes in risk monitoring and regulation costs;
— increased liability and insurance costs; and
— repercussions for other technologies, products, or places (for example, lower levels of public acceptance) and for social institutions (for example, erosion of public trust and confidence).

The consequences of risk and risk events, then, often go well beyond the direct physical harm to human beings and ecosystems to include more indirect effects on the economy, social institutions, and well-being associated with amplification-driven impacts. Alternatively, a dampening and constraining of risk effects—a shrinking of impact ripples—may attend the attenuation of risk by social processes. Assessment methodologies must take account of the full range of risk consequences, as it frequently cannot be determined a priori whether the biophysical impacts customarily included in traditional risk assessment and characterization are the predominant adverse effects or whether they reside instead in the amplification-driven impacts and ripple effects.

Recent research has vividly illustrated the significance of risk in creating ripples and secondary impacts where the potential exists for stigma to become associated with certain technologies. Negative imagery and emotional reactions can become closely associated with the mere thought of certain technologies, products, or places,[7] which become tainted objects to be shunned and avoided. The effects on public acceptance of a technology, its facilities and products, and the places in which it is located can be far-reaching. Nuclear energy and hazardous waste facilities are primary examples of stigmatized technologies or places now embroiled in controversy and public opposition. Biotechnology and chemicals also face some elements of such stigmatization. Contributing to such effects are the ingredients of the social amplification of risk—public perceptions of great risk, intense media coverage of even the most minor incidents or failures, distrust of the managers involved, social-group mobilization and opposition, conflicts over value issues, and disappointments with failed promises. In the modern risk society, amplification-driven impacts, such as stigma-related effects, appear to be marring and compromising the potential benefits to society from economic growth and technological change.

Although many cases are available with which to illustrate the processes of social amplification and attenuation of risk,[8] few events are more vivid than that which occurred at Goiânia, Brazil. That experience provides insight into the process of risk amplification and its potential to shape secondary consequences and ripple effects.

RISK AMPLIFICATION AND RIPPLE EFFECTS: THE GOIÂNIA EXPERIENCE

On 13 September 1987, two unemployed men in Goiânia, a city of 1 million in central Brazil, entered an abandoned clinic in search of scrap metal. They removed a stainless steel cylinder from a cancer-therapy machine and sold it to a junk dealer for about $25. An employee at the junkyard broke the cylinder and pried open a platinum capsule that contained cesium 137, a radioactive element. The crumbly cake of luminescent blue powder, described by witnesses as "carnival glitter," aroused curiosity, and pieces of it were passed around to family members and friends. Children playing in the junkyard spread the glowing material on their hands and bodies. One girl ate an egg sandwich with traces of the powder on her hands. The junkyard owner's wife slept in clothes dusted with the powder. Two weeks later, when Brazil's National Nuclear Energy Commission dispatched a response team, they found what was then the most serious radioactive accident to have occurred in the Western Hemisphere.[9]

The health consequences of the accident were serious. Of some 250 persons suspected to have been contaminated, 4 persons died within the first several months, 21 others required hospitalization, and one amputation

7. Robin Gregory, James Flynn, and Paul Slovic, "Technological Stigma," *American Scientist*, 83(3):220 (May-June 1995).

8. See the examples cited in Roger E. Kasperson, "The Social Amplification of Risk: Progress in Developing an Integrative Framework," in *Social Theories of Risk*, ed. Sheldon Krimsky and Dominic Golding (Westport, CT: Praeger, 1992), pp. 153-78.

9 For a thorough review of the accident, see *The Radiological Accident in Goiânia* (Vienna: International Atomic Energy Commission, 1988).

was required.[10] Eventually, seven major contaminated areas were identified in the city and isolated, and 42 residences were found to have been contaminated. Most of the other contaminated people, however, received relatively low radiation doses and the toll of the accident, albeit serious, has been exceeded by many other technological accidents, natural disasters, and acts of terrorism.

But the physical and health consequences of the accident were only part of a broader spectrum of effects that were ultimately to emerge from the social amplification of the accident.[11] Initially, the accident received only minor attention in a casual report in a local newspaper. But on 1 October, a highly sensational and lengthy São Paulo television broadcast initiated an intense period of dramatic and often exaggerated media coverage of the unfolding incidents and discoveries in the aftermath of the accident. Overnight, an army of reporters and camera crews descended on Goiânia to cover the tragedy. North American headlines spread the news of "deadly glitter," "a carnival of glittering poison," and

10. Constantine J. Maletskos, ed., *The Goiânia Radiation Accident*, special issue of *Health Physics*, 60(1) (Jan. 1991). Taken together, the articles in this special issue constitute an excellent analysis of the health effects.

11. The discussion that follows draws heavily on John S. Petterson, "Perception vs. Reality of Radiological Impact: The Goiânia Model," *Nuclear News*, 31(14):84-90 (Nov. 1988); John S. Petterson, "Goiânia Incident Case Study: Report on Follow-Up Study of Goiânia Incident" (Carson City: Nevada Nuclear Waste Project Office, 1988); Leslie Roberts, "Radiation Accident Grips Goiânia," *Science*, 20 Nov. 1987, pp. 1028-31; Bradley Graham, "Victims of Radiation Ostracized in Brazil," *Washington Post*, 8 Nov. 1987.

"playing with radiation."[12] Extraordinary public concerns accompanied this media coverage, with perceptions of enormous risk apparent even among people with no contact with contaminated persons or materials.

The amplification of the event and the rippling of effects began almost immediately. Within the first weeks of the media coverage, more than 100,000 persons, of their own volition, stood in line to be monitored with Geiger counters for indication of external radiation. Within two weeks of the event, the wholesale value of agricultural production within Goiás, the Brazilian state in which Goiânia is located, had fallen by 50 percent, due to consumer concerns over possible contamination, even though no contamination was ever found in the products. Even eight months after the event, when prices had rebounded by about 90 percent, a significant adverse impact was still apparent. During the three months following the accident, the number and prices of homes sold or rented within the immediate vicinity of the accident plummeted. Hotel occupancy in Goiânia, normally near capacity at this time of year, had vacancy levels averaging about 40 percent in the six weeks following the São Paulo television broadcast, while the Hotel Castros, one of the largest in Goiânia, lost an estimated 1000 reservations as a direct consequence of risk perceptions and stigma. Interestingly, many people chose to forfeit

12. "Deadly Glitter," *Time*, 19 Oct. 1987, p. 38; Sam Seibert, "A Carnival of Glittering Poison," *Newsweek*, 19 Oct. 1987, p. 55; Augusta Dwyer, "Playing with Radiation," *MacLean's*, 2 Nov., 1987, p. 44; Christine Gorman, "A Battle Against Deadly Dust," *Time*, 16 Nov. 1987, p. 66.

deposits rather than risk a hotel stay in a contaminated location.

The effects of the social amplification of the accident rippled well beyond Goiânia itself as extensive stigmatization took hold. Caldas Novas, a hot-springs tourist attraction located a full one-hour drive from Goiânia, experienced a 30-40 percent drop in occupancy rates immediately following the São Paulo television broadcast. Hotels in other parts of Brazil refused to allow Goiânia residents to register. Some airline pilots refused to fly airplanes that had Goiânia residents aboard. Cars with Goiás license plates were stoned in other parts of Brazil. Even nuclear energy as a whole in Brazil was affected, as several political parties used the accident to mobilize against "nuclear weapons, power, or waste" and to introduce legislation designed to split the National Nuclear Energy Commission into separate divisions. Increased public opposition to nuclear energy was apparent throughout Brazil. The stigmatization of Goiânia resembled that which characteristically attends attempts to site nuclear waste facilities.[13] Even international ramifications of the accident have become apparent as Goiânia has become a frequent benchmark and rallying cry in antinuclear publications throughout the world.

The social amplification of risk as illustrated by Goiânia provides convincing testimony of the intertwining of physical and social phenomena in the makeup of risk and why society

responds as it does to different types of risk. But risk attenuation is no less important or striking.

RISK ATTENUATION:
THE ROOTS OF HIDDEN HAZARDS

By contrast with Goiânia, other risks, it is clear, pass unnoticed or unattended by society, growing in size until they exact a serious toll. Asbestos, for example, pervaded the American workplace and schools, although its respiratory dangers had been known for decades. Despite years of worry about nuclear war, the threat of a "nuclear winter" did not become apparent until the 1980s. The Sahel famine of 1983-84 passed unnoticed in the risk-filled newspapers of the world press until we could no longer ignore the specter of millions starving. A society with a Delaney amendment and a $10 billion Superfund program has simultaneously allowed smoking to become the killer of millions of Americans. The potential long-term ecological catastrophes associated with burning coal command far less concern from the mass media and publics than do the risks of nuclear power.

Could these neglects be simply the random risks or events that elude society's alerting and monitoring systems? After all, each society selects its worry beads, the particular risks that we choose to rub and polish assiduously while we relegate others to inattention.[14] Because our assess-

13. Paul Slovic, James Flynn, and Robin Gregory, "Stigma Happens: Social Problems in the Siting of Nuclear Waste Facilities," *Risk Analysis*, 14(5):773-77 (Oct. 1994).

14. Robert W. Kates, "Hazard Assessment: Art, Science, and Ideology," in *Perilous Progress: Managing the Hazards of Technology*, ed. Robert W. Kates, Christoph Hoheneinser, and Jeanne X. Kasperson (Boulder, CO: Westview Press, 1985), pp. 258-59.

ment and management resources are finite, some risks inevitably slip through and surface as surprises or outbreaks. Or are risks simply part of the overall allocation of good and bad in a global political economy, so that the incidence of risk events is only one of many expressions of underlying social and economic forces? Alternatively, are the hidden hazards simply those that are attenuated because they occur in distant times, distant places, or distant—that is, powerless or marginal—social groups?

Some risks are attenuated because they lie entangled in society's web of values and assumptions, which either denigrates the importance of the consequences or deems them acceptable, elevates the associated benefits, and idealizes certain related notions or beliefs. Since the advent of television, violence has been an intrinsic part of news and entertainment programs, including Saturday morning cartoons aimed at children. Several decades' effort to regulate televised violence has run aground on the shoals of the political power of the networks and the belief that violence is a part of American reality and that the protection of free speech should override the need to prevent antisocial behavior.

Handguns are a similar matter. Despite an extraordinary annual national toll from handgun-related violence and the assassination or attempted assassination of a succession of the nation's political leaders, control efforts, such as the Brady bill, have failed to overcome the credo that the right to bear arms is one of the most inalienable of American rights. A different case involves un-

employment: the notion that unemployment arises from the failure of individuals rather than the shortfalls of a capitalist economic system accords this social risk a status very different from other risks to well-being. In European democracies, by comparison, social programs are enacted to correct the structural imperfections in the economy and to ensure that the victims of these imperfections can provide for basic needs.

The marginality of peoples, ecosystems, and regions is also an important source of risk attenuation. The Sudano-Sahelian drought of 1983 eventually emerged as one of the great environmental disasters of the twentieth century, yet it passed largely unnoticed by the world press, international organizations, and national development agencies until the famine reached its zenith during 1984.[15] Moreover, experts had predicted the prospect of continuing famine in the region for some time. As early as 1982, the United Nations Food and Agriculture Organization had issued alarming reports on the situation in Ethiopia. The Reagan administration, however, was clearly reluctant to deal with Marxist-Leninist regimes with whom its diplomatic relations were strained. The instability of governments, the political tensions, and the remoteness of the affected areas and fatalities also made it difficult to obtain accurate information. Within the U.S. government, policymakers debated whether the appropriate response should be humanitarian or political. Not until the

15. Paul Harrison and Robin Palmer, *News Out of Africa: Biafra and Band Aid* (Wolfboro, NH: Hilary Shipman, 1986).

NBC evening news aired a BBC special in October 1984 did the specter of emaciated, fly-ridden skeletons of starvation illuminate the scale of the calamity and trigger subsequent media coverage and public pressures that rendered a U.S. response to the disaster inescapable.[16]

An enduring media spotlight on the hollow eyes and distended bellies of starving children can command the attention and mobilize the flow of humanitarian aid from nongovernmental organizations and governments alike. The faces of famine, it seems, have news value. Not so a more unphotogenic epidemic, acquired immune deficiency syndrome (AIDS), which was a long while in capturing the attention of the media and the organizations that needed to manage the risk.[17] In the United States, the risks of AIDS were known in the early 1980s, yet years passed and the toll of infected persons mounted before the U.S. government belatedly took action. Doubtless, the marginality of the early victims and the taboo surrounding the transmission of the disease had much to do with its attenuation.

16. Lillian M. Li, "Famine and Famine Relief: Viewing Africa in the 1980s from China in the 1920s," in *Drought and Hunger in Africa: Denying Famine a Future*, ed. Michael H. Glantz (New York: Cambridge University Press, 1987), p. 415; Eleanor Singer and Phyllis M. Endreny, *Reporting on Risk: How the Mass Media Portray Accidents, Diseases, Disasters, and Other Hazards* (New York: Russell Sage Foundation, 1993), pp. 35-40.

17. James Kinsella, *Covering the Plague: AIDS and the American Media* (New Brunswick, NJ: Rutgers University Press, 1989); Charles Perrow and Mauro F. Guillén, *The AIDS Disaster: The Failure of Organizations in New York and the Nation* (New Haven, CT: Yale University Press, 1990).

The foregoing cases illustrate important contributors to risk attenuation and the phenomenon of hidden hazards: the margins are a low priority for a central authority, information flow and interaction with marginal groups are characteristically weak, ideological and political differences often underlie and accentuate distance in time and space, and the margins characteristically lack the power and resources to project the risk toll onto the national agenda or into vehicles of public scrutiny.

CONCLUSION

As modern society becomes increasingly preoccupied with eliminating risk, risk problems will more and more be the focus of society's microscope. In particular, assessment methodologies and risk management institutions will be called on to address risk in its full complexity and social context. But difficult risk issues, it is clear, are rarely about risk alone. Navigating the path toward alternative future societies and economies inevitably involves decisions about how society values the future, nature, and human well-being; the extent to which those most at risk should be protected; how risk reduction should best be balanced against economic gain and technological progress; and how much trust should be accorded to risk managers in a democratic society. As social structures and institutions process and resolve such matters, risk becomes transformed—it takes on added dimensions and new consequences, both beneficial and harmful, while the risk experience as a whole acquires new subtleties and social meanings. The challenge to the risk society is the creation of political regimes and institutions capable of meeting rising public expectations for risk containment and reduction in the face of the growing pace and complexity of risk generation and the progressive intertwining of risk with deeper questions of ethics, the social ends of government, and democratic process.

Hazard Communication:
Warnings and Risk

By W. KIP VISCUSI and RICHARD J. ZECKHAUSER

ABSTRACT: Risk information can alter risk judgments and promote sound risk decisions. Hazard warnings are critical in providing such information. Both right-to-know and duty-to-warn obligations reflect this. Evidence suggests that warnings can significantly affect risk-taking decisions, but care is needed in interpreting whether their influence leads to successful outcomes. Hazard warnings must accommodate individuals' cognitive limitations. Salient problems include recipients who suffer information overload or are unable to grasp adequately the level of risk communicated.

W. Kip Viscusi is the George G. Allen Professor of Economics at Duke University and the founding editor of the Journal of Risk and Uncertainty. *He has written widely on risk issues, including three books on hazard warnings.*

Richard J. Zeckhauser is the Frank P. Ramsey Professor of Political Economy at the Kennedy School of Government, Harvard University. He has developed a range of decision-analytic tools that are widely employed in addressing risk issues.

SITUATIONS involving risk often are coupled with shortcomings in information. Workers may not know the risk of being killed on the job. Consumers may be unaware of the hazards posed by prescription drugs, and society at large may not have the best available information on the risks of nuclear accidents. Information has the potential to promote more informed choices.

In legal contexts, the potential role of information is recognized in the duty to warn. Firms marketing hazardous products, for example, must apprise consumers of the risks associated with these products. The public's right to know risk levels has received considerable attention in regulatory contexts.

Figure 1 portrays the potential role of risk information about a potentially unsafe product. Information affects individuals' risk assessments, which in turn affect the product's expected utility benefits. The product may be employed in situations with pertinent safety precautions taken or not. Individuals must decide whether or not to use the product and, if so, whether to take precautions. In any event, the consumer will have an experience with the product, possibly leading to an injury. Such experiences will alter the consumer's risk beliefs and thereby affect future purchases of this and other products.

Hazard warnings and related types of information provision can ameliorate risk information shortcomings. People often have different preferences with respect to risk and injury, and hazard warnings facilitate decentralized risk-taking decisions, which can readily reflect such heterogeneous preferences. Hazard warnings can also be instrumental when we wish to encourage particular types of unmonitorable behavior, such as taking precautions when using household pesticides. Risk information programs increase individuals' perceived risks associated with dangerous products and activities, thereby indirectly creating market incentives for safer products.

Hazard warnings often represent an attractive intermediate policy option between a ban and doing nothing. Policymakers may have some knowledge of the risk, but insufficient grounds for taking strong action, such as a ban, against a hazard. Until the magnitude of the risk is better defined, it may be useful to employ hazard warnings to alert people to a potential risk, thereby enabling them to exercise appropriate care.

Communicating risks effectively is a challenge. Individuals have an incredibly difficult time making sound decisions under conditions of uncertainty;[1] this difficulty limits the efficacy of warnings in promoting accurate risk perceptions and fostering rational decisions. This article explores some of the principal characteristics of hazard warnings and the ways they can be designed to best promote appropriate levels of safety.

WARNING STRUCTURE
AND CONTENT

If individuals had perfect and unlimited information-processing capa-

1. A range of difficulties that people encounter is outlined in Daniel Kahneman, Paul Slovic, and Amos Tversky, eds., *Judgment Under Uncertainty: Heuristics and Biases* (New York: Cambridge University Press, 1982).

FIGURE 1
INFORMATION PROCESSING AND ECONOMIC BEHAVIOR

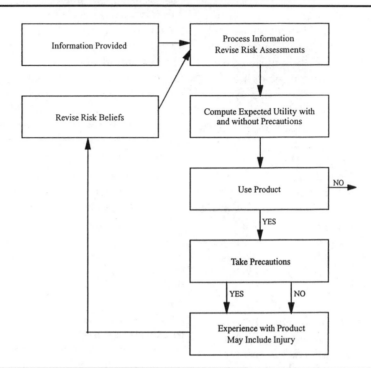

bilities, the informational task would be simple. For pharmaceutical product risks, for example, we could refer consumers to the appropriate medical literature and let them make their own judgments. The example is fanciful: specialized scientific and technical knowledge is required to interpret risk information. Moreover, people have limited ability to process all the diverse information they might receive about a great range of products and activities.

The specific language of warnings often plays an important role. Some potent words, such as "danger," "caution," and "poison," have well-defined meanings within the context of the hazard warnings vocabulary; they imply a certain risk level. For such words to retain their meaning, they should be used consistently across products and contexts. Overwarning and the overuse of such words may, for example, dilute their importance. If every product in the supermarket carries a hazard warning, no distinctions will be made. The proliferation of warnings creates a problem of information overload.

Typically, people can process reliably five to seven pieces of information; attempts to convey more information than that in a hazard warning may confuse consumers and distract them from the central message of the warning.[2] For example, warnings on some commonly marketed insecticides provide overly detailed information about how the product might be used on particular plants and about particular hazards. The net effect is that consumers are better able to make proper decisions with respect to the safe use of the product when presented with a warning that focuses on only the more important risks.[3]

The format of a warning can affect how well consumers process the information contained. Well-organized information printed in one place on the label can be read more readily than information that is dispersed. Similarly, warnings that follow a consistent organization for all products, such as the hazard warnings on pharmaceutical products, can be more easily processed. Consumers know where to find warning information about uses, adverse reactions, and the like, and this information is printed in a standardized format and written using a standardized vocabulary.[4]

2. For discussion of the limitations on human information processing, see W. Kip Viscusi and Wesley A. Magat, *Learning About Risk* (Cambridge, MA: Harvard University Press, 1987).

3. As another example, a study of consumer responses to household chemicals found that a cluttered warning actually led to increased likely riskiness of the product during use. Consumers did not accurately process product usage information if too much was provided. See Wesley A. Magat and W. Kip Viscusi, *Informational Approaches to Regulation* (Cambridge: MIT Press, 1992).

4. The importance of a standardized warning vocabulary has been recognized in legal contexts by the American Law Institute. See American Law Institute, *Enterprise Responsibility for Personal Injury: Reporters' Study* (Philadelphia: American Law Institute, 1991).

In addition to hazard warnings, risk information can be communicated through videos, educational advertising in the media, and risk training programs, among other mechanisms. It is particularly helpful to use a variety of avenues to convey complex messages. For example, the Environmental Protection Agency requires that users of very hazardous pesticides become certified pesticide applicators, for which they must undergo safety training. Consequently, the test for whether the risk information is communicated effectively does not rest on the effectiveness of only the on-product warning but, instead, examines the entire hazard communication system.

The warning context helps to define the audience for the warning. Is the recipient of the warning a sophisticated user, such as a physician or an industrial chemist? The warnings appropriate to the general consumer do not presuppose the expertise of an informed recipient. The source of the warning information is also important, particularly that source's credibility. Large companies, for example, have a strong incentive for integrity. It will help them avert unfavorable liability judgments and maintain future credibility. An information provider who develops a reputation for being systematically alarmist or complacent will find his credibility jeopardized.

The objective of a warning should not be to inspire the most cautious response possible but to enable consumers to form accurate judgments of the risk level and take appropriate action. Overwarning introduces dangers. If we exaggerate modest risks, we will have no credible mechanism for alerting people to greater hazards.

A continuing problem is how to communicate risks when there is conflicting scientific evidence, particularly since this implies that information will evolve. If we alert people to a risk now and it turns out later that there never was any risk, we could be labeled as crying wolf. At the same time, if there probably is a hazard, we do not want to be remiss in alerting people. The imprecision in our risk judgments should not lead us to undue complacency, nor should it spur us to focus on the worst-case scenario.

INFORMATION PROCESSING AND RISK PERCEPTIONS

Before warnings can have an effect, they must be received and processed by the intended recipient. Sometimes the audience for a warning is not the consumer but an intermediary, such as a physician. In these cases, the responsibility for using the risk information may be shared; the physician dispensing pharmaceuticals relies upon the risk information from the manufacturer to make the appropriate prescription and, along with the patient's package insert, alerts the consumer to the potential risks associated with the product.

In practice, warning information is hardly universally received. Heimbach, for example, found that only one-fourth of all consumers could recall the sodium content listing on food labels.[5] In addition, only 40 per-

cent of the sample recalled having read an ingredient list on a food product. More recent food information efforts may reach consumers more successfully. Information on the fiber content of cereals has had a strong effect on cereal consumption patterns.[6]

In the pharmaceutical context, however, one study suggested that many consumers do not bother to read the warning information inserted in prescription drug packages.[7] Overall, just under three-fourths of all subjects claimed to have read the leaflets; moreover, the respondents had volunteered to participate in the study, and they were told that they would be called about the information they received, both factors that would boost readership. Similarly, while 88 percent of oral contraceptive users claim to have read the patient package insert, only 69 percent could recall any information on drug usage, and only 50 percent could recall information about common drug reactions.[8] One study suggests that only one-fourth of all consumers are aware of the Reye's syndrome warnings on aspirin, and just 53 percent are aware that flu patients should not take aspirin.[9]

5. James T. Heimbach, *The Public Responds to Labeling of the Sodium Content of Foods* (Washington, DC: Food and Drug Administration, 1991).

6. Pauline M. Ippolito and Alan D. Mathios, "Information, Advertising and Health Choices: A Study of the Cereal Market," *Rand Journal of Economics*, 21:459-556 (1990).

7. See David Kanouse et al., "Informing Patients About Drugs" (Report R2800-FDA, RAND Corporation, 1981).

8. See Louis A. Morris, Michael B. Mazis, and Evelyn Gordon, "A Survey of the Effects of Oral Contraceptive Patient Information," *Journal of the American Medical Association*, 232:2504-8 (1977).

9. See Louis A. Morris and Ronald Klimburg, "A Survey of Aspirin Use and Reye's Syndrome Awareness Among Parents," *American Journal of Public Health*, 76:1422-24 (1986).

Perhaps the most successful warning effort in reaching consumers has been that for cigarettes. Surveys indicate that between 99 and 100 percent of all individuals have heard that "cigarette smoking is dangerous to a person's health" and similar admonitions.[10]

Just because a person receives information does not mean that the warning was understood. Many consumers have trouble understanding the terms used on food labels, whether the terms are bloated prose, such as "polyunsaturated fat" and "hydrogenated," or more common, such as "carbohydrates."[11] Similarly, consumers confuse salt and sodium. Warnings must be sufficiently salient and readable so that consumers will invest the time and effort to understand the information contained.

If the warning is received and processed, it will alter the consumer's risk assessments. Conveying information that will lead to appropriate risk perceptions is not a trivial task; it is too easy to encourage undue complacency or create excessive alarm. If warnings could convey quantitative risk information—say, "use of this product poses a 1/10,000 risk of an allergic reaction"—then the task would be simplified. However, people often cannot process and act on quantitative risk information in a reliable manner. Indeed, explicit quantitative information plays a prominent role only in pharmaceutical warnings, which are written for physicians, most of whom have substantial training in pharmacology. Rather than telling people the explicit probabilities involved, warnings typically use qualitative mechanisms to alert people to risk.

Evidence suggests that warnings on cigarette packaging and advertising have altered consumers' risk perceptions, though they may not have fostered pinpoint accuracy in these beliefs. In 1949, before the advent of cigarette warnings, 52 percent of all cigarette smokers believed that smoking was harmful; by 1981, 16 years after warning labels became mandatory, 80 percent of all smokers believed that smoking was harmful. Among nonsmokers, the percentage who believed that smoking was harmful increased from 66 percent to 96 percent over the same period.[12]

People seem to think that smoking is riskier than it is, however. Whereas the lifetime lung cancer mortality risk to smokers is estimated by scientists to be in the range of 6-13 percent, individuals assess this risk at 38-43 percent.[13] Overall, smoking mortality risk perceptions also appear to be exaggerated, although the discrepancy is less than that for lung cancer. Perhaps these risks are overestimated because of the substantial public attention given to smoking; however, it is unlikely that close-to-accurate risk beliefs can ever be achieved. The task for informational policies is to help consumers develop risk perceptions

10. See W. Kip Viscusi, *Smoking: Making the Risky Decision* (New York: Oxford University Press, 1992).

11. James T. Heimbach, *The Public Understanding of Food Label Information* (Washington, DC: Food and Drug Administration, 1981).

12. These statistics are based on Gallup poll results reported in Viscusi, *Smoking*, p. 50.

13. See Viscusi, *Smoking*, chap. 4, for discussion of the different smoking survey questions and the responses.

that lie within reasonable ranges, recognizing that because of the diversity of individual responses to risk and the qualitative nature of warnings, risk perceptions will seldom be highly refined.

The relatively large risks posed by cigarettes may make them comparatively easy products for crafting effective warnings. In contrast, very low-probability events—several orders of magnitude smaller than those posed by cigarettes—are more typical hazards. The state of California, for example, has attempted to warn consumers about low-probability cancer risks associated with food products. The draft warning under California Proposition 65 is, "WARNING: The state of California has determined that this product is dangerous to your health."[14] This warning pertains to risks that pose a total cancer risk of at least one in 100,000 over a 70-year lifetime. Survey respondents who assessed the implications of this warning believed that the risk was comparable to smoking 0.58 packs of cigarettes per day, which produces a lifetime risk in excess of one in 10. Many companies reformulated their products rather than have such strident language deter consumers from using the product.

Those designing warning systems face a continuing difficulty in deciding what level of risk merits warning attention. As we provide warnings about increasingly tiny hazards, we

14. For discussion of California Proposition 65 as well as the empirical evidence regarding risk perceptions pertaining to it, see W. Kip Viscusi, *Product Risk Labeling: A Federal Responsibility* (Washington, DC: American Enterprise Institute, 1993).

make it harder for consumers to notice warnings about the truly consequential ones. Moreover, warning practices patterned on cigarettes and other higher-level risks may be quite inappropriate for extremely low-probability events. On the other hand, we do not wish to ignore small probabilities; they often pertain to the risks that are least well understood by individuals, so warning information can be very helpful.

THE BEHAVIORAL RESPONSE

Warnings typically encourage two types of response. Those that alert individuals to the inherent risks of a product or activity encourage consumers not to make the purchase or not to participate in the activity. Warnings that advise individuals to take precautionary actions stimulate consumers to take care while undertaking the hazardous activity. Depending on their willingness to bear risk, some individuals may continue to purchase hazardous products even in the presence of the warning. While consumption often decreases after a hazard warning is published, it is difficult to know whether the warning's influence is too great, too little, or just right. For example, if it were truly desirable to eliminate consumption of the product, then a ban would be preferable to a warning. The role of warnings is to provide risk information when a choice to bear the risk may be rational, but some individuals once apprised of a risk will rationally forgo or take expensive action to ameliorate it.

Similar reasoning underlies many precautionary warnings. For example, those who find wearing rubber gloves onerous will not do so when using toilet bowl cleaner, even though the label urges them to do so. Most people do not wear seatbelts when driving cars, even though substantial government efforts have admonished them to do so, going so far as making nonusage subject to fine. Although not wearing seatbelts can be rational, the non-seatbelt-wearers may not accurately perceive the risks they take on, or they may be (rationally) discounting the costs that their accidents impose on society and others in the automobile insurance pool.[15]

Various sources of evidence suggest that hazard warnings do have an influence. Market data best reveal actual risk-taking decisions. For example, in 1963, hazard warnings alerted consumers to the potential tooth-staining risk of tetracycline for children under age eight.[16] Whereas the use of tetracycline by patients aged nine and older continued to increase after 1963, tetracycline use for younger children plummeted from about 400 mentions (new or continuing prescriptions by the doctor surveyed) per 1000 population in 1963 to under 100 mentions by 1974. Similarly, cigarette consumption has been dramatically influenced by the provision of risk information.[17] U.S. per capita

cigarette consumption increased steadily throughout this century up to the mid-1960s. In 1965, it became mandatory for cigarette packs to carry warning labels. In the 1970s, cigarette consumption stabilized, and since the 1980s, per capita cigarette consumption has declined. The warning for saccharin has also had an apparent effect on diet soft drink sales. The warning label alerting consumers to the potential cancer hazards for laboratory animals reduced saccharin soft drink sales by 4 percent.[18]

Consumers' responses to surveys about hypothetical products bearing warnings may also be instructive, indicating whether they would purchase the product or take the precautions listed. Evidence on consumers' handling of household chemicals suggests that individuals do take precautions in response to hazard warnings, such as wearing rubber gloves and placing poisons in a childproof location.

The optimal aggregate response to a hazard warning will yield the same response as would be made by hypothetical fully informed people capable of making rational decisions under uncertainty. Do people tend to underreact to the risk or react excessively? One study of hazard warnings in the workplace suggested that at least in some instances, appropriate warnings can lead workers to make roughly the same trade-offs between risk levels and wages for the risks

15. For discussion of the rationality and the potential errors in individual seatbelt use, see Richard Arnould and Henry Grabowski, "Auto Safety Regulation: An Analysis of Market Failure," *Bell Journal of Economics*, 12:27-45 (1981).

16. For discussion of the tetracycline evidence, see W. Kip Viscusi, *Reforming Products Liability* (Cambridge, MA: Harvard University Press, 1991).

17. The cigarette consumption trends are based on data presented in Viscusi, *Smoking*.

18. See Robert G. Orwin, Raymond E. Schucker, and Raymond C. Stokes, "Evaluating the Life Cycle of a Product Warning: Saccharin and Diet Soft Drinks," *Evaluation Review*, 8:801-22 (1984).

communicated in the warnings as for workplace risks that workers had already identified.[19] This result may not generalize to all situations, however.

As a practical matter, evaluating the success of warnings is difficult. We must ask whether consumers receive the message, whether it affects risk perceptions appropriately, and whether consumers' decisions appear to reflect cognizance of the risk levels. Observing that a warning has some effect on behavior is a useful starting point; one knows the warnings were not completely ignored. We need to delve much more deeply, however, before we can judge that an appropriate risk level is being communicated and acted on in an appropriate manner.

CHALLENGES FOR RISK
INFORMATION POLICIES

Many of the difficulties associated with hazard communication stem from the difficulties of choice under uncertainty; that is, due to our cognitive shortcomings, people do not always perceive risks accurately and make sound decisions with respect to them.

This suggests four challenges for policymakers. The first is to convey information about very small probabilities without encouraging alarmist responses. By their nature, we tend to have relatively little experience with slight hazards. When it is also unclear what the true risk level is,

19. See W. Kip Viscusi and Charles O'Connor, "Adaptive Responses to Chemical Labeling: Are Workers Bayesian Decision Makers?" *American Economic Review*, 74(5):942-56 (1984).

the relevant information is likely to change over time to reflect new knowledge. The resulting alteration of the risk message may reduce its credibility. So, too, may an indication that there is a range of uncertainty in estimates of the risk's magnitude.

A second challenge is to better utilize the various forms of hazard communication. The almost exclusive emphasis observed at present on on-product warnings, rather than other avenues such as educational programs, has made warning efforts serve as little more than informational sound bites. If we truly wish to educate the public—a task that is particularly important for complex hazards and risks for which there may appropriately be a diversity of individual responses—then greater attention must be paid to other forms of communication.

A third challenge for policy design is to develop and implement criteria for when warnings, rather than other policy options, should be used. Although warnings are well known to be an intermediate policy option between no action and explicit regulatory control, the attention given to the decision to pursue the warning option and to evaluate its success is often inadequate.

The fourth, and perhaps most important, challenge is to develop the appropriate institutional incentives for providing risk information. Excessive information tends to create problems of information overload. As a society, we should alert people to the truly important risks they face so that they understand where care is needed. Many incentives now in place promote overwarning. At present, there is no legal cost for over-warning. Hence companies err on the side of excessive warning to avoid prospective liability costs. Cautious policymakers also are prone to over-warning; for example, pesticide warnings have become increasingly lengthy over time as our knowledge of pesticide risks has improved. These officials do not devote suffi-cient attention, however, to the im-pediments that a lengthy warning may pose to people who must utilize the information.

Hazard communication policies can play an important and construc-tive role within the menu of risk poli-cies. In designing warnings, however, we must recognize that people have cognitive limitations and may make flawed decisions. The challenge to policymakers is to design warning programs to be as helpful as they can be in the presence of such limitations. Hazard warnings are one critical component of the general societal ef-fort to get citizens to confront risks appropriately.

Science, Values, and Risk

By HOWARD KUNREUTHER and PAUL SLOVIC

ABSTRACT: In the context of health, safety, and environmental decisions, the concept of risk involves value judgments that reflect much more than just the probability and consequences of the occurrence of an event. This article conceptualizes risk as a game, in which the rules must be socially negotiated within the context of a specific problem. This contextualist view of risk provides insight into why technical approaches to risk management often fail with problems such as those involving radiation and chemicals, where scientific experts and the public disagree on the nature of the risks. It also highlights the need for the interested parties to define and play the game, thus emphasizing the importance of institutional, procedural, and societal processes in risk management decisions. This contextualist approach is illustrated using the problem of siting hazardous waste facilities.

Howard Kunreuther is the Cecilia Yen Koo Professor of Decision Sciences and Public Policy and codirector of the Risk Management and Decision Processes Center at the Wharton School of the University of Pennsylvania. His current research interests focus on decision making with respect to low-probability, high-consequence events associated with natural, technological, and environmental hazards.

Paul Slovic is president of Decision Research and a professor of psychology at the University of Oregon. He studies human judgment, decision making, and risk analysis. During the past 20 years, he and colleagues worldwide have developed methods to describe risk perceptions and measure their impacts on individuals, industry, and society.

THE practice of risk assessment has steadily increased in prominence during the past several decades, as risk managers in government and industry have sought to develop more effective ways to meet public demands for a safer and healthier environment. Dozens of scientific disciplines have been mobilized to provide technical information about risk and billions of dollars have been expended to create this information and distill it in the context of risk assessments.

Ironically, as our society has expended time and money to make life safer and healthier, many in the public have become more, rather than less, concerned about risk. These individuals see themselves as exposed to more serious risks than were faced by Americans in the past, and they believe that this situation is getting worse rather than better. Nuclear and chemical technologies (except for medicines) have been stigmatized by being perceived as entailing unnaturally great risks.[1] As a result, it has been difficult, if not impossible, to find host sites for disposing of high-level or low-level radioactive wastes or for incinerators, landfills, and other chemical facilities.

Public perceptions of risk have been found to determine the priorities and legislative agendas of regulatory bodies such as the Environmental Protection Agency, much to the distress of agency technical experts who argue that other hazards deserve higher priority. The bulk of the Environmental Protection Agency's budget in recent years has gone to hazardous waste primarily because the public believes that the cleanup of Superfund sites is the most serious environmental threat that the country faces. Hazards such as indoor air pollution are considered more serious health risks by experts, but they are not perceived that way by the public.[2]

Great disparities in monetary expenditures designed to prolong life, as shown in Table 1, may also be traced to public perceptions of risk. Just as noteworthy as the large sums of money devoted to protection from radiation and chemical toxins are the relatively small sums expended to reduce routine hazards such as influenza. Other studies have shown that serious risks from national disasters such as floods, hurricanes, and earthquakes generate relatively little public concern and demand for protection.[3]

Such discrepancies are seen as irrational by many harsh critics of public perceptions. These critics draw a sharp dichotomy between the experts and the public. Experts are seen as purveying risk assessments characterized as objective, analytic, wise, and rational—based on the real risks. In contrast, the public is seen to rely on perceptions of risk that are subjective, often hypothetical, emotional, foolish, and irrational.

1. Robin Gregory, James Flynn, and Paul Slovic, "Technological Stigma," *American Scientist*, 83:220-23 (1995).

2. Environmental Protection Agency, Office of Policy Analysis, *Unfinished Business: A Comparative Assessment of Environmental Problems* (Washington, DC: Environmental Protection Agency, 1987).

3. Risa I. Palm, *Natural Hazards: An Integrative Framework for Research and Planning* (Baltimore, MD: Johns Hopkins University Press, 1995); Howard Kunreuther, "Mitigating Disaster Losses Through Insurance," *Journal of Risk and Uncertainty* (in press).

TABLE 1

**COST OF A YEAR OF LIFE SAVED
BY VARIOUS INTERVENTIONS**

Flu shots	$500
Water chlorination	$4,000
Pneumonia vaccinations	$12,000
Breast cancer screening	$17,000
All medical interventions	$19,000
Construction safety rules	$38,000
All transportation interventions	$56,000
Highway improvement	$60,000
Home radon control	$141,000
Asbestos controls	$1.9 million
All toxin controls	$2.8 million
Arsenic emission controls	$6.0 million
Radiation controls	$10.0 million

SOURCE: Adapted from T. O. Tengs et al., "Five-Hundred Life-Saving Interventions and Their Cost-Effectiveness," *Risk Analysis*, 15:369-90 (1995).

In sum, polarized views, controversy, and overt conflict have become pervasive within the domain of risk assessment and risk management. A desperate search for salvation through risk communication efforts began in the mid-1980s, yet, despite some localized successes,[4] this effort has not stemmed the major conflicts or reduced much of the dissatisfaction with risk management.

THE NEED FOR
A NEW PERSPECTIVE

We believe that new perspectives and new approaches are needed to manage risks effectively in our society. We also believe that social science research has provided some valuable insights into the nature of this prob-

lem that, without indicating a clear solution, do point to some promising prescriptive actions.

For example, early studies of risk perception demonstrated that the public's concerns could not simply be blamed on ignorance or irrationality. Instead, research has shown that many of the public's reactions to risk (including reactions that may underlie the data in Table 1) can be attributed to a sensitivity to technical, social, and psychological qualities of hazards that are not well modeled in technical risk assessments—for example, qualities such as uncertainty in risk assessments, perceived inequity in the distribution of risks and benefits, and aversion to being exposed to risks that are involuntary, not under one's control, or dreaded. The important role of social values in risk perception and risk acceptance has thus become apparent.[5]

More recently, another important aspect of the risk perception problem has come to be recognized. This is the role of trust. In recent years there have been numerous articles and surveys pointing out the importance of trust in risk management and documenting the extreme distrust we now have in many of the individuals, industries, and institutions responsible for risk management.[6] This pervasive distrust has also been shown to be strongly linked to the perception that risks are unacceptably high and to political activism to reduce those risks.

4. See William Leiss, "Three Phases in the Evaluation of Risk Communication Practice," this issue of *The Annals* of the American Academy of Political and Social Science.

5. Paul Slovic, "Perception of Risk," *Science*, 236:280-85 (1987).

6. Paul Slovic, "Perceived Risk, Trust, and Democracy," *Risk Analysis*, 13:675-82 (1993).

A third insight pertains to the very complexity of the concept "risk." We shall argue for a conception of risk starkly different from the view that is the foundation for most current approaches to risk assessment and risk management.

THE SUBJECTIVE AND
VALUE-LADEN NATURE
OF RISK ASSESSMENT

Attempts to manage risk must confront the question, "What is risk?" The dominant conception views risk as "the chance of injury, damage, or loss."[7] The probabilities and consequences of adverse events are assumed to be produced by physical and natural processes in ways that can be objectively quantified by risk assessment. Much social science analysis rejects this notion, arguing instead that risk is inherently subjective.[8] In this view, risk does not exist "out there," independent of our minds and cultures, waiting to be measured. Instead, human beings have invented the concept of risk to help them understand and cope with the dangers and uncertainties of life. Although these dangers are real, there is no such thing as "real risk" or "objective risk." The nuclear engineer's probabilistic risk estimate for a nuclear accident or the toxicologist's quantitative estimate of a chemical's carcinogenic risk are both based on theoretical models, whose structure is subjective and assumption-laden and whose inputs are dependent on judgment. As we shall see, nonscientists have their own models, assumptions, and subjective assessment techniques (intuitive risk assessments), which are sometimes very different from the scientists' models.

One way in which subjectivity permeates risk assessment is in the latter's dependence on judgments at every stage of the process, from the initial structuring of a risk problem to deciding which endpoints or consequences to include in the analysis, identifying and estimating exposures, choosing dose-response relationships, and so on.

For example, even the apparently simple task of choosing a risk measure for a well-defined endpoint such as human fatalities is surprisingly complex and judgmental. Table 2 shows a few of the many different ways that fatality risks can be framed.

An example taken from Wilson and Crouch demonstrates how the choice of one measure or another can make a technology look either more or less risky. Between 1950 and 1970, coal mines became much less risky in terms of deaths from accidents per ton of coal, but they became marginally riskier in terms of deaths from accidents per miner. Which measure one thinks more appropriate for deci-

7. *Webster's New Twentieth Century Dictionary*, 2d ed.

8. Silvio O. Funtowicz and Jerome R. Ravetz, "Three Types of Risk Assessment and the Emergence of Post-Normal Science," in *Social Theories of Risk*, ed. S. Krimsky and D. Golding (Westport, CT: Praeger, 1992), pp. 251-74; Harry Otway, "Public Wisdom, Expert Fallibility: Toward a Contextual Theory of Risk," in ibid., pp. 215-28; Nick Pidgeon et al., "Risk Perception," in *Risk: Analysis, Perception and Management*, ed. Royal Society Study Group (London: Royal Society, 1992), pp. 89-134; Paul Slovic, "Perception of Risk: Reflections on the Psychometric Paradigm," in *Social Theories of Risk*, ed. Krimsky and Golding, pp. 117-52; Brian Wynne, "Risk and Social Learning: Reification to Engagement," in ibid., pp. 275-300.

TABLE 2

SOME WAYS OF EXPRESSING MORTALITY RISKS

Deaths per million people in the population
Deaths per million people within x miles of the source of exposure
Deaths per unit of concentration
Deaths per facility
Deaths per ton of air toxic released
Deaths per ton of air toxic absorbed by people
Deaths per ton of chemical produced
Deaths per million dollars of product produced
Loss of life expectancy associated with exposure to the hazard

sion making depends on one's point of view. From a national point of view, given that a certain amount of coal has to be obtained, deaths per million tons of coal is the more appropriate measure of risk, whereas from a labor leader's point of view, deaths per thousand miners employed may be more relevant.[9]

How should we decide what measure to use when planning a risk assessment, recognizing that choice of measure is likely to make a big difference in how the risk is perceived and evaluated?

*Framing the
    risk information*

After a risk analysis has negotiated all the subjective steps of defining the problem and its options, selecting and measuring risks in terms of particular outcomes, determining the people at risk and their exposure parameters, and so on, one comes to the presentation of this information to the decision maker, often referred to as "framing." This process of presentation is also rife with subjectivity.

Numerous research studies have demonstrated that different (but logically equivalent) ways of presenting the same risk information can lead to different evaluations and decisions. One dramatic example of this comes from a study by McNeil et al., who asked people to imagine that they had lung cancer and had to choose between two therapies, surgery or radiation. The two therapies were described in some detail. Then some subjects were presented with the cumulative probabilities of surviving for varying lengths of time after the treatment. Other subjects received the same cumulative probabilities framed in terms of dying rather than surviving; for example, instead of being told that 68 percent of those having surgery will have survived after one year, they were told that 32 percent will have died. Framing the statistics in terms of dying dropped the percentage of subjects choosing radiation therapy over surgery from 44 to 18 percent. The effect was as strong for physicians as for laypersons.[10]

9. Richard Wilson and Edmund Crouch, *Risk / Benefit Analysis* (Cambridge, MA: Ballinger, 1982).

10. Barbara J. McNeil et al., "On the Elicitation of Preferences for Alternative Therapies," *New England Journal of Medicine*, 306:1259-62 (1982).

Equally striking effects result from framing the information about consequences in terms of either lives saved or lives lost[11] or from describing an improvement in a river's water quality as a restoration of lost quality or an improvement from the current level.[12]

In sum, we now know that every form of presenting risk information is a frame that has a strong influence on the decision maker. Moreover, when we contemplate the equivalence of lives saved versus lives lost, mortality rates versus survival rates, restoring lost water quality versus improving water quality, and so forth, we see that there are often no right frames or wrong frames—just different frames.

The multidimensionality of risk

As noted earlier, research has also shown that the public has a broad conception of risk, qualitative and complex, that incorporates considerations such as uncertainty, dread, catastrophic potential, controllability, equity, risk to future generations, and so forth into the risk equation. In contrast, experts' perceptions of risk are not closely related to these dimensions or the characteristics that underlie them. Instead, studies show that experts tend to see riskiness as synonymous with expected annual mortality, consistent with the diction-

11. Amos Tversky and Daniel Kahneman, "The Framing of Decisions and the Psychology of Choice," *Science*, 211: 453-58 (1981).

12. Robin Gregory, Sarah Lichtenstein, and Donald MacGregor, "The Role of Past States in Determining Reference Points for Policy Decisions," *Organizational Behavior and Human Decision Processes*, 55:195-206 (1983).

ary definition given previously and consistent with the ways in which risks tend to be characterized in risk assessments. As a result of these different perspectives, many conflicts over risk may result from the different definitions of the concept experts and laypeople have. Viewed in this light, it is not surprising that expert recitations of risk statistics often do little to change people's attitudes and perceptions.

There are legitimate values underlying the multiple dimensions of public risk perceptions, and these values need to be considered in risk-policy decisions. For example, is risk from cancer (a dread disease) worse than risk from auto accidents (not dreaded)? Is a risk imposed on a child more serious than a known risk accepted voluntarily by an adult? Are the deaths of fifty passengers in separate automobile accidents equivalent to the deaths of fifty passengers in one airplane crash? Is the risk from a polluted Superfund site worse if the site is located in a neighborhood that has a number of other hazardous facilities nearby? The difficult questions multiply when outcomes other than human health and safety are considered.

THE RISK GAME

There are clearly multiple conceptions of risk.[13] Dean and Thompson note that the traditional view of risk characterized by event probabilities and consequences treats the many

13. For a clarification of these conceptions, see K. S. Shrader-Frechette, *Risk and Rationality* (Berkeley: University of California Press, 1991).

subjective and contextual factors described earlier as secondary or accidental dimensions of risk, just as coloration might be thought of as a secondary or accidental dimension of an eye. Accidental dimensions might be extremely influential in the formation of attitudes toward risk, just as having blue or brown coloration is extremely influential in forming attitudes toward eyes. Furthermore, it may be that all risks possess some accidental dimensions, just as all organs of sight are in some way colored. Nevertheless, accidental dimensions do not serve as criteria for determining whether someone is or is not at risk, just as coloration is irrelevant to whether something is or is not an eye.[14]

We believe that the multidimensional, subjective, value-laden, frame-sensitive nature of risky decisions, as previously described, supports a very different view, which Dean and Thompson call "the contextualist conception." This conception places probabilities and consequences on the list of relevant risk attributes along with voluntariness, equity, and other important contextual parameters. In the contextualist view, the concept of risk is more like the concept of a game than the concept of an eye. Games have features such as time limits, rules of play, opponents, and criteria for winning or losing. None of these attributes is essential to the concept of a game, nor is any of them characteristic of all games. Similarly, a contextualist view of risk assumes that risks are

14. Wesley R. Dean and Paul B. Thompson, *The Varieties of Risk*, Environmental Risk Management Working Paper ERC 95-3 (Edmonton: University of Alberta, 1995).

characterized by some combination of attributes such as voluntariness, probability, intentionality, equity, and so on, but that no one of these attributes is essential. The bottom line is that, just as there is no universal set of rules for games, there is no universal set of features for describing risk. The characterization depends on which risk game is being played.

POLICY IMPLICATIONS OF THIS CONTEXTUALIST VIEW OF RISK

There has been no shortage of high-level attention given to the risk conflicts we described earlier. Proposed solutions to these conflicts tend to take one of two forms: technical solutions or process solutions.

Technical solutions

One prominent proposal by Justice Stephen Breyer attempts to break what he sees as a "vicious circle" of public perception, congressional overreaction, and conservative regulation. Breyer sees public misperceptions of risk and low levels of mathematical understanding at the core of excessive regulatory response. He feels that such regulation leads to obsessive and costly preoccupation with reducing negligible risks as well as to inconsistent standards across health and safety programs. His proposed solution is to create a small centralized administrative group charged with creating uniformity and rationality in highly technical areas of risk management. This group would be staffed by civil servants with experience in health and environmental agencies, Congress, and the Office of Management and Budget. A parallel is drawn between this group and the prestigious Conseil d'Etat in France.[15]

Similar frustration with the costs of meeting public demands led the 104th Congress to introduce numerous bills designed to require all major new regulations to be justified by extensive risk assessments. Proponents of this legislation argue that such measures are necessary to ensure that regulations are based on sound science and effectively reduce significant risks at reasonable costs.

The language of this proposed legislation reflects the traditional narrow view of risk and risk assessment based "only on the best reasonably available scientific data and scientific understanding." Agencies are further directed to develop a systematic program for external peer review using "expert bodies, or other devices . . . comprised of participants selected on the basis of their expertise relevant to the sciences involved."[16] Public participation in this process is advocated but no mechanisms for this are specified.

The proposals by Breyer and the 104th Congress are typical in their call for more and better technical analysis and expert oversight to rationalize risk management. There is no doubt that technical analysis is vital for making risk decisions better informed, more consistent, and more accountable. However, value conflicts and pervasive distrust in risk management cannot be reduced by technical analysis. Trying to address risk controversies with more science, in fact, is likely to exacerbate conflict.

Process-oriented solutions

In our view, the limitations of risk science, the importance and difficulty of maintaining trust, and the subjective and contextual nature of the risk game point to the need for a new and radically different approach, one that focuses on introducing more public participation into both risk assessment and risk decision making in order to make the risk-decision process more democratic, improve the relevance and quality of technical analysis, and increase the legitimacy and public acceptance of the resulting decisions. Work by scholars and practitioners in Europe and North America has begun to lay the foundations for improved methods of public participation within deliberative decision processes that include negotiation, mediation, oversight committees, and other forms of public involvement.[17]

An illustrative example: Siting hazardous waste facilities

One important arena in which the need for improved public-participation mechanisms has been taken

15. Stephen Breyer, *Breaking the Vicious Circle: Toward Effective Risk Regulation* (Cambridge, MA: Harvard University Press, 1993).

16. *Dole / Johnston Discussion Draft*, S. 343, 104th Cong., 1st sess. § 633 (1995).

17. Optwin Renn, Thomas Webler, and B. Johnson, "Citizen Participation for Hazard Management," *Risk—Issues in Health and Safety*, 3:12-22 (1991); Mary R. English, *Siting Low-Level Radioactive Waste Disposal Facilities* (New York: Quorum, 1992); Optwin Renn, Thomas Webler, and Peter Wiedemann, *Fairness and Competence in Citizen Participation* (Dordrecht, The Netherlands: Kluwer, 1995).

quite seriously is that of hazardous waste facility siting. Public opposition has made it extraordinarily difficult to build new disposal facilities despite a desperate need for them. For example, during the 1980s, 28 of 34 solid-waste incinerators proposed for California were canceled or postponed[18] and, of 81 applications for hazardous waste facilities, only 6 facilities were built.[19] There is no indication that the situation has changed in the 1990s. Local communities are opposed to having a waste facility in their backyard no matter how small the experts claim the risks to health and the environment are from hosting it.[20]

In the past, some state governments have attempted to overcome local opposition to siting proposals by using a preemption strategy and effectively removing local government from the official decision. This "decide, announce, defend" strategy has often backfired because the siting procedure is still subject to judicial review that may lead to discoveries of flaws in the legislation or delays in the process. The siting issue can also be raised to a high enough profile that it threatens reelection prospects of elected officials, thus prompting a revision in policy.

In order to enhance public acceptance of a facility, as well as reinforce a sense of legitimacy, practitioners and researchers have recognized the importance of establishing a fair site-selection process. At a National Workshop on Facility Siting, a set of guidelines was developed that increases the chance that the affected stakeholders would feel that their major concerns have been met in the siting process.[21]

The central feature of these guidelines is a reliance on informed public participation and consent. Residents of prospective host communities investigate the advantages and disadvantages of the facility and have the authority to negotiate the terms under which the facility will be sited. Incentives in the form of fines for violating standards as well as regular inspections are designed to ensure that public and technical safety criteria are met. The process is designed to instill trust by inviting all interested and affected parties to be players in the siting debate and enabling any community to say no if it does not want to host the facility. Empirical evidence suggests that these principles have enhanced the success of a number of siting efforts.[22]

CONCLUSION

In this article, we have endorsed what Dean and Thompson refer to as

18. Bradley Whitehead, "Who Gave You the Right?" mimeographed (Cambridge, MA: Harvard University, 1991).

19. Michael Helman, "Using Public Authorities to Site Hazardous Waste Management Facilities: Problems and Prospects," *Policy Studies Journal*, 18:974-85 (1990).

20. Doug Easterling and Howard Kunreuther, *The Dilemma of Siting a High-Level Radioactive Waste Repository* (Dordrecht, The Netherlands: Kluwer, 1995).

21. Howard Kunreuther, Kevin Fitzgerald, and Thomas D. Aarts, "Siting Noxious Facilities: A Test of the Facility Siting Credo," *Risk Analysis*, 13:301-18 (1993).

22. Anna Vari, Jeryl L. Mumpower, and Patricia Reagan-Cirincione, *Low-Level Radioactive Waste Disposal Facility Siting Processes in the United States, Western Europe, and Canada* (Albany: State University of New York, Center for Policy Research, 1993).

"the contextualist view of risk."[23] In this view, risk can be conceptualized as a game in which the rules must be socially negotiated within the context of specific decision problems. The conception of risk as a game helps illustrate why strictly technical approaches to risk management often fail with contentious problems involving hazards such as radiation and chemicals. It also highlights the need to allow interested and affected par-ties to define and play the game, thus emphasizing institutional, proce-dural, and societal processes rather than quantitative risk assessments.

Recognizing interested and af-fected citizens as legitimate partners in defining the rules of the risk game is no short-term panacea for the prob-lems of risk management. But seri-ous attention to participation and process issues may, in the long run, lead to more satisfying and success-ful ways to manage the risks posed by modern technologies.

23. Dean and Thompson, *Varieties of Risk*.

The Role of Values in Risk Management

By RALPH L. KEENEY

ABSTRACT: Values, meaning what we care to achieve, are essential to risk management. Understanding the relevant values is critical to making good decisions about risks. Thus values should be made explicit. Conceptual ideas and a few practical suggestions for building value models are discussed. Brief descriptions of several cases in which such models have facilitated decision making about important risk management decisions conclude the article.

Ralph Keeney is a professor of systems management at the University of Southern California and a private consultant on risks and complex decisions. He is the author of Value-Focused Thinking *(1992) and a coauthor with Howard Raiffa of* Decisions with Multiple Objectives *(reprinted in 1993).*

NOTE: This article was supported in part by the Electric Power Research Institute under contract no. WO-2560-03 to the University of Southern California.

R ISKS to health and safety and to the environment are among the foremost concerns of citizens in developed countries. In the United States, we spend hundreds of billions of dollars annually to improve health and safety and the environment. Numerous laws and regulations specify rules for work, requirements for product qualities, and guidelines for behavior. Individuals and families spend time, effort, and money to increase their own health and safety and reduce damage to the environment. In all these cases, risk is managed.

Risk management embraces all the decisions we make and activities we undertake with the intent of improving our health and safety and the environment. Each risk concerns the possibility of detrimental consequences and their likelihoods. The management part of risk management concerns decisions about these risks. Thousands of such decisions are made in the legislation and regulations in states and the federal government; millions are made by families and individuals.

Risk management matters because the risks we choose to manage affect how well we achieve what we value. Our values are not only philosophical principles; they also characterize the consequences of decisions that are important. For example, the health and safety risks that I care about affect the chance that I will die or suffer morbidity or injury. My values are to minimize the likelihoods of such events. Not all injuries are equivalent; I place a higher value on avoiding serious injuries than avoiding slight injuries, and it is my values

concerning these consequences that describe what I consider serious and slight.

Without values, there would be no public concern about risks, no public debate about risks, and probably no public agenda to address them. Values are at the core of all risk issues and should be explicitly accounted for in managing risks.

LIVES VERSUS DOLLARS

The quintessential problem of risk management concerns what is sometimes referred to as the "lives versus dollars" problem. A private version of this problem confronts an individual who can spend money to make his or her life safer. Should she pay to have an air bag put in her car? Should he have an expensive test to detect a possible but unlikely health concern? Should she rewire her home to reduce her family's exposure to electromagnetic fields?

The public version of the problem addresses similar issues on a grander scale. Should there be a requirement that new cars have air bags for both the driver and front-seat passenger? Should there be a national policy that subsidizes mammograms or colonoscopies for large segments of the public? Should standards for wiring or rewiring homes account for the possible but so far undemonstrated health effects of electromagnetic fields?

Your life versus your dollars

Many important issues about risk can be illustrated by using the private version of this problem. Should you spend $1600 to have a driver's-side air bag built into your car? The answer depends on your values for the $1600 and for the reduced risks if the bag is installed. The likelihood of dying in a car accident is approximately 1 in 7000 annually in the United States, or 140 chances in 1 million. Suppose the air bag would reduce your annual chance of dying in an accident by 20 chances in a million. If you plan to own the car for five more years, the cost of the air bag could be spread over five years, for $320 per year. Is it worth $320 to reduce your annual risk of dying in a car crash by 20 chances in 1 million?

You cannot make a responsible decision regarding this problem without determining your value trade-off between costs and risks of death—you must decide how much of your money it is worth to reduce your risk by 1 chance in a million. Suppose that this value trade-off is $8; hence reducing your risk of dying by 20 chances in a million has a value equivalent to that for $160 (20 times $8). This suggests that you should not purchase the air bag.

Whether $8 is a reasonable value trade-off depends on how else you might spend $8. Suppose, for instance, that driving with your headlights on reduces the likelihood of a head-on crash so much that your risk of dying next year is reduced by 20 chances in a million. If headlights and battery expenses would run $50, you may not wish to spend $320 for an equivalent benefit—and certainly not if you could afford only one of the two options. If your value trade-off were $8 to reduce the risk of death by

1 chance in a million, then leaving your headlights on would be very reasonable; you would reduce your risk by 1 chance in a million for $2.50.

This simple example illustrates some important aspects of lives-versus-dollars decisions. First, such decisions are important. They concern your life and your dollars. Second, there are significant uncertainties about the consequences of such decisions: you do not know whether you will actually have an accident with or without the air bag or with or without your headlights shining. Third, values are essential to appraise the alternatives. Fourth, it is important to make lives-versus-dollars decisions consistently. It would seem unreasonable to pay $320 for the air bag rather than pay $50 to drive with your headlights on for an identical reduction of risk.

Lives-versus-dollars decisions frequently involve values other than lives and dollars. For the car safety example, you should also consider the potential for injuries and perhaps the potential impacts of your decision on others. The main beneficiary of a driver's side air bag would be you. Driving with your headlights on to reduce the risk of head-on collisions benefits you and also your passengers and people in approaching cars.

Public lives versus
    public dollars

Many laws and regulations affect risks to members of the public and use public funds for implementation. These public risk problems have all the complexities of the private risk problems and more. Several studies have examined the costs of saving a life through different programs.[1] The range is tremendous, going from thousands to billions of dollars per life saved. Our laws and regulations are inconsistent; they require massive sums of money to save one person from potentially losing his or her life in some instances, but they do not support a modest expenditure for the same possible benefit in other situations.

There is a fundamental difference between addressing public risks and addressing personal risks. Personal risks involve identifiable fatalities and identifiable costs. That is, you know who is at risk of dying— namely, you—and you know whose money is being spent to reduce those risks—yours. With public risks, we often do not know whose life might be saved, and it is not clear whose money is used. Public programs to manage risk save statistical lives and incur statistical costs. For example, suppose a regulation is proposed that would spend a billion dollars to reduce some air pollutant that causes lung cancer. We know that a million people are exposed to the pollutant and the regulation reduces the risk to each of them by one chance in a million. Thus the regulation would save one statistical life. We never know who that individual is. The billion dollars would come from many people paying taxes and from customers paying higher prices to businesses

that also partially pay for the regulation. Thus the costs are statistical. Should we spend a billion dollars for this regulation to avoid one statistical fatality? It is this value trade-off between statistical costs and statistical lives that we need to think carefully about in order to responsibly allocate our resources for health and safety.

In many decisions that involve potential loss of life, hidden agendas play an important role. For example, some very expensive activities to reduce risks, such as the reduction of toxic material at certain industrial and military sites, ensure jobs for certain government agencies and specific industries for many years. Sometimes a risk issue is used as a means to influence an industry; for example, risks of possible loss of life are used by some parties to limit or stop the nuclear industry in the United States. Other parties justify spending large sums of money to reduce small risks; they wish to alleviate fears and promote an industry's development. The public pays massive sums for such battles, wasting both money and lives.

In the early 1980s, Aaron Wildavsky argued that richer is safer.[2] Quite simply, poverty takes lives; it is one of the largest risks in the United States. This is because individuals eventually pay to implement any regulations intended to promote our safety. Consequently, numerous individuals are poorer by a small amount and must alter their

1. John F. Morrall III, "A Review of the Record," *Regulation*, pp. 25-34, (Nov.-Dec. 1986); Tammy O. Tengs et al., "Five-Hundred Life-Saving Interventions and Their Cost-Effectiveness," *Risk Analysis*, 15(3):369-90 (June 1995).

2. Aaron Wildavsky, "No Risk Is the Highest Risk of All," *American Scientist*, 67:32-37 (Jan.-Feb. 1979); idem, "Richer Is Safer," *Public Interest*, 60:23-39 (Summer 1980).

decisions slightly. Some will not spend their money on certain safety or health items or on stress reduction, as they otherwise would have done. If your tires are bald and you drive on rain-slickened roads, you will more likely be involved in a fatal accident than if you had used an additional $40 to buy new tires. In many cases, consumers can buy health and safety more economically—and thus with less loss of life—than the government.

In the past decade, some aspects of Wildavsky's arguments have been quantified. Collectively, several studies suggest that for every $2 million to $15 million spent on public programs, one statistical life is lost.[3] These results have recently been used to appraise the net mortality due to expensive regulations. The Occupational Safety and Health Administration (OSHA) had proposed a requirement to install locks on energy devices such as circuit breakers. In *International Union, UAW v. OSHA*, Judge Williams ruled against the proposed regulation, stating that more fatalities would be induced by the costs of the regulation than would potentially be saved by the regulation. Specifically, he noted that a fatality might be induced by each $7.5 million spent and that the proposed regulation would prevent 8 to 13 deaths annually at a cost of $163 million. Thus the regulation could induce 22 additional deaths per year. As a result, Judge

Williams suspended review of the proposal and asked OSHA to investigate further its net effect, including the statistical fatalities induced by the costs of the proposed regulation.[4]

MAKING VALUES EXPLICIT

It is difficult to be clear enough about risk management decisions in our heads. By writing our values down and processing them systematically, we can make our policies consistent with our values, save lives, and improve communication. But can we express values explicitly in a meaningful manner? Yes; indeed, this has been done well for certain problems.

Making values explicit involves both qualitative and quantitative work.[5] The foundation is qualitative; one must identify objectives to specify what values are important. This task is not easy, but being explicit helps. After a list of objectives is written, it should be structured to relate means objectives, which contribute to achieving ends, to ends objectives. For instance, minimizing emissions of a certain pollutant is a means objective to reducing possible illnesses, possible deaths, and possible environmental damage.

Once the qualitative structure of the problem has been developed by stating objectives, quantification can contribute additional insight. The first step is to identify measures that can indicate the degree to which ends objectives are achieved. Important value judgments are made in this

3. Ralph L. Keeney, "Mortality Risks Induced by Economic Expenditures," *Risk Analysis*, 10(1):147-59 (Feb. 1990); Randall Lutter and John F. Morrall III, "Health-Health Analysis: A New Way to Evaluate Health and Safety Regulations," *Journal of Risk and Uncertainty*, 8(1):43-66 (Jan. 1994).

4. *International Union, UAW v. OSHA*, 938 F.2d 1310 (D.C. Cir. 1991).

5. Ralph L. Keeney, *Value-Focused Thinking* (Cambridge, MA: Harvard University Press, 1992).

process. For example, in a public risk problem to maximize lives saved, one can measure the number of lives saved or the number of years of potential life saved. With the former measure, the deaths of a 15-year-old and an 80-year-old count identically, as each is one death. With the latter measure, the 15-year-old would count six times as much as the 80-year-old if the 15-year-old has an expected lifetime of 75 years and the 80-year-old has only 10 expected life-years remaining. Which measure is more appropriate obviously requires an important value judgment.

In thinking about this value judgment and in interpreting statistical lives, it is more accurate to speak of adding years to the lives of individuals than of saving lives. This is because everyone will eventually die. If we save someone from an automobile accident at age 60, that individual may die from a heart attack at age 75; 15 years were added to that individual's life. So we only extend a person's life when we say that we save a life, and the extension is the expected additional years of life for the person whose life was saved.

Setting value trade-offs between objectives requires the quantification of judgment. Thoughtful reflection can enhance the likelihood that reasonable judgments are used. In the public risk problem, consider the value trade-off of statistical lives versus statistical dollars. How much would it be worth to extend a life by one year? Suppose the answer were $100,000. If we were looking at a pollution program that reduced the loss of life for people who were typically 55 years old, each life saved would save roughly 25 years of life. It may be worth approximately $2.5 million ($100,000 times 25) to avoid the loss of one statistical life.

But how many statistical fatalities might be induced by the cost of the program? It would not make sense to spend $50 million to save a statistical life if that money would result in taking five statistical lives by making people poorer. The induced fatalities caused by the expenditures to satisfy regulations provide an upper bound for a reasonable value trade-off between statistical lives and statistical costs.

It is also useful to be explicit about the risk attitude that should be used in the evaluation. Is the loss of life of 100 people 10 times more significant than the loss of life of 10 people? If one wishes to invest money to save as many lives as possible, the answer is yes. Is the loss of 100 lives at one time more important than the loss of 100 lives in separate accidents? They should be valued the same if the intent is to save as many lives as possible for a given cost. However, due to concerns such as the social amplification of risk, it may be reasonable to have values that account for the equity of the risks or the avoidance of catastrophes, as well as simply saving as many people as possible.[6]

In practice, how should we obtain values for risk management decisions? The idea is to build a value model using concepts similar to those used to build models of any physical

6. Ralph L. Keeney, "Evaluating Mortality Risks from an Organizational Perspective," in The Value of Life and Safety, ed. M. W. Jones-Lee (Amsterdam: North Holland, 1982), pp. 217-27.

or social process. First, analysts interview stakeholders and decision makers about values appropriate for a particular decision, convert these values into objectives, and structure them into means and ends objectives. Then analysts work with technical specialists who understand the problem to identify appropriate measures that indicate the degree to which the objectives are achieved. Next, parameters that quantify the value trade-offs necessary to combine the different measures and the risk attitudes for different levels of impacts on those measures must be defined. Judgments about these parameters might come from the public, stakeholders, and public decision makers with responsibility for the decision.

CASES INVOLVING EXPLICIT VALUES

Values have been made explicit for numerous risk management decisions. The cases summarized here indicate a range of risk management problems for which making values explicit has helped. The first case concerns personal risks; the other cases concern public risk problems.

Personal risk decisions

I have many opportunities to spend my money to reduce risks to my life. I would like to make these decisions consistently and without a great deal of time or effort. Consequently, I have carefully thought about the value trade-off between cost and risk to my life that promotes consistency in these decisions. Considering what I can use money for to influence the quality of my life, I have

decided that about $12 of my money is an appropriate amount to reduce my immediate risk of dying by one chance in a million. This is consistent with spending nearly $1700 annually to eliminate any chance of dying in a vehicular accident ($12 times the likelihood of dying in a car accident [140 chances in a million] equals $1680).

Several years ago, my former doctor suggested that I get a test for colon cancer in conjunction with a routine physical examination. I asked why I should have such a test and what the chances were that I had colon cancer and that a test would detect it. His answer was that I was now 40 years old and that I should have the test. This did not answer my question; I wanted to know what the test might do for me and to me. Eventually, another doctor told me that my chances of having colon cancer at that time were about one in a million, given other information about my health. Cancer would probably be detected by the test if I had it. Preparing for the test, going to and from the doctor's office, and having the test would take about four hours and cost about $200. This effort and cost were clearly not worth eliminating the risk of one chance in a million. Indeed, driving across town to have the test would add a risk of about one chance in a million to my life. I felt comfortable declining the test, as I could see it was the right decision.

Nuclear repository decisions

The U.S. Department of Energy was responsible for choosing a site for a nuclear repository to dispose of high-level nuclear waste from power plants in the United States. The values appropriate for this study were gathered from numerous documents that summarized public meetings and from individuals at the Department of Energy who were responsible for recommending a site. The categories of objectives that were specified from the values included health and safety, environmental effects, social effects on communities near proposed repositories, and economic costs. The value trade-offs between all of these objectives were elicited from four managers at the Department of Energy.[7] These value trade-offs were based on information available about other value trade-offs in other programs concerning the same categories of objectives. The value trade-off between statistical dollars and statistical lives was set at $4 million per life saved in the base case. To see if this mattered, a sensitivity analysis was done over a wide range, from $1 to $100 million per statistical fatality avoided.

Air pollution
in Los Angeles

The problem of reducing air pollution in Los Angeles was framed by many as a problem of costs versus the potential health benefits of better air. My colleague Detlof von Winterfeldt and I interviewed individuals from many stakeholder groups concerned about air pollution, including the American Lung Association, the

7. Miley W. Merkhofer and Ralph L. Keeney, "A Multiattribute Utility Analysis of Alternative Sites for the Disposal of Nuclear Waste," *Risk Analysis*, 7(2):173-94 (Apr. 1987).

Automobile Club of Southern California, the California Air Resources Board, the Los Angeles Area Chamber of Commerce, the Sierra Club, and the South Coast Air Quality Management District. These interviews identified a wide range of values—not only public health and safety and economic costs but also psychological and visibility impacts, the influence on lifestyles, environmental impacts, social impacts, impacts on jobs and businesses, and equity concerns.

The main measure for public health impacts was the annual number of otherwise healthy adults diagnosed as having a 20 percent impairment in lung function. The value trade-off between annual cost and one adult avoiding such a condition was assessed at between $20,000 and $125,000 by those interviewed. The annual cost of the proposed program to reduce the air pollution was estimated at $10 billion per year. Given the estimated number of individuals who might experience health effects, the equity implications for how the $10 billion were spread among individuals turned out to be more significant than the health effects.

Wastewater
treatment facilities

Victoria, British Columbia, screens its liquid waste to remove solids and pumps the liquids through two pipes into the nearby Strait of Juan de Fuca between British Columbia and Washington State. While extensive monitoring has suggested that putting this untreated sewage into the strait has had no adverse effects on human health or environmental quality, many people feel that the waste should be treated. Working with officials in Victoria, Tim McDaniels of the University of British Columbia developed a value referendum to allow the public to vote in a nonbinding vote on three options to treat liquid waste. The options were to continue the status quo, to construct a new preliminary treatment facility, and to construct a secondary treatment facility. In extensive discussions prior to the referendum, the implications of the three options were described in terms of their environmental, health, aesthetic, and economic effects. Consistent with local tradition, the referendum indicated the options and their respective costs in terms of total capital costs, new annual costs, and the estimated annual cost per $100,000 of assessed property value.

In November 1992, about 34,000 voters (24 percent of those registered) participated in the referendum, which was held with no other voting. The status quo option received 57 percent of the votes, and the other two alternatives received 21 and 22 percent, respectively. This referendum indicated a useful way to obtain thoughtful values from large numbers of the public on decisions that could significantly affect each of them.

CONCLUSION

In summary,

— values are crucial to risk management;
— there are systematic procedures that make values explicit, organized, and quantified; and
— explicit and quantified values can significantly improve risk management decisions.

Values are why people care about risk management. Thus it is natural to involve the public in decisions about their risks by asking them about their values. If we know what the public wants, we have a much better chance of providing it.

Risk management decisions are complex, so a little analysis can go a long way in providing insights. Such analyses should include models of possible consequences and models of values to facilitate the evaluation of existing alternatives and the development of better ones. In addition, if values are explicit, we can communicate why one alternative is chosen and why others are not. Greater trust in the decision processes and the decision makers should result.

ANNALS, *AAPSS*, **545**, May 1996

Rethinking Risk Management in the Federal Government

By ROBIN CANTOR

ABSTRACT: This article examines recent debates about guiding principles and implementation of risk management in the federal government. Considering influences from both political and scientific arenas, the article will highlight how changing perspectives about science, regulatory objectives, and decision models are fostering significant innovations in the conduct of risk management by federal agencies. The first part of the article summarizes several explicit signals of rethinking the federal approach to risk management at the administrative and congressional levels. The second part considers particular intellectual shifts in our understanding of risk management that are fueling contemporary debates on the science, objectives, and process. Specific agency examples are used to illustrate recent suggestions for or experience with implementing innovations for federal risk management. The article concludes with some thoughts about the future of the federal role in risk management and risk policy more generally.

Robin Cantor is the program director for decision, risk, and management sciences of the National Science Foundation. She earned a Ph.D. in economics in 1985 at Duke University. She was a member of the research staff of Oak Ridge National Laboratory for ten years prior to serving in her current position at the National Science Foundation.

A MONG the many demands for change at the federal level, few are as controversial and encompassing as recent movements to rethink the role of government in risk management. Beginning as small pockets of discontent over rules and regulations that cost too much and accomplished too little, the movement to reform risk management is now firmly linked to a general sense that the system is fundamentally flawed and in need of radical reform.

This article examines some of the factors that are fueling the discontent and demands for reform in federal risk management. Recently, a number of explicit actions to bring about risk management reforms have been initiated by the Clinton administration, Congress, and federal agencies. Many of these actions address the overall approach for analysis and risk management, but many also are aimed at prescribing methods and scope requirements for risk assessments. Disagreements about how best to proceed on risk reform often stem from concerns about the level of prescription, feasibility for agency implementation, or inconsistencies across prescribed guidelines.

Bolstering many of the federal actions are intellectual shifts about how we analyze and respond to risks as individuals and as a society. Arguments that come into the intellectual debate range from the roles of different levels of government in protecting health and safety[1] to highly tech-

nical criticisms of particular analytical methods.[2] Currently, it seems as if no aspect of risk management is free of vigorous scientific or political contention.

Federal agencies have been both catalysts and reactionaries in the risk management turmoil. While agency representatives support many changes to improve the regulatory system, agency heads have expressed strong concerns about the impacts of certain congressional reforms on their abilities to protect human health and the environment.[3] At the same time, however, agencies have made their own significant changes in the conduct of risk analysis and risk management. Innovations under development at the Department of Energy (DOE) for hazardous waste management and at the Environmental Protection Agency (EPA) for pollution control and prevention within economic sectors are notable examples.

Where is all of this rethinking, reforming, and reinventing likely to lead for risk management at the federal level? Some proponents of the reform believe it will lead to a more rational process of risk management, that is, greater grounding in established scientific principles and facts, greater peer review and scientific consensus regarding the analysis, and less politicization and manipulation

---

1. Paul Portney, "Overall Assessment and Future Directions," in *Public Policies for Environmental Protection*, ed. P. R. Portney (Washington, DC: Resources for the Future, 1990), pp. 282-84.

2. Regulatory Impact Analysis Project, Inc., *Choices in Risk Assessment: The Role of Science Policy in the Environmental Management Process* (Washington, DC: Regulatory Impact Analysis Project, 1994), pp. 25-59.

3. Office of Management and Budget, "Statement of Administration Policy on S.343 Comprehensive Regulatory Reform Act of 1995," 10 July 1995, p. 1.

of the results.[4] Others, however, worry that it reverses recent trends to broaden the dimensions of risk policy and ultimately will lead to paralyzing the federal role in risk management activities.[5] Whatever the future holds, rethinking risk management has fostered a new round of questions about the uneasy relationship between science and politics in risk policy.

PRINCIPLES FOR RISK MANAGEMENT

The Clinton administration's efforts on risk management have tended to emphasize the role of risk analysis both in setting agency priorities and in rule making. The Executive Order on Regulatory Planning and Review (No. 12866) reinforced attention to risk-based priority setting and the balancing of risk reduction and costs in the broader context of regulatory decision making.[6] This order also established a Regulatory Working Group, which launched a concerted effort across federal agencies to develop principles for risk assessment, risk management, and risk communica-

4. Lester B. Lave, "Risk Assessment Reform Is for Real," *Risk Analysis*, 15(2):107 (Apr. 1995); John D. Graham, "Verifiability Isn't Everything," ibid., p. 109.

5. Linda-Jo Schierow, "The Role of Risk Analysis and Risk Management in Environmental Protection," Congressional Research Service Issue Brief, IB94036, updated 28 Apr. 1995, pp. 3-5.

6. Previous administrations also emphasized these principles for risk-related policymaking. See Institute for Regulatory Policy, *Toward Common Measures: Recommendations for a Presidential Executive Order on Environmental Risk Assessment and Risk Management Policy* (Washington, DC: Federal Focus, 1991), pp. 28-48.

tion. The National Science and Technology Council, through its Committee on the Environment and Natural Resources, is responsible for a complementary effort to coordinate scientific research and development for risk assessment and management.

Administration guidance on risk management emphasizes the best use of scientific, technical, and economic data but readily acknowledges that risk assessment and cost-benefit analysis are inputs to a broader framework. Similarly, administration guidance is supportive of approaches such as comparative risk analysis and so-called best practice but allows considerable agency flexibility in the selection of methods and assumptions for particular risk analyses.[7]

A similar objective to develop broad guidelines for agency operations guides the President's Commission on Risk Assessment and Management. The commission was created under the Clean Air Act amendments of 1990. It is charged with reviewing policy implications and appropriate uses of risk assessment and risk management in federal regulatory programs that address human health risks of exposure to hazardous substances. Unlike a number of recent reviews of risk assessment practices, the commission has adopted a much broader perspective and will consider such issues as communicating uncertain risk estimates, cost-effectiveness and cost-benefit analysis, environmental justice and equity, comparative risk assessment, and the role of peer review.

7. Executive Office of the President, Office of Science and Technology Policy, "Science, Risk, and Public Policy," Mar. 1995, pp. 11, 13.

In contrast to these oversight efforts, specific requirements for risk analysis and cost-benefit analysis have been the hallmarks of at least eight bills introduced into Congress by mid-1995. Generally, these bills are aimed at regulatory reform, but their implications for risk management are extensive.

Provisions that are particularly relevant for the future of federal risk management include revisions to the judicial review process for regulatory actions that would alter the scope and possibly the frequency of such review for risk assessments and cost-benefit analyses. Final actions are now subject to judicial review, but agencies have been afforded considerable flexibility in conducting the supporting analysis, subject to an "arbitrary and capricious" test. Because the regulatory reform bills contain specific prescriptions for risk assessment characterization, and cost-benefit analysis, supporting analysis may increasingly face a "consistent with law" test. Additional provisions include expanded requirements for peer review, cost-benefit analysis, and reopening assessment activities for existing regulations.

Opponents of these reforms worry that the science supporting risk assessment and cost-benefit analysis is so controversial that the provisions essentially paralyze risk management at the federal level. Another possible implication of delineating so much of the analytical process in statute is that it will prevent agencies from keeping pace with rapidly evolving scientific practices and data.[8]

Finally, both the administration and congressional efforts have benefited from more than ten years of debate on sound principles for risk management. Beginning with the formal guidance provided by the 1983 Red Book,[9] reports by Federal Focus,[10] the Carnegie Commission,[11] the National Research Council,[12] the Business Roundtable,[13] and the Harvard Group on Risk Management Reform[14] mark a progression of discontent with federal approaches to risk management. While these debates center largely on the scientific rigor of risk assessment, they ultimately frame a very particular structure for risk management that is decidedly rational concerning outcomes, information intensive, and utilitarian.[15]

8. National Academy of Public Administration, *Setting Priorities, Getting Results: A New Direction for the Environmental Protection Agency* (Washington, DC: National Academy of Public Administration, Apr. 1995), pp. 48-49.

9. National Research Council, *Risk Assessment in the Federal Government: Managing the Process* (Washington, DC: National Academy Press, 1983).

10. Institute for Regulatory Policy, *Toward Common Measures*.

11. Carnegie Commission on Science, Technology, and Government, *Risk and the Environment: Improving Regulatory Decision Making* (New York: Carnegie Commission on Science, Technology, and Government, June 1993).

12. National Research Council, *Science and Judgment in Risk Assessment* (Washington, DC: National Academy Press, 1994).

13. Business Roundtable, *Toward Smarter Regulation* (Washington, DC: Business Roundtable, Jan. 1995).

14. Harvard Group on Risk Management Reform, *Reform of Risk Regulation: Achieving More Protection at Less Cost* (Boston, MA: Harvard Center for Risk Analysis, Mar. 1995).

15. Jonathan Lash, "Integrating Science, Values, and Democracy Through Comparative Risk Assessment," in *Worst Things First: The Debate over Risk-Based National Environmental Priorities*, ed. Adam M. Finkel and

Competing paradigms of risk management that emphasize process rationality, dispute resolution, individual rights, and environmental ethics have had little impact on the idealized model over this period. At best, these alternative views have secured a role for public participation and socioeconomic data, but they have done so on the basis of values and not science.

Fixing risk management

Some of the most compelling arguments for risk management reform stem from a growing understanding of how good intentions may lead to bad results. Examples such as Superfund and the Delaney Clauses under the Federal Food, Drug and Cosmetic Act highlight the complex relationships between legislation, rule making, and implementation. Case studies provide a burgeoning literature on the practices of federal risk management.[16] A number of general insights emerge from this literature that lend strong support to the calls for risk management reform.

Scientific credibility

First, risk assessment methods, assumptions, and conclusions differ dramatically across the federal government, even where agency activities and goals overlap. One of the more powerful conclusions from the case study literature is that there is

tremendous variation in the cost-effectiveness of various regulations. In 1991, the Office of Management and Budget published data in the fiscal year 1992 budget document indicating that the cost per life saved for 53 selected regulations ranged from $100,000 to $5.7 trillion (in 1990 dollars). A more recent study analyzed 587 life-saving interventions to calculate cost per life-year saved and generally found variations over 11 orders of magnitude within and across different categories of intervention.[17]

In practice, risk analysis combines information from many sources with varying degrees of scientific rigor, making judgments over analytical assumptions and methods essential. There is a long-standing tension between the use of judgment and the use of science in risk assessments. While this tension exists in every area of assessment, it represents one of the defining features of federal risk management. In 1983, the Red Book described a model for analysis that stressed attention to objective and quantitative risk measures and effectively separated idealized risk assessment from risk management. Since then, scientific debates about risk assessment have emphasized methodological issues and agency practice.[18] Scientific debates in risk management have focused on the roles of science and values in decision making but

Dominic Golding (Washington, DC: Resources for the Future, 1994), pp. 74-76.

16. For an extensive summary, see Stephen Breyer, *Breaking the Vicious Circle: Toward Effective Risk Regulation* (Cambridge, MA: Harvard University Press, 1993).

17. Tammy O. Tengs et al., "Five-Hundred Life-Saving Interventions and Their Cost-Effectiveness," *Risk Analysis*, 15(3):371 (June 1995).

18. Sheila Jasanoff, *Risk Management and Political Culture: A Comparative Study of Science in the Policy Context* (New York: Russell Sage Foundation, 1986), pp. 26-27.

have paid far less attention to the scientific credibility of the management or decision science embedded in the framework.

To encourage consistency in risk assessment practices, agencies such as EPA employ default options for key analytical assumptions, or inference guidelines. This attempt to manage judgment, however, has launched an entire area of scientific debate around the practice of using default options and whether or not these practices tend to overestimate risk.[19] Some of the more controversial default assumptions attempt to guide extrapolation from animal data to human cancer risks, selecting the most sensitive species to represent human health impacts, using no-threshold dose-response models, and using upper-bound estimates for exposure variables.

New results, methods, and data actually may further disagreement within a scientific community that strives to displace judgment with facts. Default options may not keep pace with the supporting science given the practicalities of limited agency resources and pressing responsibilities, and new knowledge may lack the level of credibility needed to displace the default options. Cross-national studies of risk management indicate that this emphasis on debating the science may have served to exacerbate protracted and inconclusive risk controversies in the United States.[20] A more subtle implication is that exces-sive emphasis on the scientific credibility of risk assessment may have inadvertently made it less responsive and relevant to the risk management task.[21] On the other hand, scientific debate about methods has brought much needed attention to the treatment of ecosystems in ecological risk assessment and population susceptibilities in health risk assessment.

A powerful belief at the federal level is that the integrity of risk assessment is inextricably linked to its scientific credibility. Consequently, nearly all proposals for improving this component of risk management emphasize peer review and reducing uncertainty through additional research. For example, EPA began collaborating with the National Science Foundation in 1995 to implement a greatly expanded effort in peer-reviewed, investigator-initiated research grants. These activities are part of a broader emphasis by the agency's Science Policy Council on the use of peer review for risk analysis activities throughout the institution.

Setting priorities

A second insight from studying current practices is that regulatory approaches and, hence, the risk management options are often constrained by the enabling legislation. Environmental laws such as the Clean Air Act and the Safe Drinking Water Act require basing standards and priorities on frameworks that emphasize health risk and the best available technology to the exclusion of other factors such as cost.

19. National Research Council, *Science and Judgment*, pp. 85-105.

20. Sheila Jasanoff, "American Exceptionalism and the Political Acknowledgment of Risk," *Daedalus* 119(4):75-77 (Fall 1990).

21. National Research Council, *Science and Judgment*, p. 260.

To a large extent, inconsistencies across risk management approaches result from the piecemeal and crisis-driven history of environmental laws. In the past 25 years, Congress has passed more than 26 principal statutes on risk regulation. Responsibilities for these regulations span nine federal agencies.

Fragmented and uncoordinated statutes are seen as an obstacle to placing risk management in the broader context of risk priorities.[22] Risk prioritization, for all its definitional problems, has emerged as one organizing approach to rationalize the existing complex and unwieldy system.

Agency studies of risk prioritization[23] have helped forge a general consensus for reform that supports shifting federal attention from simply reducing risks to a more balanced consideration of setting priorities. While methods to set risk priorities in federal agencies remain controversial, most proposals include a prominent role for the analysis of costs and benefits. Unlike earlier debates about risk that largely emphasized health and economic outcomes, current debates emphasize the roles of equity, environmental ethics, and democracy in the priority-setting process.

Risk-based priority setting is being implemented in agencies such as EPA and DOE, but with mixed results. For example, efforts in EPA have been confounded by congressional earmarks, internal changes to the budget process, court orders and consent decrees, specific statutory mandates, executive orders, and presidential initiatives.[24] Efforts at the DOE toward implementing priorities for funding remediation of hazardous waste sites have also been controversial. Public and scientific discussions about a national priority system have been strained by conflicts between risk criteria and social factors such as standing compliance agreements, cultural values, and local socioeconomic impacts.[25]

The social context

The priorities debate highlights the sometimes incompatible influences of technical approaches to risk, economics, and democracy. Despite the friction, there is a growing recognition at the federal level that risk management must be placed in its social context for better policy results. The attention to a cost-benefit analysis for proposed regulations is an obvious sign of this. But other signs are also visible. For many years, economists argued that market-based mechanisms for controlling pollution would be superior to command and control regulation. Concerns about equity

22. F. Henry Habicht II, "EPA's Vision for Setting National Environmental Priorities," in *Worst Things First*, ed. Finkel and Golding, p. 42.

23. Environmental Protection Agency, *Unfinished Business: A Comparative Assessment of Environmental Problems* (Washington, DC: Environmental Protection Agency, 1987); idem, *Reducing Risks: Setting Priorities and Strategies for Environmental Protection*, SAB-EC-90-021 (Washington, DC: Environmental Protection Agency, 1990).

24. National Academy of Public Administration, *Setting Priorities*, pp. 152-58.

25. Karen E. Jenni, Miley W. Merkhofer, and Carol Williams, "The Rise and Fall of a Risk-Based Priority System: Lessons from DOE's Environmental Restoration Priority System," *Risk Analysis*, 15(3):409 (June 1995).

and performance, however, were obstacles to using these mechanisms. In 1990, the amendments to the Clean Air Act included provisions for tradable allowances to reduce annual sulfur dioxide emissions by U.S. utility companies. Current results show that distributional impacts of the trading have been small, prices for allowances have fallen, and cost savings are evident but less than the ideal.[26] One potentially important limitation on realized cost savings derives from state regulatory rules, which vary significantly for rate setting and returns on technology investments.

In addition to economic incentives, grounding risk management in its social context highlights the importance of other decision factors. Federal risk management often creates a divide between citizens and scientific elites. Place- or geographically based and community-based approaches have emerged as concepts that attempt to capture the influence of values, as well as incentives, in the processes of selecting and managing risks. Community-based programs also emphasize the role of democracy in determining risk priorities. These approaches are dramatic contrasts to the traditional tunnel vision often attributed to federal risk managers. The 1994 EPA Common Sense Initiative (CSI) is an example of an effort to bring a more comprehensive, sector-based view to risk management. The CSI is designed to replace the adversarial model of risk manage-

26. Robert W. Hahn and Carol A. May, "The Behavior of the Allowance Market: Theory and Evidence," *Electricity Journal*, 7(2):33-34 (Mar. 1994).

ment of a specific hazard, with one based on a partnership view of environmental protection within a specific industry. Supporters of the CSI hope that a more comprehensive analysis of environmental protection will encourage industries to prevent pollution and to develop innovative technologies for meeting environmental standards. The team concept for the CSI stresses participation by high-level EPA officials, industry leaders, and national and grassroots environmental organizations, along with representatives of state environmental commissions, local government, labor unions, and environmental justice groups. The six industries participating in the first phase of the CSI are automobile assembly, computers and electronics, iron and steel, metal plating and finishing, petroleum refining, and printing.

LOOKING AHEAD

While not quite endorsing a strictly rational model of risk management at the federal level, many agency efforts are certainly aimed at a more reasoned approach to environmental protection. Practical change at the federal level, however, is fundamentally constrained by the organizational, political, and legal realities of agency operations. Intellectual shifts in our understanding of federal risk management have brought about some significant changes in the idealized framework. Scientific review of major risk assessments is now common practice by the federal agencies, as is scientific review of major assessment guidelines. But it is doubtful that the scientific credibility of risk assessment alone will ensure social acceptance of risk management. Public involvement ideals have shifted from opportunities for public comment to an emphasis on open and participatory processes. Our experience with such openness is too limited to judge if scientifically driven risk-based frameworks can coexist with social goals to build political consensus. Complicating matters further is the additional concern about consistency between political consensus and economic efficiency. The task of reforming environmental risk management is daunting, especially when reform objectives differ so dramatically. Agency willingness to try a number of risk management approaches is important. As we gain more experience in using different approaches to address a range of risk problems, we undoubtedly will discover that some innovations work better than others. More generally, this knowledge may help us understand how better to balance technocratic and democratic ideals in all areas of risk management.

ANNALS, *AAPSS*, **545**, May 1996

The Risk Management Dilemma

By RICHARD J. ZECKHAUSER and W. KIP VISCUSI

ABSTRACT: Market processes play a central and constructive role in allocating risks, but impediments such as inaccurately perceived risks and externalities create a potential role for government intervention. Individuals overestimate small risks, are averse to imprecisely understood risks, and give excessive weight to errors of commission over errors of omission. The challenge for the government is to strike an appropriate balance in its risk regulation efforts and to avoid institutionalizing common irrational responses to risk. Excessive expenditures on risk reduction, often undertaken by or required by government, not only squander resources but also may increase risks to us all; they can divert expenditures that could have been used to enhance our standard of living and, directly or indirectly, our health. Risk equity concerns often prove problematic: they may direct excessive attention to unimportant risks and hinder efforts to deploy resources to produce the greatest gains in societal health status.

Richard J. Zeckhauser is the Frank P. Ramsey Professor of Political Economy at the John F. Kennedy School of Government, Harvard University. He has made fundamental contributions to the theory of insurance, to principal-agent theory, and, most recently, to our understanding of catastrophes.

W. Kip Viscusi is the George G. Allen Professor of Economics at Duke University and the founding editor of the Journal of Risk and Uncertainty. *His estimates of the value of life and health are used throughout the federal government.*

WHEN society allocates resources, three questions must be answered: who should decide; whose values count; and who should pay? In a democratic, capitalist society, the answer is straightforward: individuals and corporate decision makers should decide and pay for themselves, making their own values the basis for decision. The government establishes property rights and enforces contracts but otherwise sits on the sidelines.

The government often participates actively, however, in decisions affecting physical risks, frequently by overriding individual choices. When bad outcomes do occur, payment is often made by insurance companies and government, whose actions may have played no role in the bad outcomes. This approach is understandable because of three common characteristics of physical risks: surrounding uncertainty, significant consequences, and externalities. Even perfectly rational individuals have difficulty making consequential decisions under conditions of uncertainty. Moreover, if adverse consequences are significant, transfer of payment responsibility (risk spreading) is desirable. Finally, in many risk-taking decisions, such as a factory choosing an emissions level, one actor may impose significant adverse effects on others (that is, externalities).

Risk management thus presents a dilemma: challenging circumstances undermine many of the justifications for self-interested decentralized choice, but when we depart from this norm, both legitimacy and efficiency are undermined. We examine this dilemma here, looking first at the sources of risk and then at challenges to decision making.

SOURCES OF RISK

Nature is the source of many risks, such as earthquakes and hurricanes. But human action—the only avenue for affecting risk costs—usually amplifies (or ameliorates) the consequences. For example, houses built near major faults or coastlines are more likely to be damaged than houses built elsewhere.

Three primary sources of risk are generated by human action: lifestyle choices, contractual arrangements, and externalities from choices by others. Lifestyle choices—drinking to excess, smoking, and failing to eat a nutritious diet or take sufficient exercise—create many of the most important risks to human health.[1] Governments try to influence these choices; for example, they provide nutrition information, punish public intoxication, and require warning labels on cigarette packages.

Other risks are contracted for voluntarily with some other economic agent; for example, people buy potentially risky products and decide to work in hazardous jobs. In return, they expect some offset: higher wages for risky jobs or lower prices for the product. Such trade-offs, and their role in promoting efficiency, have been part of economic thought since Adam Smith. Nevertheless, the rationality of trading risk for resources is often called into question, frequently by the government. For ex-

1. See Willard Manning et al., *The Cost of Poor Health Habits* (Cambridge, MA: Harvard University Press, 1991).

ample, the government intervenes to protect the well-being of those exposed to the risk through mechanisms such as product and job safety regulations, workers' compensation, and tort liability compensation for injuries.

Contracts on risk acceptance often have significant legitimacy and strength. Indeed, even when risks escalate, individuals in high-risk jobs often carry out their obligations; for example, firefighters and police officers rarely renege on their obligations when confronting an extraordinary risk. However, individuals often attempt to exploit the risk terms in a contract. For example, housing prices near toxic waste dumps are substantially depressed, but a purchaser who knows the risk and receives a discounted house price may well lobby or sue government agencies to expedite the cleanup.

In the third group of risks, externalities, actions by one party create risks or costs for others. These are the most obvious candidates for government intervention. In such situations, the firms or individuals imposing the risk have no incentive to care about the adverse external effects of their actions. Water and air pollution by firms, and drunk driving, are classic examples of externally imposed risks. The rationale for regulating externalities is clear-cut, but the optimal degree of regulation rarely is. Externality-regulating efforts can substantially redistribute resources; thus efforts to reduce pollution may benefit the politically influential rather than those who suffer the greatest harm or whose health could be saved most cheaply.

Our perception of the seriousness of a risk often depends on the risk's specific source; as a society, we tend to take some types of risks far more seriously than others. Consider now some important risks that we tend to respond to less than rationally.

Ordinary versus catastrophic risks

From the standpoint of an individual citizen, a reasonable objective would be to target risk regulation efforts to maximize the expected number of lives saved for the resources spent. Such an approach would treat equally two situations: one where one person faces a risk of 1/1000, the other where 100 people together confront a risk of 1/100,000. Yet, while the expected number of lives lost is the same in each instance, the death of 100 people in an airplane crash or natural catastrophe typically receives much more publicity than the separate deaths of 100 individuals. That is, society is especially concerned with large-scale catastrophes.

Except in wars—and recent terrorist attacks—large numbers of people rarely die at the same time in contemporary developed nations. Early in the twentieth century, a natural disaster would frequently account for hundreds of deaths in the United States, but society has adapted to these threats through design improvements, through fire-protection devices, and by locating populations away from the riskiest areas. At least as judged by insurance claims, in many of the most recent catastrophes, such as those related to hurricanes, there are greater losses from property damage than from personal injury.[2] Largely because of the high value society attaches to a life—our most fundamental source of value—we have successfully developed substantial expenditures to preserve lives.

Extensive media coverage also leads people to overestimate certain risks and give undue importance to catastrophic events.[3] Do not the lives that are lost in unheralded highway accidents merit the same preventive efforts as those that will be lost due to a highly visible catastrophe, such as a hurricane or earthquake? It is noteworthy that we have responded to the isolated automobile accident case by making various kinds of insurance mandatory, whereas our principal response to natural catastrophes has been to offer subsidized federal insurance coverage and massive ex post bailouts once the catastrophes have hit. Interestingly, for

2. The largest losses of life from disasters in the United States, for each major category apart from terrorism, occurred long ago. The largest flood disaster was the Galveston tidal wave of 1900. The most devastating hurricane occurred in Florida in 1928. The most deadly tornado was in Illinois in 1925; the most deadly earthquake occurred in San Francisco in 1906; and the most catastrophic fire was in Wisconsin in 1871. See National Safety Council, *Accident Facts* (Chicago: National Safety Council, 1993), p. 15. By contrast, the largest financial losses associated with disasters have occurred more recently. Other than the Great Chicago Fire of 1871, the most costly fire was the Oakland wildfire of 1991. The most costly insured hurricane was in 1992, and the most costly U.S. earthquake was in 1989. For data on these and other financial losses and catastrophes, see Insurance Information Institute, *Property/Casualty Fact Book* (New York: Insurance Information Institute, 1994), pp. 77-85.

3. For a discussion of the role of publicity, see Paul Slovic, "Perception of Risk," *Science*, 236:280-85 (1987).

both autos and hurricanes, those who impose the greatest risks often get subsidized; many states impose regulations to temper auto insurance rate differentials, and beachfront dwellers pay a fraction of the fair actuarial charges for flood insurance.

Lurking risks

Lurking risks are major long-term risks of particularly catastrophic consequences that we have never experienced but fear greatly. They include nuclear war, major climate change, the chance that Earth will be hit by an asteroid, and new viruses that may emerge from shrinking rain forests. There may be considerable time before these risks are resolved, and by the nature of these risks, past happenings provide little guidance to gauge their likelihood or consequences.

In lurking risks, catastrophic consequences—in some cases, possibly the end of civilization itself—are coupled with small probabilities, so that risk judgments may differ widely. In the 1960s, for example, much of the U.S. public believed that the chance of a nuclear war within a decade was about 1/3, whereas many experts estimated the annual risk to be from 10^{-3} to 10^{-5}.[4] Such differences in risk perception often cannot be resolved, yet perceived risks must largely determine the size of major national and international risk-reducing expenditures, such as efforts to cut or build nuclear stockpiles or to curb global warming. Assessing magnitudes of loss is often no easier. For example, if a potent new virus

4. Thomas Schelling, personal communication, 1995.

emerges, how likely is it to be more damaging than the acquired immune deficiency syndrome (AIDS) or more than ten times as widespread, or only a tenth? We simply do not know.

What is the source of our fears of lurking risks? One possibility is that society needs a major fear. As the threat of nuclear war has faded, fear about climate change and AIDS has taken hold. Despite increases in most measures of our well-being, we fear for survival of the planet. (Witness the "Save the Planet" motto of the pop culture Hard Rock Cafe chain.)

Yet the scientific community is substantially more worried about climate change than the public is. Its risks are linked with the pollution dangers associated with fossil fuels. And our energy mix is a Hobson's choice: significant reductions in fossil fuel can be achieved only by incurring the dangers of nuclear power. Interestingly, the lower the real risk, the relatively more important is its perception in determining its effect on welfare, for that perception will stir anxiety, which in turn creates a very real loss in utility.

Special status of health risks

Risks of property damage receive far less attention than risks to health. Indeed, this health-over-resources bias is a general phenomenon. For example, society's redistributional efforts focus on health care—Medicaid expenditures significantly exceed welfare expenditures in virtually all cities—although the same dollars might offer substantially greater benefits if spent on transport or appliances. Indeed, controlling for pertinent factors such as age, poor people visit the physician more often than do the affluent.

A desire to control externalities may explain subsidized vaccinations and certainly explains why we pay some individuals for undergoing tuberculosis treatments. It cannot, however, explain our pro-health bias. Rather, we suspect that health status plays an important signaling role: worse health or risk outcomes for the poor are visible and stir the compassion of those who determine political outcomes. Relying on willingness-to-pay to place a toxic waste dump in an impoverished community would be widely perceived as unfair, even if the associated risks were negligible. By contrast, high homicide rates among young black males are treated with relative complacency.

The costs of risks and risk avoidance

As a society, we are doing extremely well in reducing per capita risk costs. Overall death and injury rates, particularly from accidents and natural catastrophes, have fallen dramatically and fairly consistently this century, presumably due to technological advances. Nonetheless, our risk avoidance activities are woefully inefficient. Had the same resources been put where they addressed the greatest reduction, these rates would now be far lower.[5]

The costs imposed by risks are the sum of the value of the losses incurred and the resource costs of re-

5. See Richard J. Zeckhauser and W. Kip Viscusi, "Risk Within Reason," *Science*, 248(4955):559-64 (1990).

ducing risks. We throw away value whenever the same expenditures would produce greater risk reduction elsewhere. Still greater waste, indeed profligacy, is achieved if the expenditures entail such large reductions in income that lives are lost on net. Studies of the relationship between societal income and mortality suggest that a reduction of income in the range of $12 million may cost one statistical life. In addition to better housing, food, and sanitation, higher incomes are also associated with better diets and exercise habits and less of both smoking and excess drinking. Assessing merely the associated increase in risky health habits alone, the life-costing income loss is on the order of $15 million to $18 million.[6] These numbers are below the regulatory expenditures per statistical life saved for many programs, suggesting that beyond wasting dollars, such programs discard lives.

THE CHALLENGE TO RATIONAL DECISIONS

Economists argue that individuals' preferences are to be relied on and taken as given, while paternalistic critics assert that individuals do not know what they want or are easily manipulated. Yet economists, and their decision analyst fellow travelers, are the first to question the underlying rationality of individuals' choices about risks and to suggest that informed expert opinion offers a superior guide to policy.

Individuals systematically overassess small risks and underassess a range of truly consequential larger risks such as those posed by a poor diet. Increases in risk are much more salient than decreases. Ambiguous risks—ones whose probabilities are hard to estimate—are often the cause for alarm. Moreover, researchers have documented many anomalous behaviors regarding choices involving uncertainty.[7]

Yet the rational decision framework remains the appropriate normative reference point: policies should not institutionalize the errors people make but, rather, should promote the outcomes they would choose if they understood the risks accurately and could make sound decisions that reflected their values. (Individuals who are well equipped to choose between apples and oranges may have difficulty when the oranges are received only probabilistically and there is a small probability that one of the apples is poisoned.)

6. For an introduction to these issues, see Ralph Keeney, "Mortality Risks Induced by the Costs of Regulations," *Risk Analysis*, 10(1):147-59 (1994). The health-habit study is presented in Randall Lutter, John F. Morrall III, and W. Kip Viscusi, "Risky Behavior and the Income-Mortality Relationship" (Working paper, Duke University, 1995). The rationale for lower-income people to choose riskier lifestyles is examined in John Pratt and Richard Zeckhauser, "Willingness to Pay and the Distribution of Risk and Wealth" (Working paper, Harvard University, 1995).

7. The framing of risk problems has a considerable effect on how risks are viewed and what preferences are expressed. See Daniel Kahneman and Amos Tversky, "Prospect Theory: An Analysis of Decision Under Risk," *Econometrica*, 47:263-91 (1979). For example, car accident rates per trip appear negligible, but when expressed as annual or lifetime fatality rates, they seem considerable.

Omission and commission

Actions often generate risks, but sometimes inaction leads to greater risks. In theory, errors of omission and commission should be treated similarly; in practice, the latter count far more heavily. This is partly because they are framed as losses incurred rather than as gains forgone. When a treatment creates a significant risk, it may be rejected, however great the risks avoided. Estrogen-replacement therapy decreases a woman's heart attack risk, but increases her breast cancer risk. A woman should consider the relative utility costs of the two diseases, and the changes in probability entailed by the therapy, and then calculate her expected utility. (The cover story on this issue in *Time* magazine[8] omitted any risk numbers that could facilitate such a calculation, suggesting that such numbers were hardly relevant.)

The Food and Drug Administration (FDA), which regulates prescription drugs and medical devices, should balance the risks of placing potentially hazardous products on the market and the risks that sick people will suffer if these innovative technologies are not available. The consensus of outside analysts is that the agency has erred on the side of excessive caution, suggesting that society's net risk has been increased by delays in approving beneficial new drugs, such as beta blockers for heart disease.[9]

8. *Time*, 26 June 1995.
9. Asymmetric incentives help explain this. There is little penalty for not approving a drug that would have saved statistical lives, but allowing a drug that has identifiable ad-

Concepts of fairness

Human health is a special commodity. It is an ultimate source of value, and its primary production comes from nature, not people. Given these features, fairness plays a major role when risks to health are discussed. Yet what fairness in risk means is rarely clear. Differences in risk levels are perceived as unfair. For example, if the downwind town of Eastside has a greater risk than Westside, that is unfair. Yet risk increases that might balance matters—locating a toxic waste dump in Westside—are unfair as well.[10] Fairness issues are made still more intractable because money (or other compensation), however efficient an arrangement it may offer, is often regarded as inappropriate compensation for bearing risk.

Risk equity has also been a concern for trade policy. Should we prohibit imports from less developed countries that do not adhere to U.S. safety standards and environmental objectives? While this may appear to be in the best interest of these nations' citizens, it would actually decrease their employment and income, which are the main contributors to economic and physical well-being. Al-

verse effects, such as thalidomide, would impose enormous political costs. For further analysis of the excessive conservatism of the FDA, see Henry G. Grabowski and John M. Vernon, *The Regulation of Pharmaceuticals: Balancing the Benefits and Risks* (Washington, DC: American Enterprise Institute, 1983).

10. Advocates of environmental equity in Chapel Hill, NC, which has traditionally sited landfills in rural areas, have proposed balancing risks by siting a new one near heavily populated residential areas. Severely increased risk will be the inefficient outcome.

lowing such imports is likely to benefit even their health. Japan's enormous growth in per capita income from 1935 to 1975 was accompanied by age-specific reductions in mortality of over 35 percent for individuals under 65.[11]

Should companies in the United States be permitted to export products that are considered too hazardous for use in this country to other countries that may welcome them, as with many products? For example, pharmaceutical companies may not manufacture drugs in the United States for sale overseas unless they have been approved by the FDA for U.S. usage. Since the FDA drug approval process is lengthy, however, many drugs are first approved in Europe. The result is that U.S. companies have been forced to move operations abroad to supply these markets.

On an even more touchy issue, a less developed country might seek to expand its revenues by becoming a depository for nuclear wastes, as poverty-stricken but geologically blessed Equatorial Guinea was offered— and under pressure refused—just a few years ago. Should it have this privilege, or should more affluent nations interfere with its decision? Although intervention to provide information regarding risks certainly seems well founded, interfering with the actual decision appears to be a much more problematic role for a foreign government or international authority.

11. See Richard J. Zeckhauser, Ryuzo Sato, and John Rizzo, "Health Intervention and Population Heterogeneity: Evidence from Japan and the United States" (Monograph, National Institute for Research Advancement, Dec. 1985), p. 29.

The role of entitlements often affects the zeal with which we undertake risk reduction efforts. If we must pay for the reduction ourselves, there may be substantial reluctance to make the expenditures. For example, many people do not remove lead paint from their houses or asbestos insulation from their basements. However, these same individuals might insist that their children's day-care centers meet the highest safety standards; their insistence might be particularly intense if a large party such as the city or a corporation ran the center.

THE CHALLENGE TO GOVERNMENT

Ideally, society, and the government acting as its agent, should undertake the risk reduction efforts that would best promote the welfare of its citizens.

Balancing risks and costs

The benefit-cost approach, which seeks to quantify the pertinent consequences of alternative policies, can be adjusted to allow for uncertain outcomes and such factors as risk aversion. Appropriately conducted analyses must also seek valuations for such hard-to-assess outputs as damage to a unique ecological resource.

The reality of government policymaking strays far from any careful process of weighing costs and benefits. The legislative mandates of risk regulation efforts almost invariably articulate risk-based objectives and sometimes exclude the consideration of costs altogether.

Executive branch efforts to balance the competing concerns of risk and cost have had limited success. Since the Carter administration, risk regulations must meet a cost-effectiveness test that gives preference to regulations that could achieve the same objective for less money. This requirement eliminates some of the least efficient options, but it does not ensure that an appropriate balance is struck between cost and risk. Since the Reagan administration imposed a benefit-cost test requirement, agencies have undertaken more comprehensive regulatory analyses.

However, these tests are not binding; they are typically inconsistent with the more narrowly written mandates of regulatory agencies, which impose legal constraints. As a result, the U.S. Office of Management and Budget, which oversees the risk regulation agencies, has never rejected a regulation with a cost per life saved of under $100 million.[12] Most risk and environmental regulations that are adopted have costs far in excess of any established estimate for the value of life, indeed above the amounts (discussed earlier) whose expenditure leads to the loss of a statistical life. This suggests that many programs that are supposed to reduce risk actually cost lives.

As chronicled here and elsewhere in this volume, individuals have difficulty responding to risk appropriately, particularly to low-probability risks. If government responds to individuals' fears and irrationalities rather than the actual risks, we in-

12. See W. Kip Viscusi, *Fatal Tradeoffs: Public and Private Responsibilities for Risk* (New York: Oxford University Press, 1992).

crease the probability of adopting policies that achieve few risk reduction benefits in return for the expenditures made. The gains in health will be as illusory as the fears that generated the policies.

Process

The risk debate parallels the debate over the federal budget. We all want lower taxes, but we do not want to sacrifice the government programs that taxes pay for. Similarly, we all want less risk and demand a lot of improvement in all risk measures, but we do not want to spend the money to achieve these gains. Government proposals to promote energy conservation and decreased air pollution through a nickel-a-gallon gas tax, for example, created a public uproar, suggesting that the public's expressions of unbounded commitment to the environment may in fact have quite narrow financial limits.

The government also reassures the public about risk levels. The FDA, for example, does not state that our food is so safe that only 1 in 10 million Americans will be killed by bacteria contamination. Rather, it declares that our food is safe and makes unqualified commitments to maintaining this safety. In some cases such ceremonial commitments to public safety run counter to the best interests of the citizens exposed to the risk.

Government as insurer

The government also plays an important role in insuring many classes of risks. For example, the major risks of old age—lack of health and wealth—are covered by Medicare and Social Security. In addition, the government often provides humanitarian relief after major national catastrophes, such as hurricanes and tornadoes. The government also runs subsidized insurance programs for such adverse events. If the government is going to compensate people ex post for disaster-related losses, then it is in the government's interest to promote the purchase of insurance to reduce the cost of the humanitarian ex post bailout. For massive catastrophes, the government has a risk-spreading advantage over insurers; it has an enormous asset base that it can tax into the future.

Government as referee

In debates on risk issues, all affected parties have standing, making compromises and trade-offs difficult. Individuals' current endowments have legitimacy, as do claimed rights such as the right to a safe environment. Even physical entities may have rights. For example, advocates of stringent hazardous waste cleanup claim that contaminated raw land that does not undergo remediation will simply be "dead zones." That may be true, but it also may be an economically efficient outcome that gets overridden by a rights philosophy. If even undeveloped acreage has standing in the political debate, wholly apart from the potential uses of the land, then it will be difficult to forge the types of political compromises that are necessary for sound risk regulation policies.

Politics is likely to exacerbate inefficiencies. The HAZWRAP Program, which is to clean up the Department of Energy's nuclear material and weapon sites, is estimated to cost between $100 billion and $300 billion. Cleanup efforts have been recognized as public works (that is, pork barrel concerns have been legitimized), and expenditures have been spread across states rather than spent where they provide the greatest risk reduction. Significant expenditures will have no effects on human health, often providing cleaned-up land at more than ten times the local price of never-contaminated land.[13]

Risk reduction policies often have their genesis in legal actions between private parties. Many of the most significant hazards, such as those posed by asbestos, first rose to prominence in the courts. Information about these risks was not available when most individuals were exposed. As a result, thousands of people suffered from asbestos exposure. Their illnesses first became well known to legislators and regulators through the workers' compensation and tort liability claims that they filed. This litigation explosion focused public attention on asbestos and led to government regulations that dramatically curtailed exposure.

Compensation through the courts serves three functions. First, it transfers income to those in need, to meet both their medical expenses and their income losses. Second, these income transfers are funded by the parties responsible for the accident or illness, thus creating financial incen-

13. Martin Marietta Energy Systems, "An Application of an Interim Version of the Formal Priority System to Fiscal Year 1992 Environmental Restoration Planning" (Report to the U.S. Department of Energy, Nov. 1990).

tives for safety. Third, such ex post payments highlight the existence of risks not adequately handled at present through risk regulation.

Regulatory costs

In the past, most government regulations consisted of restrictions on telephone rates, restrictions on interstate commerce, and similar kinds of economic regulation. Over the past two decades, health, safety, and environmental regulation has increased in importance and now accounts for the majority of regulatory costs.[14] By 1991, total regulatory costs to the U.S. economy were estimated to be $542 billion. Of this amount, $115 billion was accounted for by environmental regulations and $36 billion by other social regulations, chiefly for health and safety. Only $73 billion was attributed to traditional economic regulations. Moreover, much of the regulatory burden consists of paperwork costs of $189 billion; a significant portion of these costs are related to compliance with risk regulations.

IMPROVING WELFARE

Singly and collectively, we have trouble responding to risks. We overrespond to many that are minuscule and ignore some hazards that have significant consequences for our lives. Public attention shifts quickly to the latest publicized hazard, and government policy often follows: wit-

ness our ready sacrifice of civil liberties in response to the terrorist threat suggested by the Oklahoma City bombing. Government policy should not mirror citizens' irrationalities but, rather, should promote the decisions people would make if they understood risks correctly and made sound decisions based on this understanding.

Making such policy is a challenge. To begin, scientific information is not always precise. Many important risks are not known with the same precision as are, for example, the familiar risks of automobiles. Scientific debates continue over the risks posed by substances ranging from cellular phones to animal fats to nuclear power.

When the magnitude of the risk is unclear, what should the government do? The current procedure is to focus on the worst-case scenario.[15] Unfortunately, this leads to policies that pay the greatest attention to the risks about which least is known. If chemical A poses a lifetime fatality risk that is known to be .00002, whereas equally widely used chemical B poses a risk that might be .00003 but probably is zero, current practice would first address the risks from chemical B, though we could save a greater expected number of lives if we focused on A. Since our imprecision is often greatest with respect to risks of new technologies, this conservatism often leads us to accept old risks and has impeded the technological and economic progress that have dramatically reduced risk in our society.

14. For a review of these trends in regulatory expenditures, see W. Kip Viscusi, John Vernon, and Joseph Harrington, Jr., *The Economics of Regulation and Antitrust* (Cambridge: MIT Press, 1996).

15. See Albert L. Nichols and Richard J. Zeckhauser, "The Dangers of Caution: Conservatism in Assessment and the Mismanagement of Risk," in *Advances in Applied Microeconomics*, vol. 4, ed. Kerry Smith (Greenwich, CT: JAI Press, 1986), pp. 55-82.

For these reasons, a flurry of congressional legislation passed in 1995 but not yet, as of this writing, signed by the president requires that federal agencies follow best-estimate risk assessment procedures. Such procedures will have the agencies assess the mean level of the risk and use assumptions regarding best estimates of the likely scenarios that will prevail, rather than focusing on worst-case outcomes.[16]

16. A number of pieces of legislation proposed or passed by Congress in 1995 would address both the mean risk and benefit-cost issues. These include Senate bill no. 333 and House bills nos. 1022, 690, 228, and 1923.

Unfortunately, the role of policy analysis within government policy-making is peripheral to much actual decision making. Whether analysis is to be done at all has become a political battle between those who would choose to promote more balanced risk regulation policies and those who wish to pursue the more absolutist approach of maximal risk reduction independent of cost.

If we are to achieve all that is possible with risk regulation efforts, we must understand how these policies will perform, and design them—based on an accurate assessment of the risks—to achieve the greatest expected health gains for the dollars spent.

Risk and Justice: Rethinking the Concept of Compensation

By PATRICK FIELD, HOWARD RAIFFA, and LAWRENCE SUSSKIND

ABSTRACT: In recent years, environmental justice advocates have made a convincing claim that risky facilities have been disproportionately clustered in poor communities and communities of color. NIMBYism (not in my backyard) has spread from predominantly white, affluent suburbs to poorer communities of color. In this article, we propose a means of addressing environmental inequities and breaking the siting impasse. We think that poor communities of color might use the proposed siting of risky facilities as a basis for negotiating substantial improvements in the well-being of their communities. We propose to embed siting negotiations in the preparation of broader development packages, jointly created with citizens of poor neighborhoods and communities of color, so that health risks are reduced, the environment is improved, and all residents are better off. As far as justice is concerned, the perceived fairness of the process by which risks are communicated and selected, and risk management strategies are devised, is as important as the actual allocation of risk.

Patrick Field is a senior associate at the Consensus Building Institute, Cambridge, Massachusetts, and a research associate with the Harvard-MIT Public Disputes Program at Harvard Law School.

Howard Raiffa is a professor emeritus of managerial economics at the Harvard Business School.

Lawrence Susskind is the Ford Professor of Urban and Environmental Planning at the Massachusetts Institute of Technology, president of the Consensus Building Institute, and director of the Harvard-MIT Public Disputes Program at Harvard Law School.

AMERICA is having a difficult time siting much-needed waste disposal facilities for toxic materials ranging from used motor oil, to industrial solvents, to biomedical waste. Despite the fact that the United States produces somewhere between 275 million and 380 million tons of hazardous waste per year—or more than 1 ton per capita—no large, fully operational, free-standing hazardous waste disposal facility has been sited since 1980.[1] The United States is even having trouble siting power plants, sewage treatment plants, and far less risky sanitary landfills. Industry spokespeople, and the critics of a selfish public unwilling to shoulder its responsibilities, have blamed the "not in my backyard" (NIMBY) phenomenon on affluent, white, suburban residents unwilling to share the burdens of their wasteful habits.

But in the early 1990s, poor people of color made a claim similar to that of white suburbanites: they, too, did not want noxious or risky facilities in their backyards. Some grassroots activists, social scientists, and attorneys had framed the NIMBY problem in a new and compelling way. One need only look at a map of the United States to see that noxious facilities are disproportionately clustered in poor communities and communities of color. To make matters worse, lax

enforcement of, and poor compliance with, existing environmental regulations coupled with slow—some would say halfhearted—cleanups of toxic waste sites in poor communities of color have increased the health and safety risks to these neighborhoods even more. Advocates also argued that, in the process of making siting decisions, poor people and people of color have not had a fair chance to be heard at public hearings, obtain adequate technical advice, or have proceedings conducted in their native language.

Last, advocates contended that proponents have explicitly referenced social characteristics such as race, culture, and income to select sites for risky facilities. Thus not only do inequities exist when we look at facilities in the aggregate over time, but as each new facility is sited, both government and industry use social factors such as race as important determinants in site selection. This is nothing less than racist. Everyone should share equally in the risks of such facilities, not just poor people or people of color. If these claims of the leaders of the environmental justice movement—that environmental decision making has been geographically, procedurally, and socially unfair—are true (and we think they are), then a remedy must be found.

---

1. Barry George Rabe, *Beyond NIMBY: Hazardous Waste Siting in Canada and the United States* (Washington, DC: Brookings Institution, 1994); Charles Piller, *The Fail-Safe Society: Community Defiance and the End of American Technological Optimism* (New York: Basic Books, 1991). A bibliography of additional sources related to this topic is available from the Consensus Building Institute, 131 Mt. Auburn Street, Cambridge, MA 01238.

SOLVING THE PROBLEM:
SUBSTANTIAL IMPROVEMENT
RATHER THAN SUITABLE
COMPENSATION

Promoters of risky facilities have made an unfortunate mistake. They set out to financially compensate people for the measurable negative impacts of risky facilities. Economic theory suggested that it could be done. After all, we all make implicit trade-offs that, when made explicit, could be used to derive an estimate of how much we value our lives. People ride motorcycles without helmets; people take on hazardous jobs in mining and nuclear waste site cleanup, to name only a few. When asked to make these trade-offs explicitly and collectively, however, people usually react with aversion and anger. Why? Compensation means to make up for, to counterbalance. But how does one counterbalance increased risk of death with financial compensation? How does one pay for putting a child at increased risk of asthma, leukemia, or even death? It seems to us that in a public and political setting, this simply cannot be done. When the question entails involuntary instead of voluntary risk, collective instead of individual risk, and involves people's homes and families and not just their workplace and themselves, financial compensation is not enough. Experts have tried to condense values, in the broad sense, into a common but disagreeable metric of dollars. If communities are going to accept risky facilities, financial compensation and mitigation are not sufficient. Unless decision makers respond to a community's sense of its own needs and priorities, unless host communities find themselves, when all is said and done, better off, citizens, especially those already unduly burdened, will continue to resist the siting of locally unwanted land uses (LULUs).

We would like to propose a means both to break the siting impasse and to improve environmental equity.

Our proposal is that the siting of noxious facilities be embedded in a broader development package, jointly prepared by citizens of poor neighborhoods and communities of color, so that their environment is actually improved, health risks are reduced, and all residents are better off.

Since we have agreed with those who have found that communities of low income and color have received unjust treatment when it comes to the siting of LULUs, readers might wonder why in the world we would propose siting a risky facility in a disadvantaged neighborhood. We think that poor communities of color might use the siting of risky and unwanted facilities as an opportunity to significantly reduce risks in their community and improve residents' lives. Poor communities of color need a practical vehicle to address inequities. The NIMBY problem might be a powerful bargaining chip to help poor communities and communities of color leverage substantial resources. Risky facilities, rather than being yet another imposition forced on disadvantaged communities, could provide an opportunity to make substantial improvements in communities that need and deserve, due to past and current inequities, substantial investment and development.

AN IMAGINED DIALOGUE

Imagine this scenario: the state is desperate. A new low-level radioactive waste facility needs to be sited. Currently, wastes of this kind generated in the state are being shipped across state boundaries for disposal, but neighboring states are discouraging this practice by progressively raising their rates. The governor fears that research facilities in hospitals, universities, and high-technology industry that generate low-level radioactive wastes will be forced to relocate out of state, and with this exodus other industries will follow. The governor has asked his trusted adviser S. Simpson to pull out all the stops to get a radioactive waste facility sited.

Simpson, an astute lawyer and master negotiator, has contacted G. Garrity, a geologist and hydrologist from the most prestigious engineering school in the state, to investigate suitable sites. Their investigation disclosed that the only part of the state with adequate subsurface geology and acceptable groundwater levels is in Kendall County. In particular, two sites were deemed appropriate: one in the wealthy, suburban community of Oakville and one in the inner-city community of Kent, home to a higher percentage of people of color than the rest of the region and also home to many low-income whites.

Simpson has invited O. Otis, a prestigious banker who years ago was a selectman from Oakville, and K. Kass, an adviser to the mayor of Kent, to join Garrity and him in what Simpson has called a facilitated joint brainstorming session about the problem of siting LULUs.

Simpson: Thanks for coming. As I mentioned to you in my letter of invitation, we're here unofficially. In confidence, let me tell you that the governor has asked me to advise him on what to do about a growing crisis in our state: opposition to the siting of what we call LULUs. The NIMBY attitude is taking its toll in our state.

Kass: I still don't understand why you invited Otis and me to this meeting— what you call a brainstorming session.

Garrity: Simpson asked me to locate some technically suitable, geologically sound sites for a low-level radioactive disposal facility, and I identified one in Oakville and another in Kent.

Simpson: I asked you to come as recognized leaders of your communities to brainstorm with me.

Otis: Well, this is going to be a short meeting if you think you're going to get me to endorse a plan to locate a waste repository in Oakville. That's just not in the cards no matter what the governor tries to do. I'll fight him all the way, and he can't win this one. People in my town will fight any such proposal tooth and nail.

Kass: Well, O., I'll be out the door ahead of you. I'm tired of my community being the dumping ground for the entire state. We've already got more than our share of LULUs. It's just not fair to ask us to suffer more. The governor is going to have one helluva political fight if he tries to ram this down our throats.

Simpson: Hold on. I think I understand and empathize. I'm not trying to force anything down your throats. We're here to see if we can think of some imaginative solution that will make everyone better off. Remember, the governor is willing to use some of the state's resources to break this impasse.

Kass: If your aim is to try to bribe us, forget it. We won't sell out!

Simpson: But, K., substantial resources could be used to redress some of the serious problems in your community. All I'm asking you to do is to brainstorm with me. Don't think of this as a threat; look at it as an opportunity. Imagine if we helped invent a solution to both facility siting and environmental injustice that made the rest of the state's citizens sit up and take notice. Tell me, what are the key concerns in your community?

Kass: We have serious problems. First, there's public safety. Our kids aren't safe. Kids are getting shot by other kids. We have no foot patrolman. Lead pipes, lead paint, and asbestos seem to be everywhere. Also, we need tennis courts and a municipal pool. We need emergency health care and care for teenage mothers. Some of our elderly citizens live in hovels and don't have any place to meet or play cards. And to top it all off, the few businesses we have are ready to leave.

Simpson: I'm telling you, K., that this may be the opportunity to do something about the litany of problems you've just mentioned. Kent needs and deserves real investment. Unfortunately, we all know, in today's political climate, how difficult that is.

Kass: We don't want to be bought off. We want things to get better. Put together a solid package that improves the health and safety of my community and creates jobs, and then we'll talk.

Otis: But if your community got cold cash, you could spend it as you wanted.

Simpson: What the governor and I have in mind is something far more inventive: a development package that will include the waste repository. It will be a package that will have to be voted up or down by the citizens of Kent, or any other town. From experience, we know citizens must be convinced that they will be better off on a host of dimensions: public health, public safety, aesthetics, taxes, jobs, and the general quality of life in the town.

Garrity: We have to be honest about this. This is not a zero-risk proposition. There are some modest risks associated with low-level radioactive waste. Of course, these added health risks could be more than offset by other remedial actions that would improve public health—by mitigating the effects of existing lead, asbestos, and radon and by providing better medical emergency facilities and drug treatment centers.

Kass: I'll have no part of this deal if the safety of the people of Kent is in jeopardy. There will be no trade-off of dollars for lives. That's unacceptable—end of story.

Garrity: That's not the trade-off we're proposing. We must create a package that the best scientists can clearly say will improve the health and safety of the people of Kent.

Kass: The package can't improve the lives of residents in my community only marginally. It must improve their lives substantially. Too many times in the past, my community has borne the cost of risky decisions. People are mad. They simply aren't going to accept a slightly better deal, not now.

Simpson: I think this brings up the important point of community acceptance. The development package can't be accepted only because some outside expert tells the community they're better off. The citizens themselves have to believe they are better off. If the perception remains that the community is not improved, that will mean the status quo, or worse, for property values, bank loans, and further economic development.

Otis: But wait! What's a really good deal? How far might this go? Why shouldn't Kent just keep demanding more from their wish list? I can imagine the holdouts saying, "We don't believe we're better off just yet. We want something in addition. . . . " What's the upper limit?

Simpson: Kent can get a lot, but not everything. We have to commission a study of what would happen if we don't locate a facility anywhere in our state. We would have to pay exorbitant prices and perhaps lose some of our best medical research facilities. That would have to be priced out. Suppose, for example, that the no-build alternative would cost us $25 million while the cost to build the facility in Kent would be $10 million. That would leave a surplus of $15 million. Say half of that were spent on developing the improvement package for Kent.

Otis: Hey, wait a second. Why not use all the savings for improvements in Kent?

Kass: Thank you, O. I never thought I'd hear a banker arguing for increased spending for the poor people of Kent.

Simpson: We need to negotiate how much will be spent. Let's not forget, this package could generate all sorts of long-term gains and losses that we cannot directly cost out: innovative partnerships, leveraging of private and public grants, and so on. All I want to point out is that there is a natural monetary upper limit, for instance, the cost of going out of state.

Kass: That doesn't follow, if I understood the governor's intent. He will get a lot of political credit if he can locate this facility amicably and at the same time help a truly disadvantaged community. He should be willing to spend more on the Kent combined package than the alternative of going out of state.

Simpson: We're beginning to negotiate, and that's not our assignment. We're supposed to be brainstorming. I take it that you feel that there's some hope that a suitable package might fly. Let's figure out some of the things that have to be done next.

Kass: Well, I would like to see a full menu of things that might be included in the package.

Otis: You should also price the cost of each item so we know what we're talking about.

Garrity: There are students in a public policy program at my university that could help. They would need a small grant.

Simpson: I can provide $5000. Can they work with you, K.? It's important that this work is kept under wraps until it's done.

Kass: Sure. But if this thing is going to fly, we'll need to be democratic about it. The voters in Kent will want a say in the specifics of any development package.

Otis: Instead of talking about a "package," let's call it an integrated development plan, an IDP. While I have the floor, let me say that there is a role for the banking community here. If the state gives us the proper incentives, we can make investment loans available so that more capital flows into the community. That will mean jobs. It would have to be designated an experimental development project. It also seems to me that we will have to assemble a consortium of developers. The state can help a lot by offering the developers tax breaks.

Kass: Why subsidize the rich?

Otis: If the developers get tax breaks, their margins will be higher and we can justify more money flowing into the integrated development plan.

Simpson: We're making great progress. Can we take stock at this point of what could block this enterprise?

Garrity: Well, for one thing, we need credibility. If safety statistics are cited by the developers or the state, there will be doubters, and for good reason, given past history. We should arrange a blue ribbon panel of experts who can attest to the fact that the combined package—excuse me, the integrated development plan— will actually improve the health and safety of the community. I can help you form such a group.

Kass: I'm troubled by the exclusivity of this planning cabal. There have to be public meetings in Kent, and, eventually, a vote will have to be taken. The people of Kent must play a significant part in the planning process.

Simpson: I couldn't agree more. We have to brainstorm the process to be followed so that the people of Kent will be convinced that this plan deserves their support.

Kass: That sounds cynical. It's really our plan.

Simpson: No, it's our initial idea, but ultimately, it must be their own plan.

Experience in other places has shown that citizens must be directly involved in the process and take ownership of the process if it is to succeed.

Garrity: So what's the timetable? Do I try to assemble a scientific committee now?

Otis: I'd wait. The idea and suggestions for the composition of such a committee should come from the community.

Simpson: K., it would be a good idea at this point, if you discreetly convened a meeting of about a dozen key people in Kent and let them describe what they might see as a fair process. I would be willing to come to such a meeting if you think it desirable.

GETTING THE SEQUENCING RIGHT

The story we have just begun to tell incorporates four key principles. They are that

— fairness does matter, including perceptions of past inequities;
— discussion about the planning, selection, and implementation of packages that include risky facilities requires meaningful input from all stakeholders;
— the community must be left substantially better off; and
— joint decision makers, including citizens, should have access to the best technical advice available, but technicians should not make policy decisions.

We think these principles should form the foundation of the IDP. These principles are not enough, however. In addition, the sequencing of events in a facility siting process is important. In the past, not only have the foregoing principles not been incorporated into the planning process but the sequence of events has either been poorly arranged or key steps simply have been missed. For example, a widespread consensus that risky facilities are needed throughout a region or state has often not been developed. Proposals have been worked out behind closed doors by only experts and a few elected and appointed officials. Compensation has been offered, but in forms that are completely unrelated to the probable risks (or the community's perceptions of those risks) or only as an afterthought to get a community to take the bait.

In contrast to those mistakes, we think an effective process ought to include the following steps.

Step 1: Principled leadership

Up front, the governor or other key leaders must make it clear that an IDP will adhere to the four principles stated previously. Unless leaders promise from the start a fair, inclusive, and technically proficient process that leaves the host community better off, they will sow the seeds of doubt and distrust that have too often blocked facility siting later on.

Step 2: Informal assessment

Prior to any full-scale assessment of the needs of a potential host community, an informal assessment should be done to ensure that the community does have significant needs that can be addressed.

Step 3: Stakeholder involvement

The state must help develop a practical means for citizens of the potential host community to have a meaningful role in developing, approving, and implementing an IDP. Here, a professional neutral, or facilitator, might be of help. The community could select a trained facilitator who can aid the community in convening all the relevant stakeholders.

Step 4: Joint assessment

Once the stakeholder group is convened, communities must help build on the informal needs assessment conducted by the state. Community problems and needs ought to be identified, practical solutions ought to be developed, and their costs ought to be ascertained, all with the aid of citizens. When discussions require technical know-how, the citizen's group should have access to such knowledge. They also ought to have access to the conclusions, assumptions, and limitations of all background technical studies.

Step 5: Citizen choice

Once the most desirable packages have been developed by the citizens' forum, the whole community ought to have the final say in accepting or rejecting the best offer. This means a vote. Because we would want to avoid substantial minorities within the community from having to bear the cost of a facility if they truly believed they would not be better off, the voting rule ought to require more than a simple majority. Before voting, however, the citizens' forum must be careful to inform and include the community in the ongoing discussion, whether through newsletters, cable access television, or continuing print, radio, and television coverage.

The reader has probably noted that we have left the developer out of the process of managing the work of the forum. While free-market advocates may cringe, we believe the state must take an active role in asserting siting principles, supporting the community in identifying its needs, and helping to develop the IDP. In our view, the citizens' group ought to have a say in the selection of the developer, rather than the developer selecting the site.

Step 6: Iterative learning

Once the IDP has been approved and the developer selected, the involved citizens should not simply disband and go on their way, satisfied that their work is done. The process, from the beginning, ought to be about seeking information (including the opinions of all stakeholders), using that information to make decisions (with stakeholders), and gathering additional information to evaluate and reassess decisions, changing course if necessary, once the results become clear. The community ought to have a continuous process for engaging the facility in decision making. For instance, a community monitoring committee could meet regularly with facility management to discuss ongo-

ing technical issues and to keep abreast of how the facility is doing with regard to meeting community improvement goals. The state must also continue to set and enforce standards that ensure public health and safety. Even with the state playing a watchdog role, the facility should be held accountable not only to state authorities but directly to the community.

CONCLUSION

In a perfect world, there would be no need to discuss risk and justice. All citizens would have a say in when, where, and how risky facilities were built. Furthermore, all citizens would benefit more equally from the activities that generate noxious side effects than they do today. Perhaps, in an even more perfect world, there would be no crisis in waste management because attention would be focused on waste prevention efforts such as recycling and toxic use reduction. But given this world and all its imperfections, we think that embedding the siting of noxious facilities in a broader development package, jointly developed by citizens of poor neighborhoods and communities of color, could improve people's lives, reduce the health risks they face, and help make all residents better off. On a much broader scale, for the benefit of everyone, such development would help to remedy environmental injustice and overcome NIMBYism. These are two goals well worth achieving.

Reforming Risk Regulation

By ROGER G. NOLL

ABSTRACT: A commonly observed characteristic of risk regulation policy is the absence of coherent prioritization of risks and inconsistencies in the stringency of controls on risks that are regulated. The purpose of this article is to examine the roots of this problem in the way both citizens and their elected representatives deal with uncertainties associated with catastrophic risks, why elected politicians respond to this problem in constructing regulatory institutions that are prone to inconsistency, and whether various proposals to reform the regulatory process would be likely to improve its performance. The main conclusions are that most reform proposals are strongly inconsistent with democratic responsiveness, which is the most important principle that elected officials use in designing programs, and that the only plausible means for making regulatory policy more coherent is to increase the resources of regulatory agencies so as to give them greater control over the public agenda in risk policy.

Roger G. Noll is the Morris M. Doyle Professor of Public Policy in the Department of Economics, Stanford University, and a visiting fellow at the Brookings Institution. His current research focuses on the economics and politics of research policy; regulation and competition in telecommunications; economic and political influences on the courts; the economics of electronic publishing; the economics and politics of western expansion in the nineteenth century; comparative regulatory policies of countries of the Organization for Economic Cooperation and Development; and privatization of infrastructural industries in developing countries.

THE nature of the policy debate concerning risk regulation is well known. Informed proponents of stronger regulation generate examples of significant threats to life and health that receive little or no attention from regulators, and advocates of less intensive regulation are equally vociferous in pointing to regulations that impose enormous costs but that have little or no beneficial effect.[1]

This article does not deal with the problem of assessing whether risk regulation is, on balance, too stringent or not stringent enough. Instead, it assumes for the purpose of argument that both criticisms of the status quo have merit. If this assumption is true, the policy problem is incoherency and unpredictability in deciding when to regulate any given risk (the prioritization problem) and how rigorous each regulation should be (the consistency problem). The purpose of this article is to offer some ideas about why these problems arise and what practical steps could be taken to improve on the present system of regulation. The focus is on decision making within regulatory agencies and the courts.

The central argument is that an important element of the problem of risk regulation arises from the difficulties citizens face in knowing whether either those who cause risks or those who are responsible for mitigating them are acting in the citizens' interest. The relationships between citizens and regulators, with elected

officials in the middle, is an especially difficult form of agency relationship, and the problems associated with this relationship are unlikely to be solved solely by either administrative reform or risk education. Most likely, the only means available for making risk regulation more coherent and avoiding some of the costly mistakes of the past is to increase the resources available for identifying risks and effective responses to them and to publicize the results of these inquiries so as to control the public debate about risk policy.

DIAGNOSING THE PROBLEM

As used in this article, the term "risk regulation" refers to a category of environmental, health, and safety issues that have four important characteristics. The point of listing these characteristics is to make precise the nature of the problem of designing a means of implementing regulatory policies that citizens would widely regard as effective, efficient, and equitable.

First, the risky event is widely perceived as potentially severe in that it could cause substantial physical damage to humans or the natural environment. This feature of risky events leads to an emphasis on prevention rather than compensation in designing policies. When the threat consists of death, injury, or disability to humans, or an environmental catastrophe, full compensation of victims is problematic. Hence reliance on, say, the system of tort liability to induce optimal due care on the part of victims of negligent acts is regarded as unsatisfactory because it is

1. For an excellent summary of this problem, with some compelling examples, see Stephen Breyer, *Breaking the Vicious Circle* (Cambridge, MA: Harvard University Press, 1994).

likely to be both inequitable and inefficient.

Second, as far as those who seek to avoid these events are concerned, the risks are widely perceived to be involuntarily imposed by either nature or other people. Obviously, some regulatory and other policies deal with voluntary risks, such as the risks associated with reckless driving or smoking; however, these are not the focus of this article. A more interesting case is voluntary exposure to a risk, such as by choosing to live in a floodplain or along an active fault. In these cases, the aspect of risk policy that is the focus here is the relationship between the damage a victim suffers and the actions of others responsible for ameliorating the risk. Examples are the effectiveness of the flood control system and the adherence to seismic building codes by those who own and maintain buildings.

Third, the nature of a risk cannot be observed by those who would suffer from it unless they exercise a degree of diligence or incur a cost that is unreasonable. Thus the involuntary nature of the risk extends beyond the fact that one human took an action that created a hazard; rather, a reasonable person cannot be expected to know that the hazard is present.

Fourth, actions to ameliorate the risk are likely to be costly, and identifying appropriate actions requires expertise that most citizens do not possess. The idea here is that arcane knowledge is required to identify the appropriate action to reduce exposure to the risk. Consequently, an informational strategy, such as a product warning, is not helpful because the person exposed to the hazard does not know how to respond to the warning without consulting an expert.

These four conditions give rise to a demand for regulatory intervention for both efficiency and equity reasons. An important feature of the problems that give rise to risk regulation is the necessity to acquire costly information to identify and to respond to the risk. Information about risks, like all information, has public-goods attributes: its use to reduce risks is nonrivalrous among all those who are exposed to them. Regulatory policy allows all citizens who may be exposed to a risk to share the costs of identifying it and designing a common response. In addition, regulation shifts some of the costs of identifying and ameliorating the risk to those who are most informed about it. As a result, regulation has a potential efficiency benefit according to the "least-cost avoider" principle[2] and has the equity property that it works to prevent the welfare transfer that arises from involuntary exposure, costly identification, and costly amelioration. Even if all of these costs are passed through to consumers, total costs to consumers will be minimized, and, arguably, the distribution of the costs will be more equitable to the extent that some people avoid extreme costs from avoidable risky events.

Unfortunately, the characteristics that define a risk policy issue lead to fundamental problems in designing an appropriate regulatory response.

2. For the classic statement of this principle and its implications for liability law, see Guido Calabresi, *The Costs of Accidents* (New Haven, CT: Yale University Press, 1970).

Elected political officials, who bear responsibility for defining the goals and methods of regulation in a statute, face the same information imperfections as do the citizens who are exposed to the risk. Elected officials do not have sufficient information to identify the precise nature of a risk (the likelihood that it will occur and the damage that it will cause) and to devise an appropriate strategy to ameliorate it. Consequently, they must delegate the responsibility to regulate risks to experts. Moreover, they cannot directly evaluate the effectiveness of a regulatory response. Likewise, judges, who are responsible for deciding whether regulators have carried out their responsibilities appropriately, are similarly handicapped.

The barrier to efficient risk regulation as defined herein is a form of a multilayered agency problem. Not only do citizens have difficulty identifying with reasonable precision the risks that they face, but they also face difficulties in knowing whether elected political officials are dealing effectively with these risks. Likewise, elected political officials have difficulty in identifying exactly what is troubling their constituents and in knowing whether their agents—the expert regulators—are putting forth best efforts in responding to these problems. Moreover, elected officials also have difficulty knowing whether the court is attempting to make certain that the regulators are carrying out the law as written or is pursuing its own agenda by being too solicitous to either those who create involuntary risks or those who suffer from damaging events that could not reasonably have been avoided by better regulation or a better product.

As described here, the problems of risk regulation are an extreme example of the bureaucratic delegation dilemma of classical public administration theory. The rise of modern bureaucracy gave rise to the question of how one could delegate day-to-day implementation of a statute to a bureaucrat without losing effective public control of policy.[3] According to the traditional idealistic approach to political science and public administration, the institutional means for resolving this dilemma were (1) intensive oversight of the implementation process by elected political officials;[4] (2) better appointments to agencies, including civil servants that are inculcated with the norm of faithful fealty to the interests of the public as expressed through elected officials;[5] and (3) redesign of the administrative system (including judicial review) to assure that bureaucratic decisions are based on facts, the legal

3. For a more complete discussion of the issues in this and the next paragraph, see Roger G. Noll, "Government Regulatory Behavior: A Multidisciplinary Survey and Synthesis," in *Regulatory Policy and the Social Sciences*, ed. Roger G. Noll (Berkeley: University of California Press, 1985).

4. On congressional oversight, see Congress, Senate, Committee on Government Operations, *Study on Federal Regulation, II: The Regulatory Appointments Process* (Washington, DC: Government Printing Office, 1977); on executive oversight, see Commission on Law and the Economy, *Federal Regulation: Roads to Reform* (Washington, DC: American Bar Association, 1980).

5. Congress, Senate, Committee on Government Organization, *Study on Federal Regulation, I: The Regulatory Appointments Process* (Washington, DC: Government Printing Office, 1977).

mandate, and core constitutional values concerning individuals' rights.[6]

Some have argued that none of these safeguards ever works very well, making three arguments. First, oversight is weak because it is carried out by politically invisible subcommittees in Congress, which are subject to capture by organized interests. Second, the norms of the bureaucracy are governed more by the professional backgrounds of civil servants than by acknowledgment of the superior political legitimacy of the values of elected officials and, in any event, are also subject to interest group capture. Third, administrative procedures are a weak line of defense against agencies that fail to adhere to the purposes and values of their statutory mandate and the Constitution because effective participation in administrative procedures is constrained by its expense and because courts are subject to the corrupting influences that infect congressional committees and agencies. According to this account, delegation to the bureaucracy constitutes abdication by elected officials.

Regardless of the merits of these arguments, risk regulation raises a separate set of concerns about the traditional means of solving the agency problem between elected officials and bureaucrats. Specifically, the informational problems associated with making policies about risks undermine these three mechanisms of injecting politically legitimate values into regulatory policymaking. Oversight is not helpful if the overseer does not comprehend the policy. Reliance on a bureaucratic norm of deference to elected leaders is not helpful when neither citizens nor elected officials can articulate informed views about the policy that the bureaucrat is supposed to implement. Finally, the administrative process will afford little protection if it is not designed to ensure that the right questions are asked and if judicial review is undertaken before an uncomprehending judge.

INSTITUTIONAL RESPONSES

Recent work applying the economic theory of organizations to government institutions, sometimes called neo-institutionalist positive political theory, has produced new insights into the design of regulatory institutions for dealing with risks to humans and the environment. This work sees the design of regulatory policies as solving the agency problem of elected officials in a somewhat different way from the traditional model. Elected political officials, recognizing that they do not and, most likely, cannot evaluate the details of regulatory policy, use the structure and process of regulation to allocate influence in regulatory proceedings among constituents.[7]

6. Examples of such proposals are to apply stricter standards to congressional delegation of rule-making authority and to return to some form of substantive due process in judicial review. Many of these proposals are discussed, usually skeptically, in Robert E. Litan and William D. Nordhaus, *Reforming Federal Regulation* (New Haven, CT: Yale University Press, 1983), pp. 100-109, 113-16.

7. See Mathew D. McCubbins, Roger G. Noll, and Barry R. Weingast, "Administrative Procedures as Instruments of Political Control," *Journal of Law, Economics and Organization*, 3(2):243-77 (1987); Terry M. Moe, "Politics and the Theory of Organization," *Journal of Law, Economics and Organization*, 7(55):106-29 (1991).

To understand this approach, one must begin with the political environment in which elected officials find themselves with respect to policies regarding substantial risks. In the absence of regulatory oversight, risk policy is inherently reactive. Like their constituents, elected officials are unable to evaluate conflicting claims about a potential risk, so they must choose between two problematic alternatives: establishing a regulatory policy before they know either the seriousness of the problem or the appropriate response, and waiting to establish policy until the consequences of the risky activity are reasonably well-known. The danger of each strategy is apparent. The first invites costly inconsistencies and waste, and the second may result in experiencing unavoidable catastrophic losses.

Most likely, elected officials will respond to dilemmas of this form by simply behaving like their supporters. If, among supporters who care about a particular risk, most feel threatened by it, elected officials will choose to regulate, whereas if most expect to bear more costs than benefits from risk regulation, elected officials will prefer not to intervene. Whereas opposition by those who would bear the costs of regulation is likely to be present in every case, political pressure for regulation is likely to be episodic and unpredictable because of its loose connection to the actual hazards that are faced.[8]

8. For more discussion of this point and its relationship to cognitive mistakes in evaluating risks, see Roger G. Noll and James E. Krier, "Some Implications of Cognitive Psychology for Risk Regulation," *Journal of Legal Studies*, 19(4):747-79 (1990).

Faced with this political environment, elected officials can minimize political opposition to their policies by creating a regulatory system that is largely reactive to problems as they arise, but relatively harsh in the regulations that emerge from it in response to a widely perceived threat to the public. In essence, the opposition-minimizing strategy is to focus on identifying the conditions under which proponents or opponents of regulation should dominate the outcome, rather than on the principles, based upon the magnitude of a threat and the costs of alternative regulatory actions, that a proactive regulator should use to set priorities and to adopt regulations.

The core characteristics of risk regulation that are elaborated in the preceding section of this article are compatible with the objective of designing an administrative process with these features. The essential feature of risk regulation is uncertainty about the probability of a damaging event, the magnitude of the damage that might occur, and the cost and effectiveness of regulatory interventions. By designing a regulatory system in which regulators are constrained to be strongly dependent on the nature of information that is provided to them, elected officials can engage in deck stacking: predisposing regulatory priorities and the stringency of regulation to reflect the intensities of political support and opposition for regulation on a case-by-case basis.

In essence, elected officials can rely on interest groups to mobilize only when they perceive a relatively intense stake in an issue. By writing statutes so that regulatory decisions are highly sensitive to the presence of mobilized groups in the regulatory process, elected officials can make advocates of stringent regulation influential only when they care a great deal about the outcome. By constructing a case-by-case decision process, elected officials can ensure that most of the time these groups will not be mobilized, so that the regulated industry will generally be relatively influential in setting standards.[9] A few examples of how legislation about the structure and process of agencies can perform this function will serve to illustrate the point.[10]

Burden of proof

Under conditions of substantial uncertainty about the nature of a risk, a regulatory statute can affect the stringency of regulation by stating whether proponents or opponents of risk-mitigating actions bear the burden of proof that regulation is desirable. The assignment of the burden of proof is important in two respects. If the effect of a regulation is genuinely uncertain, the side that bears the burden of proof is likely to lose. Moreover, even if the effects are knowable, acquiring knowledge about these effects can be very costly, so that those who bear the burden of proof may decide not to make the necessary expenditures to win their case.

9. For an application of these ideas to water pollution regulation, see Wesley A. Magat, Alan J. Krupnick, and Winston Harrington, *Rules in the Making* (Washington, DC: Resources for the Future, 1986).

10. Each of these issues is discussed in McCubbins, Noll, and Weingast, "Administrative Procedures."

For example, the Food and Drug Administration bears the burden of proof that an ingredient is hazardous and that a regulatory standard is feasible when establishing a regulation limiting the concentration of a naturally occurring toxin in foods, but the producer bears the burden of proof for safety and efficacy in introducing a new pharmaceutical. The consensus view is that the latter rule substantially reduces the rate of introduction of new drugs.[11] Initially, proponents of the Toxic Substances Control Act (TOSCA) favored assigning the same burden of proof to producers who wished to market a new chemical; however, as actually enacted, TOSCA assigned the burden of proof to the regulator, in this case, the Environmental Protection Agency.

Standing

Regulatory statutes determine within limits who has the right to be heard in a regulatory proceeding and who has the right to challenge the regulator's decision in court. If some interests are barred from presenting evidence in support of their position or from challenging a decision that ignores the facts supporting their argument, regulatory decisions are less likely to be responsive to that interest.

For example, in Japan, the only entity that can challenge a decision on telephone regulation by the Ministry of Post and Telecommunications is the company that provides the

11. For a survey of the relevant literature, see William S. Comanor, "The Political Economy of the Pharmaceutical Industry," *Journal of Economic Literature*, 24(3):1178-217 (Sept. 1986).

regulated service.[12] This arrangement means that only the firm can threaten to overturn a decision about its prices or entry into a market, which in turn requires that the Ministry of Post and Telecommunications be especially careful in satisfying the procedural and substantive rights of regulated telephone companies. This policy bias reflects the political reality that consumer groups are especially weak in Japan. Japanese administrative procedures, therefore, tend to be designed to favor producers.

An example from the United States pertains to the old Atomic Energy Commission.[13] In the early days of commercial nuclear power, ratepayers and environmentalists were denied standing in procedures for granting licenses for nuclear power plants, and as a result no license was ever significantly delayed, let alone denied. When the environmental movement became politically significant, Congress passed the National Environmental Policy Act, requiring that environmentalists be heard.[14]

The effect was to cause increases in both the duration of the licensing process and the stringency of nuclear safety regulation, both of which became so burdensome financially that nuclear power became commercially unviable.

Case initiation

In many instances, regulatory statutes place control over an agency's agenda in the hands of external interests. For example, in product safety, environmental, and workplace safety regulations, priority is assigned to petitions external to the agency that demand action against a perceived threat. This practice forces the agency to respond to the risks that are most salient to advocates of regulation, and so it serves the purpose of making agencies more responsive to advocates of regulation who have been mobilized to act.[15] But the uncertainties associated with risks, especially as perceived by the general public, cause the correlation between the magnitude of a risk and the presence of a mobilized advocate of intervention to be weak.

ALTERNATIVE INSTITUTIONAL ARRANGEMENTS

The system described in the second section of this article is designed to serve an important political func-

12. For a discussion of administrative procedures in Japanese telecommunications policy, see Roger G. Noll and Frances M. Rosenbluth, "Telecommunications Policy: Structure, Process, Outcomes," in *Structure and Policy in Japan and the U.S.*, ed. Peter Cowhey and Mathew D. McCubbins (New York: Cambridge University Press, 1995).

13. For a complete discussion of the relationship between administrative procedures at the Atomic Energy Commission and the economic viability of nuclear power, see Linda R. Cohen, "Innovation and Atomic Power: Nuclear Power Regulation, 1966-Present," *Law and Contemporary Problems*, 43(1):67-97 (Winter-Spring 1979).

14. For an interpretation of the intent of Congress in passing this act, see McNollgast, "Legislative Intent: The Use of Positive Political Theory in Statutory Interpretation," *Law*

and Contemporary Problems, 57(1):30-35 (Winter-Spring 1994).

15. For a discussion of this feature of regulation, see Terry M. Moe, "The Politics of Structural Choice: Toward a Theory of Public Bureaucracy," in *Organization Theory: From Chester Barnard to the Present and Beyond*, ed. Oliver E. Williamson (New York: Oxford University Press, 1990), pp. 116-53.

tion. Risk regulation is set up to be responsive to well-organized advocates of intervention in particular cases, but to avoid a proactive search for new risks to be regulated. Unfortunately, this system is prone to substantive incoherence as described at the beginning of this article. The condition that organized groups advocate a regulatory action is neither necessary nor sufficient for regulation to be worthwhile.

One obvious manifestation of this system is that an excited citizenry can force a relatively unimportant risk to the top of the priority list. Indeed, under conditions of considerable uncertainty about the magnitude of a risk, citizens sometimes are manipulated by groups who seek to use regulation as a means to another end. A classic example from the nineteenth century is when investors in the established direct-current electricity industry convinced several states—quite falsely—that the new alternating-current technology was more hazardous than direct current, and thereby postponed entry by the superior technology for several years.[16]

Three types of solutions to this problem have been proposed. One is a specialized court for hearing appeals from decisions by environmental, health, and safety regulators. Another is the regulatory budget, whereby an annual limit would be placed on the total costs of all newly enacted regulations.[17] The last is some sort of super-regulatory authority with the power to influence both regulatory priorities and the stringency of regulations.[18] The super-authority would be similar to the regulatory review process in the Office of Management and Budget, but it would be larger and would be given more authority, perhaps by having the power to delay or even to veto proposed regulations or perhaps by having the authority to require and to set the key parameters of cost-benefit analyses (such as the value of reduced risk to life and health).

Whereas each of these proposals has a reasonable rationale, none addresses the core of the problem: how does one deal with incoherence in demands for regulation by citizens? Each proposal would deal with incoherence after a regulatory process has been initiated, frequently in response to a mobilized group of fearful citizens. The basic idea behind these proposals is that an institution is needed to introduce more discipline into the system. The regulatory budget disciplines overregulation by limiting the financial effect of new regulations, and the other two proposals attack both underregulation and overregulation by placing greater authority in the hands of experts. But if the argument in the previous section of this article is correct, the perceived lack of coherence in regulation has a deep root: the system is designed to reflect the incoherence in attitudes about risk among citizens. A proposal that dooms elected political officials to be regarded as heart-

16. Paul A. David and Julie Ann Bunn, "The Economics of Gateway Technologies and Network Evolution: Lessons from Electricity Supply History," *Information Economics and Policy*, 3(2):165-202 (1988).

17. Litan and Nordhaus, *Reforming Federal Regulation*, pp. 133-58.

18. Breyer, *Breaking the Vicious Circle*, chap. 3.

lessly unresponsive by their constituents is unlikely to endure.

Risk regulation does not stand alone in this category of policies. Two other important examples of policies in which citizen preferences exhibit similar inconsistency are crime and health care. These three policy areas have one commonality: the potential for personal disaster combined with a strong dependence on professionals to exercise good faith in protecting against the threatening event. Any policy that causes some citizens to be denied a protection that they demand, even if their demand is based on ignorance or a cognitive pathology, will cause a political backlash from both those who are denied protection and those who fear other risks and regard this denial as further evidence of the perfidy of government officials.

A commonly proposed solution to this class of problems is to improve the informedness of the citizenry by engaging in a systematic effort to provide more objective facts about these policies and to educate people about statistical decision theory so as to reduce mistakes in reasoning about risks.[19] The premise of this proposal is that if citizens are better informed about science and how best to deal with uncertainties, they will be less prone to overreact or underreact to specific risk issues and to be manipulated by self-interested advocates of a particular risk policy.

Whereas this proposal has obvious merit, its practicality, especially in less than a decade or more, is debatable. Moreover, even if successful, citizen education is not likely to solve

19. This proposal and its problems are discussed in ibid., chap. 2.

the policy incoherence problem for two fundamental reasons. The first is that expecting citizens to be well informed about the scientific details of most catastrophic risks is unrealistic because that knowledge is both vast and uncertain. The second is that as long as knowledge is uncertain— which it is, even among technical experts—an agency relationship will exist between citizens and government officials.

In any agency relationship, agents with more complete knowledge are in a position to take advantage of the person for whom they are acting. Indeed, the only condition under which citizens could fully rely on their regulatory agents to act in their best interests would be if regulators were pure altruists and citizens were in agreement about the appropriate degree of protection that regulators should seek with respect to every source of risk. In general, then, it is perfectly rational for citizens to interpret either a failure or a denial of protection as evidence that regulation is inadequate, rather than the result of interjecting better knowledge and judgment into the policy decision.

The preceding argument implies that the problem of overreaction to perceived failures of risk policy cannot be solved by refusing to regulate them intensively after a disastrous event has created a public demand for regulation. Far more promising is to increase the capacity of the government to identify risks before they become salient and to gain greater influence over the public agenda by proactively publicizing both positive and negative findings about the magnitude of a hazard and the effectiveness of existing safeguards. If the problem of risk regulation is that it is too prone to reacting to the risk du jour that has captured the attention of the media, the best response is for government to put more effort into the selection of the risk du jour. Greater influence on the public agenda plausibly would arise if the government devoted more resources to identifying risks, evaluating the effectiveness of regulatory policies, and designing more effective regulatory instruments. In this case, more resources devoted to regulation might actually lead to a lower social cost of regulation if these resources are devoted to improving knowledge about risks.

If the preceding account of the nature of the risk regulation problem is correct, one cannot fix the problem permanently by simply regulating less, requiring more stringent technical standards for regulations, and making citizens better risk analysts. One must deal directly with the reality that risk regulation policy creates an especially difficult agency relationship between citizens and government officials. Public officials are not likely to take actions that many citizens will interpret as evidence that the government officials are unresponsive agents who persistently fail to comply with their legitimate demands.

Public education means more than making citizens more informed about the technical aspects of risks and decision theory; it also means being the entity that brings fearful threats to the attention of the public in terms that the public can comprehend and to which the public is likely to respond politically. The public's declining faith in experts is not completely irrational, given the presence of a serious agency problem between citizens and government. A comprehensive policy to improve risk regulation must deal with citizens in a manner that is consistent with the context in which political demands for risk policies now arise: the fear of dreaded consequences that are beyond an individual's control.

Risk and the Legal System

By JAMES E. KRIER

ABSTRACT: "Risk" and the "legal system" are ambiguous terms. Here they are clarified, then considered from the standpoint of the objectives, methods, and problems of legal intervention in a world of inevitable risk.

James Krier is the Earl Warren DeLano Professor at the University of Michigan Law School. A graduate of the University of Wisconsin and its Law School, he taught law at the University of California, Los Angeles, and at Stanford University before joining the Michigan faculty in 1983. His chief teaching and research interests are property law and environmental law and policy.

THE terms "risk" and "legal system" are ambiguous, so let us begin by clarifying our topic.

THE MEANING OF "RISK"

Traditionally, "risk" has referred to the chance or probability that some (usually undesirable) event will occur, with the word "gravity" used to describe the event's consequences. In current practice, however, "risk" is taken to mean an expected value arrived at by multiplying consequences by the probability that they will occur. So, for example, we might say that the risk of some chemical is that its introduction into the marketplace will result in an expected cost of one excess death per year, that is, one more death per year than is experienced in the chemical's absence. Behind this statement there might be evidence suggesting, say, that if the chemical is used, there is a one-in-one-thousand chance of one thousand extra deaths annually.

So "risk" expresses something both about probabilities and about consequences. It is worth noting here that consequences are regarded in very different ways by experts, on the one hand, and laypeople, on the other.[1] We shall consider the significance of these differences later.

THE MEANING OF "LEGAL SYSTEM"

Laypeople tend to think of the legal system as comprising only courts and judges. Actually, though, the system includes legislative and executive (administrative) bodies as well. Indeed, legislatures (including the U.S. Congress) and administrative agencies (including the U.S. Environmental Protection Agency) play a more significant role than do the courts with respect to many contemporary problems, including the problem of risk.

THE PROBLEM OF RISK: OPTIMAL RISK

What, precisely, is the problem of risk, at least from the standpoint of the legal system? Commonly, we use the word "problem" when we mean there is too much of something (like rain during a deluge) or too little (like water during a dry spell). So is the problem of risk a problem of too much risk or a problem of too little?

Strangely enough, on this question there are two schools of thought. Many people, educated laypeople in particular, think we experience too much risk in our daily lives. The risk of cancer, the health and environmental risks of new technologies, of contaminated landfills, and so on are commonly thought to be too high, too great. At the same time, however, there are other people—they tend to be people with considerable scientific training—who conclude that we have, in a way, too little risk.[2] How can that be?

Consider the idea of optimal risk, which is to say, just the right amount. The right amount of risk—the right amount of safety—might seem like a strange notion, but notice in this connection that when people say there is too much risk, they are usually also

1. See Clayton P. Gillette and James E. Krier, "Risk, Courts, and Agencies," *University of Pennsylvania Law Review*, 138:1027, 1070-86 (Apr. 1990).

2. Ibid., pp. 1032-36.

saying, implicitly, that some lesser amount would be tolerable or perhaps even desirable. Not many of us want zero risk (absolute safety), and those of us who think we do can usually be talked out of the idea, for a very simple reason: zero risk or absolute safety is impossible to achieve. It is risky not to have some measure of risk or danger in society.

Consider as an example the risk of cancer from a new drug. That risk is a disadvantage of the drug, but presumably the same drug has advantages also (if it does not, then, of course, it should not be introduced into the marketplace). Suppose the drug guards against a serious disease more effectively than does the existing stock of drugs. If society decides that the drug is not to be used because it is risky, the cost of that decision is the incidence of disease that could have been reduced had the drug been employed; if the drug is used, the cost of that choice is an increase in the incidence of cancer. Should the drug be used or not?

Quite clearly, it depends on a comparison of the relevant risks and benefits. Since both risk and the absence of risk can be costly, what society should try to do is minimize the sum of the costs of risk and the costs of avoiding risk. In the case of our hypothetical drug, we want to approve the drug if the disease it helps cure is more serious than the increase in cancer that comes with the cure, and disapprove it otherwise. To express the idea in dollar terms, we want every dollar we spend on avoiding risk to yield a benefit larger than that dollar. Put differently, we want every dollar of risk that we introduce

to be offset by at least one dollar of some other risk avoided.

If this notion still sounds contentious, consider that it guides everybody's everyday activities. It is risky to cross the street, to drive a car, to fly in commercial (let alone private) aircraft, to eat peanut butter (a natural carcinogen), to have children. Yet we do cross the street, drive, and so forth, and with even less than perfect care, because giving up such activities, or even being very, very careful in how we conduct them, is at some point worse—more risky—than the alternative, a cure worse than the disease.

Now we can clarify the reason that some people, scientific experts in particular, tend to think we have too little risk. What they are saying is that society in general has irrational fears of new technologies and synthetic drugs and so on. Most such innovations, in the view of many experts, reduce old (background) risks in amounts greater than the new risks they introduce. Nuclear power, for instance, is certainly risky, but pollution from fossil-fueled power is, in one view, riskier yet, especially given the threat of global warming. If so, then nuclear power is the less risky of the two (necessarily risky) alternatives and also less risky than a world without power. (One would go on, of course, to consider other alternatives as well, such as solar power and hydropower, but few authorities believe that either or both of these are a sufficient power source.)

In sum, it seems clear enough, on a moment's reflection, that an optimal amount of risk—neither too little nor too much but always some—is the appropriate objective. The problem of risk arises not so much in this connection but from the fact that people—laypeople versus experts in particular—disagree in given cases about where the greater risk lies.

MORE ON THE PROBLEM OF RISK: MARKET FAILURE

It is instructive to ask why market forces—considerations of supply and demand—do not effectively control risk. The market, after all, sees to it that, by and large, we do not have way too many tomatoes or too few, too much steel or too little. So why too much risk or too little?

This is an issue that economists discuss in terms of so-called externalities, meaning costs and benefits of activities that for some reason a relevant actor fails to take into account. For example, when a steel company makes steel, it considers the cost of inputs into the manufacture of steel: the cost of raw materials like iron and coal, the cost of operating the mill, the cost of labor, and so on. What the company is unlikely to consider, however, unless forced to do so, is another cost of making steel: air pollution and its adverse effects on neighbors of the steel mill. Air pollution is costly, and it is a necessary cost of making steel. If the company neglects that cost, it is likely to make too much steel, more than would be worthwhile were the costs of air pollution figured in, rather than left external to the steel company's deliberations.

How to force the company to consider the cost of air pollution? The cost of iron it considers because the iron mines charge a price that has to be paid; so too for the coal, for electricity, for labor. Suppliers of these inputs will provide them only if payment is made, and they will withhold them otherwise; the price forces the steel mill to consider the costs of its decisions to others. But who in the marketplace can withhold the air from the steel mill's pollution? Air is something the company can take without paying, so it neglects the fact that air pollution imposes costs upon society.

In short, in the case of inputs like air and peace and quiet and, in our case, safety, the unregulated market might, in a word, fail.

THE CASE FOR INTERVENTION IN THE RISK MARKET

It is this problem of market failure that generally justifies intervention to control environmental pollution and also to control risk. Notice that not all kinds of risk require control outside the market. Chain saws might be risky, but we can count on consumers, given some instruction and common sense, to use them with due care—because the costs of carelessness will be visited on the consumer! But noise from chain saws is quite another matter. True, users of chain saws will consider the noise from the standpoint of their own interests—it can be easily avoided with earplugs and the like—but they might well ignore the interests of bystanders, who also value peace and quiet.

To deal with this noise problem, regulations have been instituted that require mufflers and other noise controls, whether producers and consumers want them or not, just as we see regulations that deal with the risks of pollution. These regulations— these instances of intervention—are provided through the legal system.

THE OBJECTIVES OF INTERVENTION

Perhaps the chief objective of legal intervention in the risk market has already been suggested. If the ideal is an optimal level of risk, and if the unregulated marketplace ordinarily fails to yield this level, then the objective is to intervene in such a way as to achieve appropriate degrees of risk in the society. Where there is too much risk, deterrence is necessary; where there is too little, the objective is encouragement. Both amount to risk management, the purpose of which, ideally, is to minimize the sum of risk costs and risk avoidance costs.

Management is not the only objective, however. As much as we might try to manage risk wisely, there will be instances where risk falls, inappropriately, on victims. People can be risk victims simply because they are exposed to threats they should not have to endure: they might have to live, for example, knowing that one of their parents used a drug that can have serious negative effects on offspring, at some probability. People— and environments and so forth—can be risk victims because some threat eventually manifests itself: a drug that threatens to cause cancer actually does result in the disease in some drug users; a chemical that threatens to pollute the environment actually does enter, say, a body of water. As to these actual consequences, deterrence is beside the point because the harm has already occurred. But compensation is possible. Victims can be awarded money or other goods and services to help provide for their loss; environments can be restored. Moreover, compensation bears a relationship to deterrence. If risk producers know that they will be liable for compensation to victims, the producers will tend to take that obligation into account in deciding how to do their business—they have an incentive to take due care. If victims know they have a right to compensation, they will have an incentive to enforce that right by bringing lawsuits, the threat of which, in turn, provides incentives for care on the part of producers.

THE MEANS OF INTERVENTION

As already suggested, society can and does draw on various legal institutions to manage risk and provide compensation. Putting the matter in the most general terms, it can resort to the courts, legislative bodies, and administrative agencies at both the state and federal levels.

Our focus here is on the courts, though we shall consider legislative and administrative activity toward the end of our discussion.[3]

RISK AND THE COURTS

Courts in the United States play two different sorts of roles in the regulation of risk. One role is to oversee administrative agencies to ensure that the agencies fulfill regulatory responsibilities prescribed by legislation. For example, the Sierra Club Legal Defense Fund might claim that the Environmental Pro-

3. These matters are covered in more detail in other articles in this volume.

tection Agency is not properly enforcing the laws regulating hazardous waste sites and sue the agency in federal court, asking the court to instruct the agency to proceed as directed. This, for our purposes, is a secondary judicial role that we will consider, but only briefly, in our later discussion of legislative and administrative activity.

The way the courts play a primary role is through what is called the law of torts, and here several kinds of lawsuits are of interest. First, risk victims might go to court seeking compensation (damages) from a risk producer, claiming that the producer acted unlawfully in a way that harmed victims. An example would be a claim that a factory let toxic chemicals seep into groundwater, leading eventually to health problems for neighbors.[4] Alternatively, victims might seek damages not for actual physical injuries but on the ground that the factory's operations have unlawfully exposed them to the threat—the risk—of future injuries.

For a variety of reasons, these sorts of lawsuits are troublesome for the courts. They commonly involve technical and scientific complexities thought by many to unduly tax the courts' capacities and also the victims' capacities. Generally speaking, victims must prove the risk producer's wrongdoing and the resulting injuries, meaning that the victims must show these things to be "more probable than not" (that is, a proba

bility greater than 50 percent). Because of the uncertainty that surrounds modern risk problems, this burden of proof can be daunting. Moreover, there is the problem of just what injury the risk producer caused. Say some victims get cancer. They might have gotten cancer in any event, at some probability. Should the risk producer be liable for all the cancers that resulted, more probably than not, from its activities and for none of the other cancers, even though there might be a 49 percent chance that those cancers resulted also from the producer's activities? On this question the courts—and the experts—differ.[5]

The problem under discussion becomes even more difficult when victims seek compensation for risk alone, without manifested injury. Suppose a risk producer's activities result in a 20 percent increase in the expected number of cancers in a given area over the next 30 years (there will be 120 rather than 100). A 50 percent cutoff (based on the more-probable-than-not standard) would deny the award of damages in all cases, meaning too little compensation and too little deterrence. Yet, if the producer were required to pay for all 120 cancers, it would be held liable for cancers it did not cause. There would be too much compensation and deterrence. A contentious—and, to date, barely used—solution to this problem is to hold the producer liable for the additional 20 percent risk it creates for everyone, whether anyone gets cancer or not.[6]

4. Instead of or in addition to seeking damages, risk victims might ask for injunctive relief, a court order that the risk producer abate its risky activities. See Richard A. Epstein, *Cases and Materials on Torts*, 6th ed. (Boston: Little, Brown, 1995), pp. 714-15.

5. Ibid., pp. 487-88.
6. See Glen O. Robinson, "Probabilistic Causation and Compensation for Tortious

At present, it is not at all clear how to resolve debates about the foregoing matters. People, mostly laypeople, who tend to think society is too risky would wish the courts to err in the direction of enhanced liability, whereas others, mostly experts, who believe we seek irrationally high levels of safety would want them to err in just the opposite direction. Given the great uncertainty surrounding the actual facts of the matter, one might believe that the general question is a political one, best solved by a political body like the legislature, with the solutions implemented through administrative agencies.

RISK LEGISLATION AND ADMINISTRATION

On this issue, too, the picture is murky, and we can see why by dwelling on the courts for just another moment.

Consider the obvious, that it is expensive for risk victims to bring lawsuits in the courts. Given this, it might well be that many victims do not find it worthwhile to proceed, the result being (again) too little compensation and deterrence. If risk is spread rather thinly over thousands (or more) of people, there could be huge aggregate risk costs that are never brought to bear on risk producers through the courts.

One might at first regard this as a powerful motivator for legislative and administrative intervention, but again the matter is complicated.

Risk," *Journal of Legal Studies*, 14:779 (1985); Bill Charles Wells, "The Grin Without the Cat: Claims for Damages from Toxic Exposure Without Present Injury," *William & Mary Journal of Environmental Law*, 18:285 (Spring 1994).

Most contemporary political theorists think that legislative and administrative bodies are driven to a significant degree by political pressures of various sorts. Political pressure, in turn, is largely a product of the ability of constituents to organize. If, then, risk producers are better organized than risk victims, legislative and administrative measures will go too easy on the producers; if victims are the better organized, the opposite is likely to hold.

Consider now that just as risk victims might not find it worth their while to bring costly lawsuits, so they might not find it worth the effort to organize political activity. The per capita stakes are usually relatively small, and in any event each victim will tend to reason that if other risk victims campaign for legislative and administrative protection, then passive victims will benefit as well. For example, legal measures that require safer workplaces will mean safer conditions for all employees, not just for those who helped to get the legal measures enacted. Finally, the experts in administrative agencies probably tend to disagree with the common lay view, mentioned earlier, that there is too much risk. The experts will look at expected mortality and morbidity statistics and see that many modern technologies are relatively safe. Laypeople, on the other hand, will look beyond the expected mortality and morbidity numbers at, for example, the worst possible case that could result in the event of a mistake. Nuclear power might look safer, on average, than fossil-fueled power, but at the same time a nuclear accident might be much worse than an accident at a conventional power plant. Laypeople tend to focus on these worst-case possibilities and on other features of high technology that appear to be threatening.

A model like this suggests that just as the market and the judicial system might provide too little protection to victims, so, too, will the legislative and administrative systems. In this view, we should err, as with the courts, in the direction of enhanced protection. But opponents say we have already erred too much. They look at the large stock of legislative and administrative risk protection regulations in place and conclude that society has gone too far. It spends far too much money guarding against evils so unlikely to materialize as to be trivial. The opponents therefore urge legislative and administrative bodies to back away from stringent controls, in the name, ironically, of greater safety. In addition, they urge courts, when they are called on to review the actions of legislative and administrative bodies, to have more respect for expert views about how much safety is enough and what kind of safety is best.

Which, again, is the right outlook? Modeling exercises suggest, to me anyway, that over the long run, society will regulate too little. Hence it should tend to err, systematically, in favor of enhanced liability in court and in favor of stringent legislative and administrative regulations. At the same time, however, it is a fact that the courts are often very hard on modern technology and that the existing legislative and administrative controls are oftentimes amazingly, perhaps foolishly, stringent.[7] Figuring out whether we are anywhere near the optimal point seems an almost foolhardy exercise.

So what do we do? There is considerable evidence that the legal system (or any other system) responds to uncertainty by stumbling along, making guesses some of which are right and some wrong, learning from mistakes, stumbling on again, and so on. Problems are resolved by trial and error, by "muddling through."[8] This method works well enough if the costs of mistakes are not too terribly high, but that condition becomes harder and harder to satisfy. Modern technology has an enormous capacity to make life on the planet better but also, in the worst case, to cause catastrophic losses. In such a situation, the legal system, and society in general, should pursue the prudent path. Unhappily, however, just what is prudent will often become clear only with experience, and the experience itself could prove very costly.

7. The reasons for this, having to do in part with the so-called salience of certain kinds of risk threats, are considered in other parts of this volume.

8. See Gillette and Krier, "Risk, Courts, and Agencies," pp. 1107-8.

Book Department

INTERNATIONAL RELATIONS AND POLITICS

HAMMOND, GRANT T. *Plowshares into Swords: Arms Races in International Politics, 1840-1991*. Pp. xviii, 342. Columbia: University of South Carolina Press, 1993. $42.95.

With the recent demise of the Soviet-American Cold War, the subject of arms races might seem to have become a bit anachronistic. Such a judgment would be unfair, however, to two interesting and related questions: Under what conditions do arms races emerge, and when do they sometimes lead to war? Despite a great deal of analysis, it is not clear that we have made much collective headway on the answers to these questions. This conclusion pertains equally well to the Cold War, to any type of arms race between states in general, and, unfortunately, to the book under review.

Grant Hammond is interested in these questions. Presumably, the conventional approach to addressing them would have started with some review of the extensive pertinent literature that explores the basic questions about arms races and the less extensive evidence that might help to answer them. Some exercise in defining what arms races are and are not would be inevitable. All of these preliminaries would then set up the author's reasonably rigorous analysis of some sample from the arms race population that would have been predicated on an a priori set of arguments that could explain the onset of arms races and their possible relationship to intensive conflict.

We get some of this in the Hammond book. A lengthy definition with as many as eight criteria is offered. Some useful distinctions between military competitions, panics, and arms races are discussed. But we never really get the discussion of previous work or a new, rigorous analysis of arms races. Instead, there are discursive chapters on arms races before World War I, before World War II, and during the Cold War, as well as a foray into arms control. Eventually, Hammond decides to focus on four arms races: Japan-Russia, 1895-1904; Germany-Britain, 1902-12; France-Germany, 1911-14; and Japan–United States–Britain, 1916-22. We are told that Hammond wishes to focus exclusively on major power contests and on only those that occurred between 1840 and 1991. Why these four cases are selected or even whether they fit the eight-step definition are questions that are not raised. For instance, one criterion requires an ex-

184

traordinary and consistent increase in defense levels of at least 8 percent per year, yet no examination of military spending is supplied. Nor is the critical reciprocal nature of military planning, in which one side's moves correspond to the other side's move(s), ever established. As a consequence, it is difficult to know what to make of the analysis or its conclusions.

Ultimately, Hammond concludes that genuine arms races are rare and unlikely to cause wars. He may very well be right on both counts. Unfortunately, his analysis is not as helpful as it might have been in systematically laying an empirical foundation that would have allowed him and his readers to arrive at such a conclusion—or any conclusion about the causal roles of arms races. Where and when arms races have occurred, and whether they influence the outbreak of war, remain worthwhile but open questions.

WILLIAM R. THOMPSON

Indiana University
Bloomington

HARDIN, RUSSEL. *One for All: The Logic of Group Conflict.* Pp. xiv, 288. Princeton, NJ: Princeton University Press, 1995. $24.95.

In this ambitious volume, Russel Hardin looks at the bleak landscape of collective politics at the end of the millennium. It is not a pleasant picture: again and again he refers with sadness and revulsion to events in Bosnia, Rwanda, Israel, and Northern Ireland. The book becomes an attack upon community and upon the collective action that makes it possible. In chapter 1, "Individuals and Groups," Hardin explores how collective action comes about. This is developed further in chapter 2, "Group Power," which takes an overview of political philosophy and the question of power. The third chapter, "Group Identification," explores

the rational foundations of group formation; the fourth deals with "norms of exclusion"; and the fifth focuses on "universalistic norms." In chapter 6, Hardin explores "violent conflicts," and in the seventh he discusses "Einstein's dictum [do not stop questioning] and Communitarianism." The book concludes with an eighth chapter, titled "Whither Difference?"

It is clear that the scourge of ethnic violence is deeply disturbing and not part of the post–Cold War world that was heralded with "the end of history." There is no question that Hardin is scarred by what he sees around the world, be it in Crown Heights or on the Shankill Road. Yet the erudition that he brings to the task of explaining this violence is curiously out of alignment with the task at hand. Hardin is fond—very fond—of arguing by analogy. While this can be helpful, the analogy has to be relevant in some way, and here it is often hard to know why he has chosen the tales and examples that he has. Pygmy Ota Benga, Turgenev's *Spring Torrents*, Corsican marriage formalities, *The Merchant of Venice*, Franz Kafka, and the Mafia all rub shoulders here and rarely to great effect. In the case of the Mafia, it makes little sense to me to suggest that the organization in southern Italy is a "group-level analog of the state," given that the organization has itself been formed in opposition to an extant state apparatus. Furthermore, I would challenge any reader to award the following passage high marks for style:

Omertà fits the paradigm of functional explanation in Chapter 4. If F is the greater power of G, the Mafia, that follows from omertà, X, then omertà contributes to the power of the Mafia (condition 1), this greater power is beneficial for virtually all members of the Mafia (condition 2), which therefore becomes even more capable of enforcing omertà against the occasional miscreant (condition 3). Omertà is similar to the norm of honor in Mérimée's story, "Mateo Falcone." (P. 132)

While Hardin suggests that "revolutions happen in a vacuum," it is clear that they, and indeed, all events, are really to be understood in specific contexts—as he himself writes, "I am a citizen of my time and place." Though he writes with great sincerity about the horrors of ethnic cleansing, it is the case that we need to place these (and other events discussed in the book) into a historical geography if we are to analyze them. For example, it is too simplistic to suggest that in the United States, whites have "begun to leave their neighborhoods . . . more or less in reaction to previous departures." Drawing on the scholarship of urbanists in many disciplines, we need to note at least the following: that the trend has been in evidence since the 1950s; that it is linked to massive alterations in the home finance system, which implicates the U.S. Treasury in this phenomenon; and that it is connected to many facets of public service provision, such as the costs and quality of school districts.

By treating all events as simple n-person games, Hardin dazzles us with the possibility that equally simple alternatives may exist. But the world is complex, and it is, to take another instance, nothing but an abdication of intellectual responsibility to dismiss Waco as an instance of "induced insanity." It is this kind of trite ideology that has left analysts scrambling to comprehend the aftermath of Waco (most notably the Oklahoma City bombing, which occurred after the book's publication). In his introductory remarks, Hardin notes that we are "sorely in need of practical understanding of the actual and the possible." What we see around us at present is a complicated social, political, and economic restructuring, somewhat akin to throwing the global Monopoly game up in the air. People are fighting to leave some squares and move to others. An appeal to the analytical powers of ra-tional choice theory does little, on this evidence, to help us understand these events or to move us toward practical alternatives.

ANDREW KIRBY

Arizona State University West
Phoenix

SIMMONS, BETH A. *Who Adjusts? Domestic Sources of Foreign Economic Policy During the Interwar Years.* Pp. xiii, 330. Princeton, NJ: Princeton University Press. $39.50.

The economic disasters of the interwar years have always been blamed to some extent on the destabilizing interaction of national economic policies. The relation between these policies and the politics of the countries concerned has been investigated only in an ad hoc manner, however; examples include the French political "strings" in June 1931 to a loan in support of the Reichsmark, the crisis over unemployment benefits, and the Bank of England's negotiations with foreign banks during the sterling crisis of August 1931. Recent developments in the theory of political choice and the theory of market reaction to economic policy, both strongly informed by the idea of rationality, are brought together in this groundbreaking statistical and systematic study of the relation of foreign economic-policy actions to domestic politics in more than twenty countries. These consist of the United States, Canada, Japan, and most European countries other than the USSR.

Displaying a sound grasp of monetary economics, Beth Simmons shows that regressions that also include variables representing cabinet instability, political complexion of governments and parliaments, degree of independence of central banks, and industrial conflict have more power to explain the international variance of currency depreciation and protection than do regressions confined to the traditional economic variables. As far as depreciation is concerned, she concludes that it is associated with lack of credibility of parity commitments in the eyes of the financial markets, due to the "time inconsistency" of the policy targets of weak governments and to the clash between the claims of labor on left-wing governments and the claim of the parity if the latter entails deflation. Most generally, she traces the problem of the interwar gold standard to pressures of the transition from elite to mass politics.

Although this cannot be an exhaustive political economy of the interwar gold standard (the dimension of international diplomatic uncertainty surely cannot be eliminated), it is certainly a stimulating conceptualization of one vital dimension. Questions regarding the deeper rationale of Simmons's findings remain; in particular there are unresolved questions, both empirical and theoretical, about the role of the Left. But the merit of the study is to have focused on and clearly identified certain empirical relations between politics, policies, and markets that need to be explained, and thus to raise research in the interwar international political economy to a new level.

T. BALDERSTON

University of Manchester
England

AFRICA, ASIA, AND
LATIN AMERICA

BRACHET-MARQUEZ, VIVIANE. *The Dynamics of Domination: State, Class, and Social Reform in Mexico 1910-1990*. Pp. vi, 251. Pittsburgh, PA: University of Pittsburgh Press, 1994. $59.95.

Offered as a tonic to "top-down" analyses of the Mexican political system, *The Dynamics of Domination* focuses instead on the ability of subordinate groups—especially, but not exclusively, organized labor—to influence the terms of their own domination. For Brachet-Marquez, the timing and implementation of major social reforms targeted at organized labor (the subject of the book)—social insurance, profit sharing, and public housing, adopted in 1943, 1961, and 1972, respectively—can be understood not in terms of models that stress elite rationality or the supposedly corporate or authoritarian nature of the Mexican state but as resulting, at least in part, from pressure from below. In her analysis, then, it is the vulnerability of the Mexican state, rather than its strength, that stands out.

The central concept around which her book is organized is that of the "pact of domination." A process rather than a fixed structure, the pact-of-domination construct is an attempt to capture both how power is wielded by the state and the means that dominated classes have to modify the terms of their subordination. Pacts, then, are the institutional arrangements that result from this process of conflict and negotiation. According to Brachet-Marquez, between 1910 and 1990 Mexico experienced six such pacts or, better, a continuously changing pact marked by the following periods: the first, from the Revolution to the Great Depression; the second, from 1934 to 1940; the third, from 1940 to 1954; the fourth, from 1954 to 1970; the fifth, from 1970 to 1982; and the last, starting after 1988. Only by understanding workers' struggles during these periods, she argues, can the emergence of Mexico's welfare system be understood.

While Brachet-Marquez is to be commended for stressing the agency of subordinate groups in her analysis of state policy, a few concerns remain. First, as

THE ANNALS OF THE AMERICAN ACADEMY

she herself recognizes, her exclusive reliance on secondary works leaves her at the mercy of her sources. This is apparent in the early sections on the Porfiriato and the Revolution, where she presents as fact interpretations that are often contested. It is of greater consequence in her analysis of the role of organized labor. Despite the fact that her argument hinges on the importance of demands made by the rank and file, as opposed to labor leadership, she can do little more than portray the rank and file as a unitary whole driven by economic self-interest. Second, while disagreeing with the approaches of many of those seeking to understand the political "rules of the game" in Mexico, Brachet-Marquez shares with them a reified conceptualization of the state as an entity unto itself. Recent work on the everyday forms of state formation has begun to call this into question.

WILLIAM E. FRENCH

University of British Columbia
Vancouver
Canada

ECKSTEIN, SUSAN EVA. *Back from the Future: Cuba Under Castro.* Pp. xix, 286. Princeton, NJ: Princeton University Press, 1994. $29.95.

EVENSON, DEBRA. *Revolution in the Balance: Law and Society in Contemporary Cuba.* Pp. xiii, 235. Boulder, CO: Westview Press, 1994. $65.00. Paperbound, $21.95.

Anyone who has ever studied Cuba has felt the frustration of a dearth of information in the public domain. While conducting research on the sports system in the 1980s, I was told bluntly by an official of the National Institute of Sports, Physical Education, and Recreation that the Cubans "amass champions, not sta-

tistics." Yet Susan Eva Eckstein and Debra Evenson have shown that, with patience, perseverance, and analytical skill, a tenacious scholar can circumvent the problem. With *Back from the Future: Cuba Under Castro*, Professor Eckstein has written a comprehensive evaluation of the Cuban revolution that is meticulously documented and chock-full of detail. Likewise, Professor Evenson's *Revolution in the Balance: Law and Society in Contemporary Cuba* is a thorough description and analysis of the evolution of the legal system in revolutionary Cuba.

Both authors present an evenhanded view, not likely to please the Cuban émigré community precisely for the balanced treatment of the revolution's pluses and minuses. As described in her preface, Eckstein's book is a "study of economic and social policy under Castro: not specifically of who makes policy and the personal motivations of policymakers but of contextual factors influencing policy choices and, above all, policy outcomes." Indeed, the subtheme of the book is that, contrary to the conventional wisdom, "Castro and Cuban communism have been circumscribed by global political and economic dynamics, by formal and informal state dynamics, and by forces in civil society." According to Eckstein's revisionist interpretation, for example, policy under Castro was driven as much—if not more in some instances—by U.S. policy as it was by Soviet policy.

Evenson's effort is the culmination of four years' work, which includes numerous interviews with active jurists in Cuba. *Revolution in the Balance* tracks the evolution of the legal profession since 1959 and, in the process, clearly evaluates the institutionalization of revolutionary ideals and points out where the process has fallen short. Evenson deftly uses a comparative approach, contrasting the Cuban legal system with that in the former Soviet Union. As in so many other areas of Cuban society, the legal system is clearly modeled after that in the Soviet Union but still contains characteristics that are distinctly Cuban.

Both books accomplish what they set out to do. *Back from the Future* does not seek to replace an anecdotal treatment of contemporary Cuba such as *Castro's Final Hour* by Andres Oppenheimer, nor is it a comprehensive history of revolutionary policy such as *The Cuban Revolution: Origins, Course, and Legacy* by Marifeli Pérez-Stable. Rather, it provides the reader with a clear framework and copious data to assess the "revolutionary experiment."

Revolution in the Balance, on the other hand, is likely the definitive work, as the subtitle suggests, on "law and society in contemporary Cuba." Evenson's legal focus provides fascinating interpretations of well-known events, such as Castro's "History Will Absolve Me" speech, the trial and execution of General Ochoa, and the Abrantes trial. Rather than discuss the political implications, as has been done repeatedly before her, she describes the events as they were interpreted by the Cuban legal community.

The books are not, however, without their weaknesses. The sheer volume of information compiled and analyzed by Eckstein sometimes slips into a repetitious treatment of specific subjects and terms. Further, endnotes could have been consolidated in many cases within paragraphs, rather than citing every sentence, which can prove distracting if not downright irritating. Her use of the term "islanders" instead of "Cubans" also seems pointless, unless it was meant to distinguish them from the many Cubans who have left the island. Such problems are likely editorial oversights.

Evenson's most glaring weakness is a tendency toward a dry style of prose, which is likely typical of work with a legal focus. Her rich analysis and research also deserve a conclusion, which is omitted for no obvious reason.

In general, however, Eckstein and Evenson have written valuable monographs for the serious researcher as well as for the undergraduate student in the classroom.

PAULA J. PETTAVINO

Arlington
Virginia

HARRISON, MARK. *Public Health in British India: Anglo-Indian Preventive Medicine 1859-1914*. Pp. xvii, 324. New York: Cambridge University Press, 1994. $69.95. Paperbound, $29.95.

This work examines selected themes related to public health in India during the ascendancy of the British Raj (1859-1914). The substance of the book lies in the interplay between the contemporary concepts of Western science, British colonial attitudes, and the multireligious Indian society. Within this context, Harrison uncovers reasons for the somewhat underwhelming progress of public health in British India.

Harrison rejects the popular allegation that preventive medicine was a tool of the British Empire. Instead, he implicates the Indian urban rentier class for opposing adequate expenditure on public sanitation. Apprehensive of alienating the rising Indian urban elite, the British rulers, argues Harrison, failed to carry out coherent public health policies. Sanitary reforms languished due to an inadequate urban tax base. Exceptions were the military cantonments and also the civil lines, where the British civil authorities resided. Bureaucratization of the Indian Medical Service and conflicting ideas about the epidemiology of communicable diseases in the tropical environment, especially cholera, malaria, and plague, also retarded preventive medicine policy. Significant progress was, however, made in the smallpox vaccination program. Harrison reveals remarkably well the interaction between colonial medical views, various Indian religions, and politics at the international and local levels. Using the case of Muslim pilgrimage (hajj) to Mecca, Harrison shows in chapter 5 how the epidemiological concept of quarantine and the pan-Islamic self-image clashed. At the local level, Calcutta, then British India's capital, provides Harrison an arena for analyzing conflicting interests of the resident British population, the growing politically conscious Indian urban elite, and the Indian government. British colonialism, with its cultural arrogance, paternalism, and spatial segregation, confronted Indian society in the cities. Ironically, it was in Calcutta that the emergent elite, the very class fostered by British colonialism, frustrated the implementation of public health policies. In turn, the deplorable sanitary conditions in the British Indian cities engendered a negative perception about tropical health in general.

Public Health in British India is a commendable work marked by its substantial scholarly apparatus—fifty pages of notes, extensive utilization of primary sources, several graphs, and illustrations (including one of an Indian privy). In spite of occasional overcrowding of textual details, each chapter has clearly stated conclusions. Arguably, the book's eight public health themes might be more clearly integrated. Yet this is a work of solid scholarship and should spawn historiographic research in the British colonial context. It is highly recommended for scholars and students of the Indian colonial history of preventive medicine.

SURINDER M. BHARDWAJ
Kent State University
Ohio

JACKSON, ROBERT H. *Indian Population Decline: The Missions of North-*

western New Spain, 1687-1840. Pp. xii, 229. Albuquerque: University of New Mexico Press, 1994. No price.

This monograph studies the decline—indeed, the devastation and collapse—of the Indian populations of a large number of mission communities of northwestern New Spain (colonial Mexico) and of the regions known as the Primería Alta in northern Sonora, Baja California, and Alta California. This study has comparative analyses of regional mission communities' demographic collapse, along with some comparison of these community populations with the nonnative mission populations of the larger region being studied. Also included are some comparative analyses of the mission community populations and contemporary American and non-American populations.

The central finding of this excellent work is that the demographic collapse of the mission communities studied was not strictly biological. It was not simply the result of recurring epidemic diseases, such as measles, smallpox, and syphilis, but was due also to the imposition of colonial social controls and physical dislocation of the peoples, as well as the systematic, conscious, and intended destruction of the surviving elements of the Indians' culture, worldview, and social and economic organization.

Jackson reports that in northern Sonora and Baja California,

periodic epidemics of contagious disease significantly increased death rates, and clearly accelerated the process of demographic collapse by carrying off adults of child-bearing age, thus reducing the ability of the populations to reproduce. Moreover, epidemics exacerbated the frightfully high infant and child mortality rates, and virtually destroyed the populations of Indians congregated in the missions in a short period of time.

On the other hand, few epidemics broke out in the Alta California missions, and yet the populations of these missions had chronically high mortality rates particularly among infants, children, and women. Jackson believes that this was because there was little or no prenatal care provided women in the missions. Women were conscripted for the mission workforce, making pregnancies dangerous. The wiping out of native cultures may have denied young women traditional support and child-care knowledge. Many children were stillborn or died shortly after birth due to complications of birth, syphilitic congenital illness, and dehydration resulting from endemic gastrointestinal diseases. "Finally," Jackson writes,

qualitative evidence also suggests that abortion was commonly practiced in the mission communities; and the response by missionaries to apparent or real instances of provoked abortion contributed to the humiliation of Indian women, raised levels of stress, and only exacerbated the social conditions that had led women to abort in the first place.

Many of Jackson's data on life expectancies at birth for the Indian Alta California or other mission populations for various years—ranging from 0.4 years for the Comondu Mission in 1783, to 26.6 years for the San Luis Rey Mission in 1830—indicate that these communities must have experienced extremely high rates of infant and child mortality. Such data, along with low birthrates, clearly indicate that many Indian mission populations had very low net reproduction rates (NRRs); some extreme examples may be noted: the San Francisco Mission's NRR was 0.00 to 0.04 for each of quinquennial years from 1793 to 1828, and corresponding NRRs for the Santa Cruz Mission ranged from 0.01 to 0.09 over the 1798-1838 period. With such low NRRs, these populations could be sustained only by addition of Indians, often forced, from outside the missions.

Other factors that led to the extremely high mortality rates of the Indian mission populations were the climate of coercive social control and the use of corporal punishment by the missionaries which "humiliated and physically injured the individual punished."

Such violently coercive means did not always achieve the ends desired by the missionaries. It was not infrequent for the Indians to flee from the missions to escape the harshness of life, and they sometimes

did not accept corporal punishment and other forms of social control as passively as the Franciscans believed. In 1812, for example, a group of converts at Santa Cruz mission murdered missionary Andrés Quintana, O.F.M., because of his plans to punish Indians in an especially sadistic form, with cat-o'-nine-tails with barbed metal on the ends of the leather strips.

Some Franciscans believed that the converts' suffering facilitated their entry into heaven. Young men were often locked up at night to prevent their escape from the mission. It was a common practice to lock women and girls in damp and filthy dormitories at night, particularly the wives of Indians who had fled from the missions. Mission sanitation was often abysmal, housing was deplorable, and overcrowding was common.

"The missionaries themselves understood epidemics and the high mortality rates in the missions as God's punishment for the resistance of Indians to the mission program, or as punishment of Spanish colonists for their sins by depriving them of Indian laborers and tribute payers." Mortality rates were high also among the colonist and soldier populations of the missions.

Readers of this book need to be alerted to two minor points. At the end of a chapter (p. 162), Jackson writes, "The following chapter outlines the growth of the non-Indian, soldier-settler population in northern Sonora and the Californias." The chapter referred to is not on this subject but is a section covering the conclusions of the study of the Indian mission populations. We might also mention that a net reproduction ratio of 1.0 does not indicate a doubling of the population, as Jackson states (p. 11), but a replacement of the population over a generation.

This monograph is excellent. The research is carefully and judiciously carried out, the exploration of the relevant literature is sagacious, the findings are very interesting, and the book is very well written.

SURINDER K. MEHTA

University of Massachusetts
Amherst

KATO, JUNKO. *The Problem of Bureaucratic Rationality: Tax Politics in Japan.* Pp. xiii, 327. Princeton, NJ: Princeton University Press, 1995. $39.50.

For some years now, there has been a lively debate between pluralists and corporatists over the respective power of the bureaucracy and political parties in Japanese policymaking. One of the key issues of the debate is whether the bureaucracy uses its monopoly on technical expertise as a means of controlling political parties. Junko Kato's book makes it clear that perceiving the debate in the terms of a zero-sum game is as erroneous as the focus on the bureaucracy's supposed hold on technical expertise.

Her analysis of the Japanese consumption tax demonstrates a complex interplay between the Ministry of Finance (MOF) and the Liberal Democratic Party (LDP) that was influenced by many factors including the organizational context within which bureaucrats selected their policy options, the role of opposition parties in the legislature, and the intraparty maneuverers of the governing party. Central to her thesis is the concept of bounded rationality, namely, that bureaucratic rationality is flexible and changes with changing needs and circumstances.

The consumption tax is well chosen as the subject of the study as it demonstrates the strengths and strategies of a variety of players over an extended period of time. For ten years the MOF attempted to convince the LDP to introduce a value-added tax as a means of rationalizing the Japanese taxation system. Although the MOF failed twice in its attempts to gain LDP support for the policy, it finally succeeded in 1989. The ability of the LDP to withstand the MOF's pressure and its eventual capitulation constitute the story that unfolds.

This study is also well researched. The data are drawn from interviews with Japanese bureaucrats, politicians, journalists, and academics, as well as a wide-ranging survey of Japanese- and English-language sources.

The only substantial criticism I have concerns Kato's assumption that the adoption of the consumption tax by the LDP was the main reason for the loss of the LDP's 38-year rule. This is a critical point, as it would then ask us to explain why the LDP committed political suicide. However, it may have been that the presentation of the policy by the LDP—for example, Nakasone's having lied to the public about the tax—was the real reason for the public's turning against the LDP, along with the LDP's refusal to get serious about political reform.

This book is highly recommended for those interested in bureaucratic rationality, corporatism, and pluralism in Japanese policymaking, or Japanese tax policy.

BRUCE STRONACH

International University of Japan
Yamato-machi

VAN STAAVEREN, JACOB. *An American in Japan, 1945-1948: A Civilian View of the Occupation.* Pp. xvii, 286. Seattle: University of Washington Press, 1995. $35.00.

For me, it was especially interesting to read this account of the doings of a rival organization in Occupied Japan, in this case, Civil Information and Education (CI&E), to which the Supreme Commander for the Allied Powers (SCAP), MacArthur, assigned positive things, such as reforming the Japanese educational system away from militarism and emperor worship. My organization was Civil Censorship Detachment, which was assigned to make sure bad things, like assassinations, did not happen. We sometimes thought we had to watch CI&E a little to be sure they were not being taken in by Japanese Imperial Rule Assistance Association (IRAA) types. Also, my view was from Tokyo—specifically, the Central Telephone and Telegraph Office—while Van Staaveren's was from Kofu, Yamanashi prefecture, 100 miles out in the countryside.

Overall, it is clear from Van Staaveren's account that CI&E worked hard and did a good job in trying to democratize Japan's prewar ultranationalist educational system, all the way from combating rote-memory teaching at the primary school level to decentralizing the Tokyo- and Kyoto-dominated university system by having a national university in every prefecture. The job was never completed, but not because CI&E people were duped by IRAA ultranationalists. In fact, Van Staaveren describes how his inspection team monitored teachers who had been IRAA members, even to resisting a petition to reinstate one of them "signed in blood." Rather, their failures were the result of SCAP's change of direction from democratization to economic recovery with the Dodge Plan of 1949 and thereafter. This resulted in budget cuts for schools and a downsizing that permitted—indeed, encouraged—the elimination of "radical" teachers, on the grounds of Communist infiltration of the Japan Teachers Union (Nikkyoso). These over-

all results are well described in the chapter 19 epilogue, with "Yamanashi's teachers' unions" discussed in more detail in chapter 8.

Other chapter topics include "assignment to Japan" (chapter 1), which involves Van Staaveren's personal experience in obtaining his appointment and preservice training in Seattle and Tokyo before his assignment to Yamanashi prefecture. There are descriptions of his "team and its task" (chapters 2 and 3), followed by details of school inspection experiences (chapters 5 and 6). Chapter 10 analyzes "the conundrum of religious freedom," with a follow-up in chapter 18, "Additional Religion and State Problems." The religion problem was particularly delicate because, although SCAP had clearly ordered separation of church and state, including religion and schools, there were architectural matters like Shinto and Buddhist statuary on school grounds and social problems like funerals. Moreover, SCAP seemed to neglect its own orders in permitting—and encouraging—Japanese Christians like Dr. Kagawa Toyohiko to visit schools.

As Van Staaveren says in his preface, this is "an autobiographical account of the occupation 'from below,' " and he deserves to be congratulated for organizing a great assortment of detailed information from notes, letters, and reports kept from those Occupation days and reviewing it in long-range perspective. Also, as Harvard Professor Akira Iriye, who was a schoolboy in Japan at the time, asserts in his introduction, this book presents "a wholesome antidote" to those "skeptics and cynics" who may think "the Japanese, and even the American occupiers themselves, were merely going through the motions, both of them anticipating that once the occupation ended, things would go back to their traditional ways." Rather, it "contains ample evidence of the earnestness with which both Americans and Japanese sought to change the country." To a considerable extent they succeeded.

HILARY CONROY

University of Pennsylvania
Philadelphia

EUROPE

McALEER, KEVIN. *Dueling: The Cult of Honor in Fin-de-Siècle Germany.* Pp. xiii, 268. Princeton, NJ: Princeton University Press, 1994. $24.95.

In undertaking the study of dueling in late nineteenth-century imperial Germany, Kevin McAleer analyzes the essential features of a nominally marginal phenomenon, and he explores its relevance in understanding certain key issues of German historiography, particularly the nature of the dynamics of Wilhelmine society and the disturbing uniqueness of Germany's Sonderweg (Separate Path).

McAleer makes a convincing case for the essentially aristocratic character of the German duel, which exemplified an attempt to recapture the illusory purity of the medieval chivalrous ethos, an ethos whose quest was rendered coextensive with the search for the defining parameters of German identity.

McAleer examines in detail the origins of the dueling process, the provisions of the dueling codes, the choice of weapons (the overwhelming preference for pistol duel over saber duel), the honor court system, which in many cases accentuated rather than contained the propensity for violent resolution of disputes, and the role of key institutions—primarily the army and university dueling associations—in fostering the correlation of status with masculinity and the latter with the ability "to dispense satisfaction in a duel."

What emerges is the picture of an activity whose lethal character, coupled with the seriousness exhibited in its pursuit by its proponents, reinforced the hierarchically structured weltanschauung of Wilhelmine Germany's ruling classes. In the exclusive milieu of upper-class men of honor, the reassertion of feudal-type bonds signaled both their imperviousness to the values of neohumanism and their confused—often outright contradictory—perceptions of the nature of their commitments.

Nothing exemplified the latter better than the duelists' views on gender relations. In one of the best chapters, McAleer shows how sexual honor was perceived, articulated, challenged, and defended. At the center of each potential dispute stood the female figure, whose vulnerability to predatory male advances was the source of simultaneous adoration and scorn. The former reinforced the need for protection, while the latter the need for monitoring; their intersections reasserted male primacy, with the requisite moral and physical attributes to guarantee the appropriate response to all challenges.

It was this commitment to elite male primacy that rendered dueling such an influential activity. It reflected the growing militarization of German life, the perfect vehicle for sustaining the cult of war in everyday life. It contributed—in conjunction with a whole set of other institutional arrangements—to the debilitating effects of the conservative reaction to the liberal interlude of the 1860s and 1870s, an interlude whose impact was too shortlived.

This raises the fascinating question of dueling's role in the unique path of Germany's polity and, in particular, in the rise of national socialism. This is a question that every student of that era must tackle no matter what the subject matter is. I wish that McAleer would have dealt with it in a more comprehensive manner, given the fact that the linkages are there and that he offers some intriguing glimpses to that effect. Having said that, this book is a very solid piece of work that deals with an activity much more representative of the character of fin de siècle Germany than many would have thought was the case.

GEORGE ANDREOPOULOS

Yale University
New Haven
Connecticut

UNITED STATES

AVRICH, PAUL. *Anarchist Voices: An Oral History of Anarchism in America*. Pp. xiii, 574. Princeton, NJ: Princeton University Press, 1995. $25.00.

This remarkable work, the materials for which were collected by the author over a period of nearly thirty years, has preserved interviews with, or about, leading American anarchists. By 1963, when Paul Avrich started this collection, the anarchist movement had dwindled down to virtually a sect. Some of the interviewees were in their seventies, eighties, and even older. Some were children or grandchildren of anarchist leaders.

This volume is intended as a sourcebook for students and scholars. It is divided into six parts: "Pioneers," "Emma Goldman," "Sacco and Vanzetti," "Schools and Colonies," "Ethnic Anarchists," and "The 1920s and After." Each part has a several-page introduction, and each interview is preceded by a paragraph of headnote. The book includes over 600 footnotes, a 12-page bibliography, and a 30-page index that lists more than 1700 people references.

Interviews are not presented in question-answer format, but rather in statements, averaging perhaps two pages, rarely over five. The words are those of the interviewee, with some editing for clarity. Several elements are common in the statements, doubtless reflecting Avrich's questions that guided their answers more or less. The questions seem to have addressed what kind of people they were; why they became anarchists; what their goal was and how they expected to achieve it; and why the movement faded.

Mostly the anarchists were immigrants from eastern and southern Europe, workers feeling oppressed in part by their regimented life here. Some carried their anarchism with them when they arrived. What they sought was freedom, to become what they could, with no authority over them, and no underlings below—to do what they might without impinging on the rights of others. How was this to be achieved? There the movement splintered. Individualists tolerated only those organizational restraints that were inherently moral; collectivists were to accomplish their goal in voluntary cooperation; syndicalists called for organization by functions; Communist anarchists wanted the withering away of the state. Some, perhaps most, were pacifists; others believed in the bomb, to destroy the state, to punish the wicked oppressors. Contradictions are easily seen. Ultimately, by the 1920s, the immigrant flow contracted. The good life within capitalism tended to satisfy at least the next generation. Wars and totalitarianism smothered anarchistic fires.

And yet, is not our society now adulating libertarianism, a watchword of the anarchists? Now prune the state, reverse regulation, protect individual rights—could these be characterized as free-market anarchism?

GEORGE BLYN

Rutgers University
Camden
New Jersey

FAILLE, CHRISTOPHER. *The Decline and Fall of the Supreme Court: Living Out the Nightmares of the Federalists.* Pp. xvi, 204. Westport, CT: Praeger, 1995. $52.95.

The title of this book is not a clear indication of its contents, except that the provocative title promised an intriguing thesis. The book has a great deal of merit, but its value is reduced by its polemic tone (the discussion of Clarence Thomas's nomination, for instance) and occasionally rambling style (the relevance of the discussion of Hugo Black's career and Lyndon Johnson's election to the House is not clearly established).

The thesis of the book is that the advent and spread of judicial realism has politicized the Supreme Court and the nomination process. Christopher Faille decries technical formalism, which, because of its facial absurdity, opened the door to realism. Judicial realism did not arise as a normative prescription so much as an empirical description of the way that justices made decisions. According to judicial realists, judges who advocated rigid formalism were merely shrouding policy-oriented decisions in the cloak of objective decision making.

Faille maintains that the Framers of the Constitution meant for the nomination process to be apolitical. In particular, he argues that factions should not be involved and the Senate's role of "advice and consent" was to be sharply limited. The central argument can be summarized in the last sentence of the first chapter: "The Constitution, with its advice and consent clause, was not intended for a world in which the Supreme Court is called upon to do all that social democracy requires."

Given the nature of checks and balances and other provisions of the Constitution, Faille does not make a convincing case that the Framers intended a minor role for the Senate in reviewing judicial nominees. Implicit in the argument is that aggressive Senate review and politicized nominations are recent phenomena and that after 1937 the Court became a political actor. His study ignores the confirmation process during the nineteenth century, when a relatively high percentage of Court nominees were rejected, some on the basis of their stands on a single issue. Indeed, many of the Framers were still active in politics when the Jeffersonians attempted to impeach Justice Samuel Chase, with Chief Justice John Marshall as the ultimate target. While 1937 represents a watershed year for the Court, the argument that the Court is now a "mere collection of nine power seekers and power keepers" ignores the impact of the justices who gutted the Fourteenth Amendment after the Civil War and those who used substantive due process to protect business.

Faille ignores the argument that the confirmation process is, in some ways, a sham in which nominees shamelessly claim they have no agenda or preconceptions about any issue. With some justification, the author criticizes senators for their politicized and often exaggerated evaluations of the candidates for the bench, but the presidents who make lofty and misleading claims about their nominees are not held to a similar standard. In some ways, those arguments would buttress his claims.

RICHARD PACELLE

University of Missouri
St. Louis

JEWELL, MALCOLM E. and MARCIA LYNN WHICKER. *Legislative Leadership in the American States.* Pp. viii, 232. Ann Arbor: University of Michigan Press, 1994. $39.50.

Legislative Leadership in the American States was published prematurely. Although the book makes some useful contributions, it is incomplete both as an empirical study and as a conceptual design.

The authors, Professors Malcolm Jewell and Marcia Lynn Whicker, acknowledge that they have not collected or analyzed the data necessary to regard their work as a finished product. Their research efforts were limited to interviewing between one and eight legislative leaders in 22 of the state capitals during 1991. This inquiry did not include rank-and-file legislators, governors, lobbyists, or others who interact with legislative leaders. There are no discussions of how the partial data might affect findings, but Jewell and Whicker do, repeatedly, call for further research.

This begs for an assessment of whether this book provides a useful foundation for additional study. Jewell and Whicker do present some leadership factors and categories that seem promising, and they pose some hypotheses of relationships between variables. However, they have not developed a general theory or conceptual framework. The major problem here is that the dependent variable of effective leadership is not defined or used. Like others who have toiled in the vineyard of leadership studies, Jewell and Whicker fail to help us know when we will recognize an effective leader when we see one.

The authors suggest the task of defining and working with the dependent variable for a future project. In this book, they rely primarily on logic and common sense for identifying salient factors and for speculating about how they might relate to one another. While Jewell and Whicker demonstrate that they are bright and do have common sense, the book shows clearly that attention to effective leadership or a similar concern cannot be postponed. The authors, for example, recognize that some factors are probably more important than others. They assign a higher possible score for whether or not

a party caucus can bind its members to a vote than they assign to the size of the leadership staff. Missing is any explanation of how or why the values are weighted differently. Ideally, one would have hypothesized or demonstrated the impacts of these factors on effective leadership.

Similarly, after suggesting a scheme for categorizing leadership styles and leadership goals, the authors state, "A legislative leader can be effective only if his or her style of leadership is acceptable to the membership." That simple observation plus the general preference shown by the authors for consensual leadership seem to contradict all that was said elsewhere about the powers that come from authority over committee assignments and legislative calendars and the capacity of some legislative leaders to dole out funds and assistance in campaigns. There may be a way of reconciling these perspectives, but not without discussing what determines leadership effectiveness.

Legislative Leadership in the American States is filled with observations and speculations by two savvy, informed scholars. We can be grateful for that. To gain a more complete understanding of state legislative leadership, we will have to wait for them—or someone else—to finish the study.

DENNIS L. DRESANG

University of Wisconsin
Madison

KAZIN, MICHAEL. *The Populist Persuasion: An American History.* Pp. x, 381. New York: Basic Books, 1995. $24.00.

While the word "Populist" with a capital "P" is commonly used to describe the agrarian political movement of the late nineteenth century, Michael Kazin has substantially broadened populism's scope. He has substituted a lowercase "p" and defined leaders of the "populist persuasion" more broadly. Populists, writes Kazin, are charismatic leaders who "speak for the people."

The leaders about whom Kazin writes range from the Left to the Right, from agrarian reformers to fundamentalist Protestants, from labor leaders to red baiters.

Kazin's populists are a mixed bag. He notes a distinct movement in more recent years from Left to Right. Anger and resentment among fundamentalist Protestants, disillusionment with crime, increasing uncertainty in the labor force, and a new emphasis on high taxes and the prospect of an uncertain economic future are creating the ideal environment, Kazin writes, for the populism of the Right. Historically, he adds, populists have been able to build mass movements out of discontent, resentment, unrest, loss of security, and fear of an unknown future.

Kazin is particularly effective in recounting the careers of Father Coughlin, Senator Joseph McCarthy, George Wallace, and the Congress of Industrial Organizations' John L. Lewis. Some who equate Populism with Robert LaFollette, William Jennings Bryan, and George Norris may regret the inclusion of so many newcomers in what had been a relatively exclusive society.

The use by populists of increasingly sophisticated communications technology is included but probably not accorded the attention it deserves. Kazin observes, for example, that Father Coughlin thrived on radio but was diminished by newsreels. On radio he spoke with "the pleasantly modulated rhythms of a friendly parish priest." In newsreels he was "harsh and feverish . . . ranting on the stump."

Television was brutal to Senator McCarthy except when he was able tightly to control the scene, but it was a godsend to Ronald Reagan, whom Kazin also describes as a populist. The influence of the old-fashioned Chautauqua is missing. Without Chautauqua, the agrarian populists would have lacked a made-to-order podium from which to exercise their platform skills.

An aspect to which Kazin gives relatively short shrift is the lasting legacy of the Populism with a capital "P." The agrarian Populists of the 1890s have faded into history, but their impact on government is still much in evidence. One has only to note the widespread use of initiative and referendum in state government; in addition, many federal regulations governing commerce and industry owe their existence in large part to Populist efforts.

In this book, Kazin provides a significant historical view of a complex phenomenon that has had a profound impact on American life. He deserves credit for enlarging the panorama and furnishing a fresh outlook on a significant aspect of American history.

SIG MICKELSON

San Diego
California

KERBEL, MATTHEW R. *Edited for Television: CNN, ABC, and the 1992 Presidential Campaign*. Pp. vii, 246. Boulder, CO: Westview Press, 1994. $59.95. Paperbound, $18.95.

SCHMUHL, ROBERT. *Demanding Democracy*. Pp. vii, 149. Notre Dame, IN: University of Notre Dame Press, 1994. $22.95. Paperbound, $10.95.

Few social scientists would still quibble with the assertion that presidential campaign politics today are media politics. In recent years, the discussion, demonstration, and evaluation of media political influence have taken center stage not only among campaign pundits and popular commentators but among academics of various disciplines as well. The main difference between the popular and academic accounts lies in the quantity and precision of empirical evidence each demands before being comfortable with the value of resultant inferences. More often than not, each is also subject to very distinct biases emanating from the very natures of their vocations—the rigorous and self-effacing academic is inclined to offer very qualified and fairly couched research conclusions; the self-referential pundit, on the other hand, tends to fixate on one cogent observation, which is then passionately contended.

Professors Schmuhl and Kerbel focus their analyses of the 1992 presidential election on a shared concern: the normative implications of a pervasive and ubiquitous, albeit increasingly multifaceted, media for democratic praxis. Both also share an engaging talent for prose. Once the question of media consequence for politics and political culture is raised, however, Schmuhl and Kerbel quickly part company. Not only do they disagree on an answer to the foregoing question; they starkly diverge in style and method of inquiry as well. Schmuhl, a self-described "citizen-critic," uses personal observations of and exposure to the popular media to argue that, in 1992, the political media environment was broadened, and, as a consequence, the distance between the politician and the potential voter was reduced. This, it is inferred, holds the promise of a democratic renaissance. Kerbel, on the other hand, grounds his inferences in extensive and detailed content analyses of the campaign as conveyed by the ABC and CNN television networks. He concludes that the content and process of television reporting breeds, among other things, a cynical citizenry and, far from serving the cause of democracy, serves only to feed its own commercial appetite. Kerbel's case is admirably documented and his research uncovers critical insights into the media–

political culture interface; Schmuhl seems to have one point to make, and it rests on fairly transparent and, arguably, ephemeral supports.

Schmuhl's essential point, that a broadening of the mediated campaign environment from the evening news to the talk-show circuit, broadcast town halls, infomercials, and "New News" (popular culture political information) represents a qualitative improvement in voter education, is highly debatable. A specialist in American studies at Notre Dame, his earlier work, *Statecraft and Stagecraft: American Political Life in the Age of Personality* (University of Notre Dame Press, 1990) focused on the convergence of political life, popular communication, and popular culture to the detriment of substantive democratic discourse. The current volume purports to demonstrate a reversal of this process; an opening of the campaign into wider media formats is seen as a response to the demands of citizens for less packaged and more unfiltered information about the presidential candidates.

The point that Schmuhl misses, and Kerbel soberly infers, is that there may be very important differences between a citizen and a consumer. A consumer—no matter what the marketing schools teach—is essentially a passive creature who is cultivated for consumption. The commodity precedes the creation of a market for its need. The notion of citizen, however, if it ever was a reality, implies a sense of active political empowerment at the mass level. The question then becomes, Did the media in 1992 embrace citizen demands for unadulterated civics information, or did they move to more fully capitalize on the commercial viability of presidential electioneering? Watching a presidential aspirant play the saxophone on a late-night talk show may not be helpful information for the voter-as-citizen; however, it does entertain an audience on many, mostly trivial, levels.

Mass media are, after all, a commercial endeavor, and it would be irrational for them to behave otherwise. Schmuhl may argue that what sells is what audiences (read "citizens") demand. It is just as plausible to maintain that a population nurtured on the offerings of a commercial media, whether the offerings be political or nonpolitical in content, has very limited possibilities for demand articulation. This is even more plausible if the issue of media consonance is raised. Kerbel, a political scientist at Villanova, demonstrates many times over that there is little difference between two apparently incomparable campaign news sources—ABC, an old-style broadcast network, and CNN, the perpetual news cable operation. Just like ABC, which, along with the other two traditional networks, CBS and NBC, placed its news bureau under the creative control of its entertainment division a few years ago, CNN "relies on the entertaining quality of information to attract an audience that finds fulfillment in tuning in to accounts of the latest events." Given this shared orientation, Kerbel finds that CNN and ABC covered the 1992 election in a similar fashion, delivering more entertainment than information and more trivia than substance. As an example, from primaries to election day, the horse race still dominated election coverage and, when that was combined with image, process, and purely nonissue reports, campaign issue coverage was thoroughly overwhelmed.

Both Schmuhl and Kerbel are very engaged and reflective observers of the political drama that has characterized media coverage of presidential campaigns in recent decades. Their penetrations into the details of the 1992 campaign are valuable in their own right. The difference is that Schmuhl's work lacks a certain depth in analytic rigor and remains essentially a popular commentary. Kerbel's analytic labors, however,

resurrect the provocative notion that, in presidential campaigns as in all mass-targeted information, the media may very well be the message.

SILVO LENART

Purdue University
West Lafayette
Indiana

LADD-TAYLOR, MOLLY. *Mother-Work: Women, Child Welfare, and the State, 1890-1930*. Pp. x, 211. Urbana: University of Illinois Press, 1995. $39.95. Paperbound, $14.95.

LINDSEY, DUNCAN. *The Welfare of Children*. Pp. ix, 404. New York: Oxford University Press, 1994. $29.95.

In the first paragraph of her thoroughly researched and extremely well-written book, Molly Ladd-Taylor clarifies the meaning of mother-work. It does not mean the paid work of mothers outside of the home. What it does refer to is the unpaid work of mothers engaged in the important work of reproduction and caregiving. With this as her starting point, Ladd-Taylor traces an engrossing history of "maternalism" in the late nineteenth and early twentieth centuries.

Mother-Work: Women, Child Welfare, and the State, 1890-1930 explores the inextricable bond between the private experience of mothering and the public political events that influence this experience. The reader is introduced to three groups—sentimental maternalists, progressive maternalists, and feminists—and is given an intimate look at their ideals, convictions, rhetoric, and prejudices. Their individual successes and failures at attempting to shape public policy dealing with mothers and their children are marvelously detailed.

Examined in a historical context, these groups, composed primarily of women, were active at a time when help from the state for families was considered radical. In fact, as Ladd-Taylor tells it, such ideas were often easy targets for those who fought against the Communist element. In this environment, the maternalist groups labored to give birth to their different visions of the motherhood-state communion. The sentimentalists desired to protect dependent mothers and children who were without a male breadwinner. The progressives, who helped create and shape the U.S. Children's Bureau, emphasized the right of women to choose between marriage and a career. The feminists, who advocated the Equal Rights Amendment, rejected the maternalist notion that a woman's duty was to care for her family.

In her conclusion, Ladd-Taylor observes that, "unfortunately, maternalism and its compromises continue to shape U.S. family policy." This is where Duncan Lindsey's book, *The Welfare of Children*, picks up. Lindsey argues that our current system for ensuring the welfare of children and families, which to a large extent evolved from some of the compromises made by the maternalists, is inadequate. It is a system that emphasizes a "residual approach," and began by providing orphanages and then foster homes for abandoned and neglected children. Currently, it vacillates between attempting to preserve families through intensive casework services and protecting children from abuse through mandatory reporting and investigation. Lindsey makes the point that the effectiveness of preservation services is open to question and that the issue of child abuse is a red herring that consumes resources and misuses the talent of child welfare professionals.

What we are left with is a child welfare system that misses the mark. Lindsey asks why so much attention is paid to the child abuse that takes place inside the walls of our nation's homes and so little attention is given to the societal inequities that allow 20 percent of our nation's

children to live in poverty. The core question Lindsey proposes is, If the primary mission of the child welfare system has become to target child abuse, why not aim at the massive suffering caused by child poverty? He hits the target when he places responsibility for many of our social problems on the inescapable reality that too many of our children grow up without "hope or opportunity." As a society, to contemplate that fact should cause us shame and send a shudder along our collective spine. What nihilistic depths have we reached when one-fifth of our children are considered expendable? A child welfare system, if it is true to its mission, should be engaged in the process of imbuing all of our children with a sense of possibility. Essentially, this is the challenge that Lindsey poses. He also offers proposals to get there. To those who study the field, some of the proposals are familiar; nonetheless, the material that Lindsey presents in *The Welfare of Children* must be included in any future discussions of child welfare.

JAMES X. BEMBRY

University of Maryland
Baltimore

LIGHT, PAUL C. *Thickening Government: Federal Hierarchy and the Diffusion of Accountability*. Pp. xiii, 217. Washington, DC: Brookings Institution, 1995. $29.95. Paperbound, $11.95.

According to Paul Light, the federal bureaucracy in its current form cannot do its job well because of a bulging, overweight hierarchy. In other words, there are too many layers of management between the top and the bottom, which causes a diffusion of responsibility and a lack of accountability. In 1960, there was a 17-layer pyramid at the top of the federal hierarchy. By the 1990s, this had grown to 32 layers, increasing from 451 senior executives and presidential appointees to almost 2400, a jump of 430 percent.

Light carefully documents why bureaucratic thickening occurred, tracing it from Luther Gulick's 1937 principles of span of control to the 1949 Hoover Commission's recommendations for greater secretarial leadership in the departments through more assistants. New cabinet departments in the 1960s and 1970s added to the thickening, as did the growth of the presidential and congressional bureaucracies. Both Democrats and Republicans expanded the size and weight of the bureaucracy.

As the federal government has expanded outward and upward, the key question is whether anything can or should be done about it. Would a lighter and more efficient bureaucracy be any more effective in delivering services? Light believes that it would, thereby offering alternatives to advocates of eliminating departments and agencies altogether through privatization, contracting out, or devolving functions and services from Washington to state and local governments.

Light's solutions call for an assertion of strong presidential leadership. More efficient federal bureaucracy may be possible if federal field offices are reduced, departmental spans of control are increased, and analyses of departmental layering can establish height and weight limits for hierarchies. Light admits the costs and problems of achieving these goals. But he argues that they can be achieved by creating an orthodoxy of thinning and raising the price for thickening by congressional oversight and better monitoring by the Office of Management and Budget.

At a time when the idea of reinventing government and Vice President Gore's National Performance Review are advocating large reductions in federal management positions, Paul Light's insightful arguments and recommenda-

tions should be carefully considered by the federal government's top policymakers. Only a comprehensive approach can result in a more efficient and effective bureaucracy for the twenty-first century.

ALAN SHANK

State University of New York
Geneseo

LOOMIS, BURDETT A. *Time, Politics, and Policies: A Legislative Year*. Pp. xv, 199. Lawrence: University Press of Kansas, 1994. $29.95. Paperbound, $12.95.

MATHEWS, DAVID. *Politics for People: Finding a Responsible Public Voice*. Pp. 229. Chicago: University of Illinois Press, 1994. No price.

In some ways, these two recent books on American politics are mirror images. Burdett Loomis's *Time, Politics, and Policies* recounts in great detail executive and legislative politics in the state of Kansas during the 1989 legislative session. David Mathews's *Politics for People*, on the other hand, articulately makes the case that governmental behavior per se is only one part of democratic politics, that public deliberation through community-based associations is closer to the essence of what it means to be a self-governing people.

By restricting his study to one legislative year in one medium-sized state, Loomis, a professor of political science at the University of Kansas, is able to examine the whole range of major issues that constituted the state legislative agenda and how the outcomes in each case were influenced by the "three basic components of political time: trends, cycles, and deadlines." Loomis pays particular attention to the interplay of electoral considerations (for the lawmakers as well as the incumbent governor) and policy aims. He concludes that Kansas legislators "were concerned, but not consumed, with their own electoral survival." Policy preferences "that spanned many years" had an independent effect on political behavior.

Those who decry the tendency of electoral calculations and policy goals to drive up governmental spending in democracies will find support for their concerns in Loomis's careful delineation of the "spending spree" engaged in by the 1989 legislature: "almost every time a problem came up, it was resolved by throwing money at it. . . . When in doubt, legislators avoided conflict by spending more money."

As the title *Politics for People* suggests, David Mathews, president of the Kettering Foundation and secretary of the Department of Health, Education, and Welfare during the Ford administration, is much less interested in what legislators do than in how to promote communitywide public deliberation outside of the formal institutions of government. Building upon an old political tradition and a renewed scholarly interest in political deliberation, Mathews maintains that it is only by deliberating together about common interests that a collection of diverse individuals becomes a true political community, a *polis* in the words of the ancient Greek philosophers. In this respect, his book is both a refutation of the view that Americans are apathetic, cynical, and merely self-interested and an effort to reinvigorate an active democratic citizenship that does not simply defer to the governing institutions to set the public course (a view that others have identified as the classical republican tradition).

Of the two books, Mathews's is the more readable and embraces a much broader scope. It is, on the other hand, a much more derivative work, drawing especially heavily from the writings of political scientist Benjamin Barber (particularly *Strong Democracy*), although without Barber's philosophical depth or his detailed practical recommendations. In this respect, Barber is much clearer than Mathews on the necessary tension between representative democracy and participatory deliberative democracy. Although in the first half of his book, Mathews does a commendable job of articulating the difference between rule by public officials and true popular self-government, in the end he does little to sort out the respective spheres of each kind of politics (communitywide associations, he notes, "do not attempt to do the work of formal institutions") and apparently sees no danger to representative democracy from an embrace of the principles of Jeffersonian ward democracy, the New England town meeting, or Athenian participatory politics.

Loomis's work, by contrast, is the result of extensive firsthand research and observation. Yet readers who, compared to the author, have less intrinsic interest in and fascination with the machinations of Kansas's politics may find his detailed account less than fully engaging. Indeed, fans of Loomis's previous insightful study of the U.S. Congress, *The New American Politician*, may well be disappointed by the narrower scope and less compelling arguments of the present work.

JOSEPH M. BESSETTE

Claremont McKenna College
California

MAY, DEAN L. *Three Frontiers: Family, Land, and Society in the American West, 1850-1900.* Pp. xi-xiii, 313. New York: Cambridge University Press, 1994. $44.95.

Dean L. May's *Three Frontiers* is a volume in the series of interdisciplinary perspectives on modern history edited by Robert Fogel and Stephen Thernstrom. Making an intensive study of three farming communities settled in the Far West during the second half of the nineteenth century, May presents the thesis that the "roots of American capitalism lie not in the cities but on the farm." He further maintains that the goals of the settlers he discusses were shaped by their place of departure and that the communities they formed were the product of these goals; that is, "the frontier did not greatly alter the people who went there [to the Far West], but rather it made it possible for them to realize the deepest aspirations of the cultures from which they came." Thus he presents interesting contrasts to Arthur M. Schlesinger, Sr.'s concept of the role of cities in the development of American civilization and to certain aspects of the Turner thesis.

In the first of the communities examined, Sublimity, Oregon, May depicts the 1840s' quest of small, independent farmers primarily of southern and midwestern background. These sought, in the Willamette Valley, good farmland and family continuity that they felt they could not attain in their place of origin.

Next, May deals with a group of Mormon migrants of the 1850s, largely drawn from Europe, especially Liverpool, England, who settled in Alpine, in the Utah Valley, near Salt Lake City. Seeking escape from the breakup of home and family created by the industrial revolution, they brought a cooperative, communal spirit motivated by the establishment of a new religion. Personal discipline was important to them, plus a desire to live apart from the mainstream of society. Analysis here centers on negative values of materialism, although May does touch on other differences and practices.

The third settlement, Middleton, near Boise, Idaho, came into being in the 1860s. It was composed of a mixed group, predominantly midwestern and southern. In contrast to the Alpine and the Sublimity communities, these were people much more interested in mobility.

Some came to flee the ravages of the Civil War, some for the gold rush, some to sell for commercial gain rather than sustenance the products of their land and of their labor. The promise of the intercontinental railroad was a strong lure, and prosperity was more important than remaining within the confines of the community with the expectation that the next generations would do so also. Thus May sees Middleton as a society more like ours in its materialism and self-centeredness than those of Alpine and Sublimity. Modifications are charted in the latter two as well, tending toward a more commercial outlook and less stability in terms of values, despite efforts to retain their original concepts.

May uses U.S. census figures, tax rolls, minutes of Farmer's Clubs meetings, court records, wills, funeral customs, and documentaries in the form of autobiographical and biographical sketches of key individuals in their respective settlements. He also considers the type of land, market and labor accessibility, and the reliability of the sources available. Within its announced scope, this is a meticulous study, laden with revealing family portraits and copious amounts of statistics to illustrate the characteristics of three nineteenth-century settlements of the Far West.

Students of American civilization, particularly those interested in the rural settlements of the Far West and their role in establishing contemporary attitudes of modern American society, will find *Three Frontiers* a valuable source.

                              DOROTHY RUDY
Montclair State University
Upper Montclair
New Jersey

SCHNEIDER, MARK and PAUL TESKE with MICHAEL MINTROM. *Public Entrepreneurs: Agents for Change in*

American Governments. Pp. xi, 263. Princeton, NJ: Princeton University Press, 1995. $39.50.

A central issue in social science revolves around the question of whether it is the intentional actions of individuals or broader social structures that should be given explanatory primacy in the analysis of societal change. This book makes a spirited case for the former perspective. Conceptualizing the individual actions of political entrepreneurs as the crucial variable at work in the process, the authors view themselves as "laying the micro foundations for understanding [broader] systemic change" in society.

In a refreshing contrast to several other analyses embracing this methodological individualism, Schneider, Teske, and Mintrom present a much more sophisticated variant of this perspective. In their story, the political entrepreneurs driving the dynamic of sociopolitical change are not isolated atomistic cowboys and cowgirls on lonely quests to alter the status quo. Instead, these actors "are embedded in social networks that help them discover opportunities and help them develop and implement strategies to achieve their goals."

Despite the book's somewhat misleading title, its empirical focus is on political entrepreneurs operating at only the local level of American government. This focus is justified by the authors' belief "that these communities are small enough for entrepreneurial individuals to make an important difference." Rather than looking at all local-level governments in the United States, one particular type is chosen for study: the suburbs. Therefore, this book will be especially of interest to scholars of local—and more specifically, suburban—politics.

To make thoroughly convincing the case that individual actions are key factors behind the social changes they observe, the authors must demonstrate that their political entrepreneurs "help radically transform economic and political systems." Unfortunately, this point is merely asserted and not subject to rigorous empirical scrutiny. The evidence that is supplied is largely anecdotal. Early in the book, this deficiency is recognized: "We are not yet able," the authors admit, "to test the long-term dynamic impact of entrepreneurship on local government systems."

Instead, what is offered is a comprehensive test "to identify the conditions that affect the emergence of [political] entrepreneurs" on the local level. Based on this empirical work, the authors argue that the emergence of these entrepreneurs in local communities is not simply a random process; rather, it is "a function of specific political, fiscal, economic, and demographic factors that influence the supply and demand for entrepreneurs." Where the local conditions provide for a high level of potential benefits from political entrepreneurship relative to the potential costs, political entrepreneurs are more likely to emerge.

By carefully delineating the conditions under which certain kinds of political change are likely to occur, Schneider, Teske, and Mintrom have made a solid contribution to our understanding of local politics. It is not clear, however, what their individualist approach adds to the analysis. To take one example, the study specifies the conditions favorable to the emergence of an "antigrowth" entrepreneur, that is, one who works toward limiting the rate of economic growth in a community. Yet it could have just as easily focused on the conditions favorable to the development of an antigrowth movement, rather than on the emergence of antigrowth entrepreneurs. Of course, such a movement will be led by individual political entrepreneurs responding to incentives structured by a given context. (After all, even Marx understood that "men make their own history.") But, to repeat, this insight adds little to our power to explain and predict political change.

In sum, absent the authors' almost superfluous commitment to methodological individualism, this book provides a useful examination of some current dynamics at work in local political-economic processes.

DAVID IMBROSCIO

University of Louisville
Kentucky

TOLNAY, STEWART E. and E. M. BECK. *A Festival of Violence: An Analysis of Southern Lynchings, 1882-1930.* Pp. xiv, 297. Chicago: University of Illinois Press, 1995. $49.95. Paperbound, $19.95.

A Festival of Violence is a competent blend of research and analysis of southern lynchings that roughly extends from post-Reconstruction to pre–Great Depression. It examines lynchings in the American South against a backdrop of existing social and economic data and theory, aided by a new inventory of lynching developed by the authors for the present research.

In a concluding chapter, Tolnay and Beck set out how their conclusions agree and disagree with important scholarly works that preceded their study, principally Arthur Raper's *Tragedy of Lynching* (1933), Joel Williamson's *Crucible of Race: Black Relations in the American South Since Emancipation* (1984), and Edward L. Ayers's *Vengeance and Justice: Crime and Punishment in the Nineteenth-Century American South* (1984).

None of the major conclusions of this study are truly surprising to anyone familiar with this area of study. For example, Tolnay and Beck find an apparent inverse relationship between lynching and economic conditions. But some conclusions do run counter to hypotheses advanced by some theorists. Thus, Tolnay and Beck conclude that there is no systematic support for the hypothesis that lynching is linked to shortcomings of the formal legal system. In addition, their research shows little support for the commonly advanced hypothesis that lynchings served to neutralize the potential political control of Afro-Americans through their proportionately large numbers.

A Festival of Violence would benefit anyone interested in Afro-American studies and the American South. The principal contributions of this study, however, are to serious researchers. They would benefit from an examination of an appendix that critiques existing inventories of lynching—those developed by the National Association for the Advancement of Colored People, the *Chicago Tribune*, and Tuskeegee University. They also will want to examine an appendix that details the development of the Tolnay-Beck inventory.

The book contains 11 pages of references and an 8-page index that should be more than adequate to the needs of most readers.

GEORGE R. SHARWELL

University of South Carolina
Columbia

SOCIOLOGY

TIANO, SUSAN. *Patriarchy on the Line: Labor, Gender, and Ideology in the Mexican Maquila Industry.* Pp. ix, 260. Philadelphia: Temple University Press, 1994. $44.95. Paperbound, $18.95.

Early feminist research on the role that gender plays in the export zones, or maquiladoras, focused on the social construction of biological and emotional differences by corporate managers and state governments to explain the disproportionate hiring of women in the electronics and textile industries. This research often concluded that despite the immediate economically liberating effects of maquiladora hiring for women, the overall impact of such hiring was physically, emotionally, socially, and economically negative. A 1990 article by Linda Lim titled "Women's Work in Export Factories: The Politics of a Cause" (in *Persistent Inequalities*, edited by I. Tinker) critiqued feminist writing for methodological flaws. According to Lim, ideological blinders, lack of empiricism, absence of updated comparative data sources, and sloppy methodology led feminist scholars to reiterate conclusions that were drawn from the experiences of women in the early years of the maquiladora experience. Susan Tiano's work, *Patriarchy on the Line*, like much of her previous work, is not only a timely and cogent response to Lim's critique, but it is also an invaluable resource for scholars assessing the impact of global economic restructuring on workers, women workers in particular, in the maquiladora industry in Mexico.

Tiano's study is rich in empirical resources, a result of survey research and information-seeking interviews carried out in Mexicali, the capital of Baja California, for various lengths of time in June 1981 and the summers of 1982, 1983, and 1984. The summer of 1990 was used to explore the changes in the maquiladora policies since the survey research was carried out. Her sample compares women workers in the electronics and garment industries. Since the small garment industry is often Mexican owned and operated—contrary to the electronic industry, which is owned and operated by big foreign capital—her study also compares the impact of different ownership and scale of capital on women's hiring, well-being, and consciousness. Tiano utilizes the integration, marginalization, and exploitation perspectives on women in development to evaluate "an empirically

grounded portrait of women's roles in the maquila industry."

Tiano's findings and analysis are insightful. Women in Mexicali, like their counterparts in Juarez and Tijuana, are entering the labor force in unprecedented numbers and continue to remain in full-time employment for most of their adult lives.

In the first decade and a half of maquiladoras in Mexicali, corporate managers hired young, single, and childless women, thereby reinforcing "patriarchal relations embodied in the ideology of reproduction that defines women in terms of their wife-mother roles and views employment as incompatible with their domestic responsibilities." Maquila industry expansion, the increasing need for labor, and an insufficient labor supply "forced" Mexicali corporations to revise their hiring practices and allow older, married women with children to enter the workforce. Accompanying the demographic changes of the female labor force is the change in ideology. Now corporate managers declare that the wife-mother role makes older women a more reliable workforce and that these positions are "complementary and mutually reinforcing." Integration into the capitalist economy has not challenged the patriarchal structures of production and reproduction; rather, it has created a compatible ideology that sustains both. The book may have benefited from a lengthier discussion of the centrality of ideology in maintaining relations of production and reproduction and how ideology buttressed economic necessity in "forcing" women into the workplace.

The empirical results of Tiano's survey also show that the victimization of women in maquiladoras has not abated. Although for some women, wages provide the means to struggle against domestic patriarchal relations, they fail to provide the means to struggle against the corporate or other public patriarchal relations.

However, Tiano documents that these women are not "necessarily passive" but struggle against their oppression in a variety of ways. She concludes by suggesting that in the coming decades, Mexican women workers will struggle to change the exploitive aspects of their work. Overall, this is a methodologically and theoretically sophisticated book addressing gender issues in the maquiladora industry.

GEETA CHOWDHRY

Michigan State University
East Lansing

ECONOMICS

ASLUND, ANDERS. *How Russia Became a Market Economy*. Pp. xviii, 387. Washington, DC: Brookings Institution, 1995. $39.95. Paperbound, $16.95.

The economic transformation of Russia since 1991 is one of the most stirring stories of this century. Few Westerners have better qualifications to tell it than Anders Aslund, a noted Swedish economist who served as a diplomat in Moscow during the final years of the old regime and then as an economic adviser to Russia's reformers during the opening phase of the new democratic government. Aslund's detailed insider study of Russia's transition to a free market is a useful antidote to the pessimism about that country's prospects currently at large in the West. But it contains some somber warnings of its own.

The main argument of the work, as its title makes clear, is that Russia has successfully made the leap from a planned, centralized system to what any student in the West would recognize as an open economy. Ironically, the passage was made easier by the vacuum of authority created by the failure of Communist economics. By the 1990s, the Kremlin was presiding over a corrosive budget deficit of 30 percent of the gross domestic product, and the system had become so remote from economic realities that one ton of crude oil sold domestically for the equivalent of a package of Marlboro cigarettes: about 30 rubles.

The vacuum opened what Aslund calls a "window of opportunity" for the reformers brought into the new government by President Boris Yeltsin. If they could move quickly and decisively enough to shatter what remained of the old system, Russia's vast natural resources and the skills of its people would be freed for rational development. This was the intellectual underpinning for the "shock therapy" program developed by Yegor Gaidar, new Russia's first economic mandarin, with the help of a team of Western advisers that included Aslund and Harvard economist Jeffrey Sachs. As Aslund ruefully admits, Russian political realities played havoc with the plan, and the "window of opportunity" was smaller than anyone expected.

Nevertheless, fundamental changes were achieved between December 1991 and December 1993 that Aslund believes are now irreversible. A drastic reduction of bank credits and subsidies broke up the largest concentrations of state economic power. The byzantine state-administered system of prices and artificial exchange rates was abolished, unleashing a flood of consumer goods and cash onto the market. Under the steady pressure of privatization laws, more than two-thirds of the Soviet economy passed out of state control.

These were monumental achievements, and Aslund maintains they resolved the long-running academic dispute about whether Russia represented a unique case for which standard economic theory was inapplicable. However, Aslund ends his account in 1994, when Russia seemed recovered from its bout of hyperinflation and political chaos. Subsequent developments such as the catastrophically expensive Chechen war and the government's embrace of neo-Communist authoritarianism are troubling departures from the path charted by Aslund's reformers.

Aslund insists that while the price of the transformation might be high, Russians have built the foundations of a "normal" entrepreneurial economy. He argues that the decline in the standard of living and the huge gap between the very rich and the very poor—both used by opponents of reform as proof that the so-called Westernization of the Russian economy has been a disaster—are less serious than they seem. Western and Russian fears about an explosion of popular unrest, he notes, never materialized.

Yet forbidding problems remain. The reformers failed to neutralize state enterprise managers who, after transforming themselves into powerful industrial lobbies, now effectively run the government and have helped fuel organized crime and corruption. The new government's overeagerness to accommodate the old nomenklatura elite explains why a full dose of shock therapy was in fact never administered, as Aslund admits. Aslund's optimism is therefore tempered by the knowledge that the story is not over, and he is scathing toward Western institutions such as the International Monetary Fund, whose help was often too little and too late. The world might have paid closer attention to the profound changes under way in Russia if the end of the Cold War "had left millions of corpses" behind, Aslund dryly observes. His book, however, is a significant contribution to our understanding of the forces and personalities that emerged from the ruins of Soviet communism.

STEPHEN HANDELMAN

Columbia University
New York City

CALDER, KENT E. *Strategic Capitalism: Private Business and Public Pur-* *pose in Japanese Industrial Finance.* Pp. xxii, 372. Princeton, NJ: Princeton University Press, 1993. $35.00.

The common view of a Japanese economy driven and guided by state funding and strategy is challenged by Kent Calder in this carefully researched book. The picture he paints is one where the policies of the "strategic" organizations like the Ministry of International Trade and Industry (MITI) have been limited by "regulatory" bureaucracies like the Bank of Japan and the Ministry of Finance. These regulatory organs were frequently risk averse in their policies, with a preference for stability over innovation. State credit power was weakly centered, with different organizations sometimes pursuing counter objectives. Moreover, financial credit allocated by the state was frequently directed at welfare or infrastructure rather than at targets that might provide economic growth.

Calder finds that most of the strategic initiative for industrial modernization came from the private sector and that most funding for sectors like steel, machine tools, and computers came from private sources. In part, this was because Japanese corporations enjoyed close relations with Japan's large private banks, which were a major source of their funds. More important, the larger banks—like the Industrial Bank of Japan—served as strategists of high growth, particularly during the Banker's Kingdom era of the 1950s and 1960s.

Calder uses Albert Hirschman's "exit, voice, and loyalty" typology to investigate how Japanese private borrowers responded to public credit controls in Japan. Although loyalty might be assumed to be the Japanese norm, Calder finds that while the auto parts industry played that option, Kawasaki Steel used the exit option by turning to the World Bank for funds, and Sasebo Heavy Industries utilized voice, mobilizing support from Prime Minister Fukuda after the Bank of Japan refused to provide a needed loan. But the Sasebo case also demonstrates a point that runs through Calder's book, namely, that nonstrategic clientelism at the state level can drive investment decisions, and this is not an atypical case.

For Calder, the Japanese economy is characterized by corporate-led strategic capitalism, neither laissez-faire nor state dominated. This view differs from the MITI-influenced economy described by Chalmers Johnson, but Calder makes a convincing case for it. This book will be of considerable value not only to scholars of Japanese politics but also to those interested in comparisons between Japanese strategic capitalism and that practiced in other industrial states.

DAVID S. SORENSON

Air War College
Maxwell Air Force Base
Alabama

GRAHAM, CAROL. *Safety Nets, Politics, and the Poor: Transitions to Market Economies.* Pp. xiv, 378. Washington, DC: Brookings Institution, 1994. $28.95.

Safety Nets, Politics, and the Poor addresses the timely issue of the political sustainability of transitions to market economies. In particular, Carol Graham examines the use of safety nets as a tool to enhance the sustainability of economic reform. When governments institute market-oriented reforms, they are necessarily reducing the role of the state in microeconomic decisions. Specifically, the state withdraws from the provision of purely private services. This generates a conflict between recipients of state-provided services. Graham divides the recipients into two groups, the "well organized and vocal" and the "poor and vulnerable." If the state can co-opt the poor and vulnerable, and give them a stake in the economic reform effort through ser-

vice provision, the reform effort will be more sustainable. Graham concludes that demand-based social funds, as exemplified by Bolivia's Emergency Social Fund (ESF), are best suited for "alleviating poverty and insuring sustainability." For ESFs to be effective, Graham notes, there needs to be an open political environment and ESF management must be free from partisanship and clientelism. Graham uses six case studies—Chile, Bolivia, Peru, Senegal, Zambia, and Poland—to illustrate her point.

Although Graham gives a short explanation on case study selection, the reader walks away with a feeling that her cases were chosen to weigh evidence on the side of ESFs as opposed to evaluating their efficacy. This feeling is intensified when Graham excuses the ESF failure in Senegal to partisanship. The argument for ESFs would have been stronger had the countries selected had similar political environments. It is impossible to disentangle the sustainability of economic reform from the pure popularity or legitimacy of the government. Additionally, Graham's assumption that poverty alleviation is per se efficient is wrong. To the extent that the state uses market-distorting devices to provide private services, a social welfare loss exists, and economic growth is sacrificed. Graham tempers her stand on poverty alleviation at the end when she notes that the administrative costs of reaching the poorest can be prohibitive. When the government is weak, the very poor may be sacrificed on the altar of consensus.

Overall, the book is a good read and the topic is timely. Graham's work can stand as a springboard for more systematic investigations into the role of safety nets and the sustainability of market-oriented reforms.

DEAN DUDLEY

United States Military Academy
West Point
New York

LEHMAN, TIM. *Public Values, Private Lands: Farmland Preservation Policy, 1933-1985*. Pp. xii, 239. Chapel Hill: University of North Carolina Press, 1995. $39.95. Paperbound, $16.95.

In this book, Tim Lehman outlines the politics of agricultural land use planning from the New Deal through the end of the first Reagan administration. The book begins with a summary of New Deal programs, beginning with the Agricultural Adjustment Act of 1933 and the subsequent establishment of the Soil Conservation Service. The intellectual and political precedents for national land policy, including the arguments of George Perkins Marsh, Gifford Pinchot, Theodore Roosevelt, and especially L. C. Gray, are noted. Chapters 2 through 5 outline the reemergence of federal regulatory policies in the 1970s and early 1980s, after a retrenchment in the 1950s and 1960s. Lehman points to heightened concerns about urban sprawl, the loss of prime farmland, uncontrolled population growth, and an increasing sense of resource limitations for economic growth as the source of renewed political activity for more intensive land regulation. He describes the formation of tenuous political coalitions between agricultural and environmental interests in maneuvering for cropland quality assessments and regulatory legislation. Coalition formation between heterogeneous groups, however, required compromise, weakening the results of land use planning initiatives. Lehman concludes in chapter 6 with a call for greater reliance on policy history case studies to place land use regulations in the larger scope of federal and state policies.

Lehman's book is thoroughly documented with extensive endnotes and a lengthy bibliography. Its contribution lies in discussing the politics of land use regulation after 1970. Lehman clearly sympathizes with the objectives of the various policies considered—and in some cases, adopted—to regulate farmland use between 1933 and 1985. A more critical analysis of the positions taken by the special interests involved (including politicians, ambitious bureaucrats, professional technicians, environmentalists, and agriculturalists) would have strengthened the book. Moreover, despite Lehman's call for placing farmland controls in the broader picture of federal and state policies, he fails to link these regulations to overall economic, social, and environmental regulation. Indeed, the United States has experienced two distinct government regulatory waves in the twentieth century, one during the New Deal and one in the late 1960s and early 1970s. The regulations adopted during these periods account for much of the price and entry restrictions, environmental controls, and social welfare policies that exist today. Examining land policy within this more comprehensive perspective suggests that other broader forces likely were behind the adoption of farm preservation regulation, such as the political ascendancy of activist professionals, rather than the emergence of the specific land use problems that Lehman emphasizes.

GARY D. LIBECAP

University of Arizona
Tucson

OTHER BOOKS

ABADINSKY, HOWARD. *Law and Justice: An Introduction to the American Legal System*. 3d ed. Pp. x, 446. Chicago: Nelson-Hall, 1995. Paperbound, $26.95.

ALLISON, DAVID B., ed. *Handbook of Assessment Methods for Eating Behaviors and Weight-Related Problems: Measures, Theory, and Research*. Pp. xx, 634. Thousand Oaks, CA: Sage, 1995. $65.00.

ALLUM, PERCY. *State and Society in Western Europe*. Pp. xxii, 627. Cambridge: Polity Press, 1995. Distributed by Blackwell, Cambridge, MA. $59.95.

ANDREOPOULOS, GEORGE J. and HAROLD E. SELESKY, eds. *The Aftermath of Defeat: Societies, Armed Forces, and the Challenge of Recovery*. Pp. vii, 195. New Haven, CT: Yale University Press, 1994. No price.

ANDREWS, CLINTON J., ed., *Regulating Regional Power Systems*. Pp. xii, 405. Westport, CT: Quorum Books, 1995. $65.00

ANTHONY, IAN, ed. *The Future of the Defence Industries in Central and Eastern Europe*. Pp. vii, 142. New York: Oxford University Press, 1994. $39.95. Paperbound, $26.00.

ARCHIBUGI, DANIELE and DAVID HELD, eds. *Cosmopolitan Democracy: An Agenda for a New World Order*. Pp. viii, 190. Cambridge: Polity Press, 1995. Distributed by Basil Blackwell, Cambridge, MA. $44.95.

ARMSTRONG, SUSAN, ed. *Using Large Corpora*. Pp. viii, 349. Cambridge: MIT Press, 1994. Paperbound, $37.50.

ARNETT, ERIC, ed. *Implementing the Comprehensive Test Ban: New Aspects of Definition, Organization and Verification*. Pp. viii, 128. New York: Oxford University Press, 1995. $39.95. Paperbound, $26.00.

ARONSON, RONALD. *After Marxism*. Pp. xiv, 321. New York: Guilford Press, 1994. $40.00. Paperbound, $18.95.

ARTHUR, JOHN and AMY SHAPIRO, eds. *Campus Wars: Multiculturalism and the Politics of Difference*. Pp. vii, 279. Boulder, CO: Westview Press, 1994. $55.00. Paperbound, $17.95.

BALL, TERENCE. *Reappraising Political Theory*. Pp. xv, 310. New York: Oxford University Press, 1995. $59.00. Paperbound, $19.95.

BANUAZIZI, ALI and MYRON WEINER, eds. *The New Geopolitics of Central Asia and Its Borderlands*. Pp. 284. Bloomington: Indiana University Press, 1995. $39.95. Paperbound, $15.95.

BARROW, JOHN D. *The Origin of the Universe*. Pp. xv, 150. New York: Basic Books, 1994. $20.00.

BEETHAM, DAVID, ed. *Defining and Measuring Democracy*. Pp. vii, 228. Thousand Oaks, CA: Sage, 1995. $69.95. Paperbound, $24.95.

BELL, DAVID S. and ERIC SHAW, eds. *Conflict and Cohesion in Western European Social Democratic Parties*. Pp. ix, 202. London: Pinter, 1994. Distributed by St. Martin's Press, New York. $49.00.

BERKOWITZ, EDWARD D. *Mr. Social Security: The Life of Wilbur J. Cohen*. Pp. xx, 396. Lawrence: University Press of Kansas, 1995. $34.95.

BERRY, JEFFREY M., KENT E. PORTNEY, and KEN THOMSON. *The Rebirth of Urban Democracy*. Pp. xiv, 326. Washington, DC: Brookings Institution, 1993. $36.95. Paperbound, $16.95.

BEST, GARY DEAN. *Witch Hunt in Wise County: The Persecution of Edith Maxwell*. Pp. 186. Westport, CT: Praeger, 1994. $49.95.

BORDERS, REBECCA and C. C. DOCKERY. *Beyond the Hill: A Directory of Congress from 1984 to 1993*. Pp. xv, 215. Lanham, MD: University Press of

America, 1995. $46.50. Paperbound, $19.50.

BOTELHO, RICHARD. *The New Individualism: Personal Change to Transform Society.* Pp. ix, 151. Danville, CA: Windstream, 1995. $19.95. Paperbound, $12.95.

BOWLES, PAUL and GORDON WHITE. *The Political Economy of China's Financial Reforms: Finance in Late Development.* Pp. xiii, 206. Boulder, CO: Westview Press, 1993. $49.95.

BREAKWELL, GLYNIS M., SEAN HAMMOND, and CHRIS FIFE-SCHAW, eds. *Research Methods in Psychology.* Pp. xi, 418. Thousand Oaks, CA: Sage, 1995. $75.00. Paperbound, $21.95.

BRINKLEY, DOUGLAS. *Dean Acheson: The Cold War Years, 1953-71.* Pp. xiv, 429. New Haven, CT: Yale University Press, 1995. Paperbound, $18.00.

BULLARD, ROBERT D. *Dumping in Dixie: Race, Class, and Environmental Quality.* Pp. xx, 195. Boulder, CO: Westview Press, 1994. $55.00. Paperbound, $19.95.

BUTLER, DAVID, ANDREW ADONIS, and TONY TRAVERS. *Failure in British Government: The Politics of the Poll Tax.* Pp. x, 342. New York: Oxford University Press, 1995. $39.95. Paperbound, $12.95.

CAIDEN, NAOMI and JOSEPH WHITE, eds. *Budgeting, Policy, Politics: An Appreciation of Aaron Wildavsky.* Pp. 143. New Brunswick, NJ: Transaction, 1995. $29.95.

CHARTERS, DAVID A., ed. *The Deadly Sin of Terrorism: Its Effect on Democracy and Civil Liberty in Six Countries.* Pp. 246. Westport, CT: Greenwood Press, 1994. $55.00.

CHEHABI, H. E. and ALFRED STEPAN, eds. *Politics, Society, and Democracy: Comparative Studies.* Pp. xxii, 414. Boulder, CO: Westview Press, 1995. $64.95.

CHRISTIE, KENNETH. *Problems in European Politics.* Pp. ix, 276. Chicago: Nelson-Hall, 1995. Paperbound, $21.95.

COOK, MARIA LORENA and HARRY C. KATZ, eds. *Regional Integration and Industrial Relations in North America.* Pp. 284. Ithaca, NY: ILR Press, 1995. Paperbound, $28.95.

COUTIN, SUSAN BIBLER. *The Culture of Protest: Religious Activism and the United States Sanctuary Movement.* Pp. xiv, 250. Boulder, CO: Westview Press, 1993. $55.00. Paperbound, $18.95.

CUTHBERTSON, IAN M. and JANE LEIBOWITZ, eds. *Minorities: The New Europe's Old Issue.* Pp. xii, 322. Boulder, CO: Westview Press, 1994. $39.85.

D'AMICO, FRANCINE and PETER R. BECKMAN, eds. *Women in World Politics: An Introduction.* Pp. xiii, 230. Westport, CT: Bergin & Garvey, 1995. $59.95. Paperbound, $19.95.

DARCY, R. and RICHARD C. ROHRS. *A Guide to Quantitative History.* Pp. viii, 323. Westport, CT: Praeger, 1995. $65.00. Paperbound, $24.95.

DAVIES, PAUL. *The Last Three Minutes: Conjectures About the Ultimate Fate of the Universe.* Pp. xiii, 162. New York: Basic Books, 1994. $20.00.

DeMUTH, CHRISTOPHER and WILLIAM KRISTOL, eds. *The Neoconservative Imagination: Essays in Honor of Irving Kristol.* Pp. xv, 249. Washington, DC: AEI Press, 1995. $24.95. Paperbound, $12.95.

DORNBACH, ALAJOS. *The Secret Trial of Imre Nagy.* Pp. xvii, 194. Westport, CT: Praeger, 1994. $59.95.

DWIVEDI, O. P. and DHIRENDRA K. VAJPEYI, eds. *Environmental Policies in the Third World: A Comparative Analysis.* Pp. xii, 233. Westport, CT: Greenwood Press, 1995. $59.95.

ESTEVA-FABREGAT, CLAUDIO. *Mestizaje in Ibero-America.* Pp. xii, 378.

Tucson: University of Arizona Press, 1995. $55.00.

FARLEY, REYNOLDS, ed. *State of the Union: America in the 1990s.* Vol. 2, *Social Trends.* Pp. xvii, 377. New York: Russell Sage Foundation, 1995. $39.95.

FAUBION, JAMES D., ed. *Rethinking the Subject: An Anthology of Contemporary European Social Thought.* Pp. xii, 227. Boulder, CO: Westview Press, 1995. $55.00. Paperbound, $18.95.

FRIEDGUT, THEODORE H. and JEFFREY W. HAHN, eds. *Local Power and Post-Soviet Politics.* Pp. xv, 292. Armonk, NY: M. E. Sharpe, 1994. $49.95. Paperbound, $19.95.

FRIEDMAN, EDWARD, ed. *The Politics of Democratization: Generalizing East Asian Experiences.* Pp. xi, 276. Boulder, CO: Westview Press, 1994. $59.95. Paperbound, $21.95.

GALTUNG, JOHAN. *Human Rights in Another Key.* Pp. vi, 184. Cambridge, MA: Blackwell, 1994. $49.95.

GARFINKEL, IRWIN, SARA S. McLANAHAN, and PHILIP K. ROBINS, eds. *Child Support and Child Well-Being.* Pp. xx, 361. Washington, DC: Urban Institute Press, 1994. $69.50. Paperbound, $32.50.

GEARY, PATRICK J. *Phantoms of Remembrance: Memory and Oblivion at the End of the First Millennium.* Pp. xiv, 248. Princeton, NJ: Princeton University Press, 1995. $29.95.

GILLON, STEVEN M. *The Democrats' Dilemma: Walter F. Mondale and the Liberal Legacy.* Pp. xxix, 468. New York: Columbia University Press, 1995. Paperbound, $17.00.

GOODWIN, CRAUFURD D. and MICHAEL NACHT, eds. *Beyond Government: Extending the Public Policy Debate in Emerging Democracies.* Pp. ix, 481. Boulder, CO: Westview Press, 1995. $65.00. Paperbound, $24.95.

GORDON, WENDELL. *The United Nations at the Crossroads of Reform.* Pp.

ix, 285. Armonk, NY: M. E. Sharpe, 1994. $49.95. Paperbound, $19.95.

HARBESON, JOHN W. and DONALD ROTHCHILD, eds. *Africa in World Politics: Post–Cold War Challenges.* Pp. ix, 340. Boulder, CO: Westview Press, 1995. $74.00. Paperbound, $21.95.

HART, H.L.A. *The Concept of Law.* Pp. xii, 315. New York: Oxford University Press, 1994. $26.00.

HASTIE, REID, ed. *Inside the Juror: The Psychology of Juror Decision Making.* Pp. vi, 277. New York: Cambridge University Press, 1994. Paperbound, $19.95.

HAZAREESINGH, SUDHIR. *Political Traditions in Modern France.* Pp. viii, 355. New York: Oxford University Press, 1994. $55.00. Paperbound, $19.95.

HEIBEL, YULE F. *Reconstructing the Subject: Modernist Painting in Western Germany, 1945-1950.* Pp. x, 207. Princeton, NJ: Princeton University Press, 1995. $45.00.

HEPER, METIN and AHMET EVIN, eds. *Politics in the Third Turkish Republic.* Pp. xi, 270. Boulder, CO: Westview Press, 1994. $59.00.

HIMMELFARB, GERTRUDE. *Victorian Minds: A Study of Intellectuals in Crisis and Ideologies in Transition.* Pp. xiii, 392. Chicago: Ivan R. Dee, 1995. Paperbound, $16.95.

HIPPLER, JOCHEN. *Pax Americana: Hegemony or Decline.* Pp. xii, 212. Boulder, CO: Westview Press, 1994. $61.95. Paperbound, $17.95.

HOFFMANN, STANLEY. *The European Sisyphus: Essays on Europe, 1964-1994.* Pp. x, 326. Boulder, CO: Westview Press, 1995. $69.95. Paperbound, $19.95.

HOLMES, ROBYN M. *How Young Children Perceive Race.* Pp. xi, 132. Thousand Oaks, CA: Sage, 1995. $49.95. Paperbound, $24.00.

HONIG, BONNIE. *Political Theory and the Displacement of Politics.* Pp. xiv,

269. Ithaca, NY: Cornell University Press, 1993. $35.00. Paperbound, $15.95.

HOSLER, DOROTHY. *The Sounds and Colors of Power: The Sacred Metallurgical Technology of Ancient West Mexico.* Pp. x, 310. Cambridge: MIT Press, 1995. $50.00.

HUTTNER, HARRY J. M. and PIETER VAN DEN EEDEN. *The Multilevel Design: A Guide with an Annotated Bibliography, 1980-1993.* Pp. viii, 276. Westport, CT: Greenwood Press, 1995. $69.50.

KELLY, ELIZABETH A. *Education, Democracy, and Public Knowledge.* Pp. xv, 168. Boulder, CO: Westview Press, 1995. $49.95. Paperbound, $17.95.

KING, LINDA. *Roots of Identity: Language and Literacy in Mexico.* Pp. xii, 193. Stanford, CA: Stanford University Press, 1994. $37.50.

KLEY, ROLAND. *Hayek's Social and Political Thought.* Pp. viii, 248. New York: Oxford University Press, 1995. $39.95.

KRAMER, STEVEN PHILIP. *Does France Still Count? The French Role in the New Europe.* Pp. xiii, 113. Westport, CT: Praeger, 1994. $45.00. Paperbound, $12.95.

LAMOREAUX, NAOMI R. and DANIEL M. G. RAFF, eds. *Coordination and Information: Historical Perspectives on the Organization of Enterprise.* Pp. viii, 337. Chicago: University of Chicago Press, 1995. $68.00. Paperbound, $22.50.

LANDY, MARC K., MARC J. ROBERTS, and STEPHEN R. THOMAS. *The Environmental Protection Agency: Asking the Wrong Questions from Nixon to Clinton.* Pp. x, 341. New York: Oxford University Press, 1994. Paperbound, $17.95.

LANGLEY, WINSTON E. and VIVIAN C. FOX, eds. *Women's Rights in the United States: A Documentary History.* Pp. xxxiii, 356. Westport, CT: Greenwood Press, 1994. $49.95.

LAWSON, KAY, ed. *How Political Parties Work: Perspectives from Within.* Pp. xiv, 317. Westport, CT: Praeger, 1994. $59.95.

LEAKEY, RICHARD. *The Origin of Humankind.* Pp. xvi, 171. New York: Basic Books, 1994. $20.00.

LEFF, ENRIQUE. *Green Production: Toward an Environmental Rationality.* Pp. xix, 168. New York: Guilford Press, 1995. $36.95. Paperbound, $16.95.

LEWIN, ELLEN. *Lesbian Mothers: Accounts of Gender in American Culture.* Pp. xviii, 232. Ithaca, NY: Cornell University Press, 1993. $34.95. Paperbound, $13.95.

MAGNUS, BERND and STEPHEN CULLENBERG, eds. *Whither Marxism? Global Crises in International Perspective.* Pp. xxiii, 253. New York: Routledge, 1995. $55.00. Paperbound, $17.95.

MAISEL, L. SANDY. *The Parties Respond: Changes in American Parties and Campaigns.* 2d ed. Pp. xviii, 445. Boulder, CO: Westview Press, 1994. $68.50. Paperbound, $22.95.

McCHESNEY, FRED S. and WILLIAM F. SHUGHART II, eds. *The Causes and Consequences of Antitrust: The Public-Choice Perspective.* Pp. xi, 379. Chicago: University of Chicago Press, 1995. $66.00. Paperbound, $32.95.

McCORMICK, THOMAS J. *America's Half-Century: United States Foreign Policy in the Cold War and After.* 2d ed. Pp. xix, 291. Baltimore, MD: Johns Hopkins University Press, 1995. $38.95. Paperbound, $13.95.

McFAUL, MICHAEL and TOVA PERLMUTTER, eds. *Privatization, Conversion, and Enterprise Reform in Russia.* Pp. xi, 228. Boulder, CO: Westview Press, 1995. $59.95.

MIGDAL, JOEL S., ATUL KOHLI, and VIVIENNE SHUE, eds. *State Power and Social Forces*. Pp. x, 333. New York: Cambridge University Press, 1994. $59.95. Paperbound, $19.95.

MILANI, MOHSEN M. *The Making of Iran's Islamic Revolution: From Monarchy to Islamic Republic*. Pp. xxv, 268. Boulder, CO: Westview Press, 1994. $62.00. Paperbound, $21.95.

NIVEN, JOHN, ed. *The Salmon P. Chase Papers: Correspondence, 1823-1857*. Vol. 2. Pp. xxv, 489. Kent, OH: Kent State University Press, 1995. $35.00.

O'CONNOR, MARTIN. *Is Capitalism Sustainable? Political Economy and the Politics of Ecology*. Pp. xiv, 283. New York: Guilford Press, 1994. $40.00. Paperbound, $17.95.

ORLOVSKY, DANIEL, ed. *Beyond Soviet Studies*. Pp. xi, 349. Washington, DC: Woodrow Wilson Center Press, 1995. Distributed by Johns Hopkins University Press, Baltimore, MD. Paperbound, $24.95.

OVENDALE, RITCHIE. *British Defence Policy Since 1945*. Pp. xv, 218. Manchester, England: Manchester University Press, 1994. Distributed by St. Martin's Press, New York. $49.95. Paperbound, $24.95.

PEREZ, LOUIS A., JR. *Essays on Cuban History: Historiography and Research*. Pp. xiv, 304. Gainesville: University Press of Florida, 1995. $44.95.

REDNER, HARRY. *A New Science of Representation: Towards an Integrated Theory of Representation in Science, Politics and Art*. Pp. x, 486. Boulder, CO: Westview Press, 1994. $59.50.

RIEFF, DAVID. *Slaughterhouse: Bosnia and the Failure of the West*. Pp. 240. New York: Simon & Schuster, 1995. $22.00.

RIESELBACH, LEROY N. *Congressional Politics: The Evolving Legislative System*. 2d ed. Pp. xx, 500. Boulder, CO: Westview Press, 1995. $75.00. Paperbound, $29.95.

ROGERS, PETER and PETER LYDON, eds. *Water in the Arab World: Perspec-*

tives and Prognoses. Pp. xix, 369. Cambridge, MA: Harvard University Press, 1995. Paperbound, $25.00.

ROOF, WADE CLARK, JACKSON W. CARROLL, and DAVID A. ROOZEN, eds. *The Post-War Generation and Establishment Religion: Cross-Cultural Perspectives*. Pp. xx, 291. Boulder, CO: Westview Press, 1995. $65.00.

RUSH, MARK E. *Does Redistricting Make a Difference? Partisan Representation and Electoral Behavior*. Pp. x, 172. Baltimore, MD: Johns Hopkins University Press, 1993. $32.50.

SCHECTER, DARROW. *Radical Theories: Paths Beyond Marxism and Social Democracy*. Pp. x, 205. Manchester, England: Manchester University Press, 1994. Distributed by St. Martin's Press, New York. $69.95. Paperbound, $19.95.

SCHNEIDER, ROBERT A. *The Ceremonial City: Toulouse Observed 1738-1780*. Pp. x, 202. Princeton, NJ: Princeton University Press, 1995. $24.95.

SCHUTTE, GERHARD. *What Racists Believe: Race Relations in South Africa and the United States*. Pp. xiii, 381. Thousand Oaks, CA: Sage, 1994. $49.95. Paperbound, $24.00.

SHEA, DANIEL M. and JOHN C. GREEN, eds. *The State of the Parties: The Changing Role of Contemporary American Parties*. Pp. xi, 395. Lanham, MD: Rowman & Littlefield, 1994. $57.50. Paperbound, $21.95.

SHIHATA, IBRAHIM F. I. *The World Bank Inspection Panel*. Pp. xiv, 408. New York: Oxford University Press, 1995. $24.95.

SHINGLETON, A. BRADLEY, MARIAN J. GIBBON, and KATHRYN S. MACK, eds. *Dimensions of German Unification: Economic, Social and Legal Analyses*. Pp. xv, 254. Boulder, CO: Westview Press, 1995. $49.95.

SIMMONS, A. JOHN et al., eds. *Punishment: A Philosophy and Public Affairs Reader*. Pp. xii, 335. Princeton, NJ:

Princeton University Press, 1995. $45.00. Paperbound, $14.95.

SIMON, RITA J. and JAMES J. FYFE, eds. *Editors as Gatekeepers: Getting Published in the Social Sciences.* Pp. x, 275. Lanham, MD: Rowman & Littlefield, 1994. $53.50. Paperbound, $22.95.

SIMONS, HERBERT W. and MICHAEL BILLIG, eds. *After Postmodernism: Reconstructing Ideology Critique.* Pp. x, 258. Thousand Oaks, CA: Sage, 1994. No price.

SKOCPOL, THEDA. *Social Revolutions in the Modern World.* Pp. viii, 354. New York: Cambridge University Press, 1994. $49.95. Paperbound, $16.95.

SMITH, J. W. *The World's Wasted Wealth 2: Save Our Wealth, Save Our Environment.* Pp. xviii, 558. Cambria, CA: Institute for Economic Democracy, 1994. $27.95. Paperbound, $17.95.

SMOKE, PAUL J. *Local Government Finance in Developing Countries: The Case of Kenya.* Pp. 223. New York: Oxford University Press, 1994. Paperbound, $19.95.

STOCK, ROBERT. *Africa South of the Sahara: A Geographical Interpretation.* Pp. x, 435. New York: Guilford Press, 1995. $45.00.

SULEIMAN, MICHAEL W., ed. *U.S. Policy on Palestine from Wilson to Clinton.* Pp. vi, 263. Normal, IL: Association of Arab-American University Graduates Press, 1995. Paperbound, $15.95.

SUTTERLIN, JAMES S. *The United Nations and the Maintenance of International Security: A Challenge to Be Met.* Pp. xii, 146. Westport, CT: Praeger, 1995. $55.00. Paperbound, $16.95.

SZPORLUK, ROMAN, ed. *National Identity and Ethnicity in Russia and the New States of Eurasia.* Pp. xiii, 328. Armonk, NY: M. E. Sharpe, 1994. $49.95. Paperbound, $19.95.

TACHAU, FRANK, ed. *Political Parties of the Middle East and North Africa.*

Pp. xxv, 711. Westport, CT: Greenwood Press, 1994. $125.00.

TEMPLETON, MALCOLM. *Ties of Blood and Empire: New Zealand's Involvement in Middle East Defence and the Suez Crisis 1947-57.* Pp. xi, 278. New York: Oxford University Press, 1994. Paperbound, $32.00.

TETREAULT, MARY ANN, ed. *Women and Revolution in Africa, Asia, and the New World.* Pp. viii, 456. Columbia: University of South Carolina Press, 1994. $39.95.

TIFFT, LARRY L. *Battering of Women: The Failure of Intervention and the Case for Prevention.* Pp. xiv, 230. Boulder, CO: Westview Press, 1993. $56.00. Paperbound, $17.95.

TILLY, CHARLES and WIM P. BLOCKMANS, eds. *Cities and the Rise of States in Europe, A.D. 1000 to 1800.* Pp. v, 290. Boulder, CO: Westview Press, 1994. $65.00. Paperbound, $21.95.

VINING, JOSEPH. *From Newton's Sleep.* Pp. xvii, 398. Princeton, NJ: Princeton University Press, 1995. $24.95.

VOOS, PAULA B., ed. *Contemporary Collective Bargaining in the Private Sector.* Pp. iv, 548. Ithaca, NY: ILR Press, 1995. Paperbound, $29.95.

WALKER, JENONNE. *Security and Arms Control in Post-Confrontation Europe.* Pp. ix, 182. New York: Oxford University Press, 1994. $29.95.

WEITZMAN, EBEN A. and MATTHEW B. MILES. *Computer Programs for Qualitative Data Analysis.* Pp. x, 369. Thousand Oaks, CA: Sage, 1995. $65.00. Paperbound, $29.95.

WHITEBROOK, MAUREEN. *Real Toads in Imaginary Gardens: Narrative Accounts of Liberalism.* Pp. x, 152. Lanham, MD: Rowman & Littlefield, 1994. $47.50. Paperbound, $19.95.

WOLIVER, LAURA R. *From Outrage to Action: The Politics of Grass Roots Dissent.* Pp. xi, 195. Champaign: University of Illinois Press, 1993. $36.95. Paperbound, $16.95.

INDEX

It's tough being a lone wolf. Besides, joining the pack is more affordable.

Being part of a large group means you can get excellent group rates. On things like health care insurance. Of course, many people get that where they work.

But when you choose AAPSS insurance, you get affordable group rates, but you're free to run, too. You see, AAPSS insurance goes where you go, from job to job. And it has been tailored specifically to your needs.

To learn more about this exclusive benefit of membership, call 1 800 424-9883, or in Washington, DC (202) 457-6820, between 8:30 a.m. and 5:30 p.m. eastern time to speak with a customer service representative. Then see if the numbers add up.

 AAPSS Insurance

Term Life • Excess Major Medical • In-Hospital
High-Limit Accident • Medicare Supplement Insurance

The term life plan is underwritten by the New York Life Insurance Company,
51 Madison Avenue, New York, NY 10010.

The German-American Academic Council Foundation

together with the Alexander von Humboldt Foundation is awarding **TransCoop Program** grants for transatlantic research cooperation in the humanities and social sciences.

Funds are available to support cooperative projects among and between German, U.S., and/or Canadian scholars and/or groups of scholars (Ph.D. required), above all from universities. Projects in the humanities and social sciences, including law and economics, selected for funding can receive up to $60,000 each over a three-year period. Prerequisite is that the amount applied for from Transcoop be matched by funds from U.S. and/or Canadian sources, which must be identified in the application. Project funds can be used to finance short-term research visits, special conferences and workshops, material and equipment, printing costs, and research assistance.

The **application deadline** for Transcoop projects to begin no earlier than December 1996 is **30 June 1996**. The next deadline will be in December 1996 for projects to begin in the summer of 1996.

Applications can be requested from the:

German-American Academic Council Foundation
1055 Thomas Jefferson St., N.W., Suite 2020
Washington, D.C. 20007
Tel.: (202) 296 2991   Fax: (202) 833 8514
gaac@nas.edu

The information you need to make intelligent judgments regarding the issues affecting you. . . your work. . . your society. . . and your world. Subscribe to

THE ANNALS

OF THE AMERICAN ACADEMY OF POLITICAL AND SOCIAL SCIENCE

Subscription Order Form

	Individual			Institution		
	One Year	Two Years	Three Years	One Year	Two Years	Three Years
Hardcover	❑ $74	❑ $148	❑ $222	❑ $229	❑ $458	❑ $687
Softcover	❑ $51	❑ $102	❑ $153	❑ $197	❑ $394	❑ $591

Name / Institution _____

Address _____

_____

City _____ State _____ Zip _____ Country _____

❑ My check or credit card information is enclosed.　　❑ Bill me.

Charge my:　　❑ MasterCard　　❑ Visa　　Exp. Date _____ Phone _____

Account # _____ Signature _____

Prices effective through August 31, 1996. Institutional checks for personal orders cannot be accepted. Phone number must be included with bill-me and credit card orders. In Canada, add 7% GST (#R129786448). On subscriptions outside the United States, add $12 per year for foreign postage. All foreign orders must be paid in U.S. funds. Make checks payable to:

Ⓢ **SAGE Publications, Inc.** • P.O. Box 5084 • Thousand Oaks, CA 91359 • (805) 499-0721　　**T5686**

The information you need to make intelligent judgments regarding the issues affecting you. . . your work. . . your society. . . and your world. Subscribe to

THE ANNALS

OF THE AMERICAN ACADEMY OF POLITICAL AND SOCIAL SCIENCE

Subscription Order Form

	Individual			Institution		
	One Year	Two Years	Three Years	One Year	Two Years	Three Years
Hardcover	❑ $74	❑ $148	❑ $222	❑ $229	❑ $458	❑ $687
Softcover	❑ $51	❑ $102	❑ $153	❑ $197	❑ $394	❑ $591

Name / Institution _____

Address _____

_____

City _____ State _____ Zip _____ Country _____

❑ My check or credit card information is enclosed.　　❑ Bill me.

Charge my:　　❑ MasterCard　　❑ Visa　　Exp. Date _____ Phone _____

Account # _____ Signature _____

Prices effective through August 31, 1996. Institutional checks for personal orders cannot be accepted. Phone number must be included with bill-me and credit card orders. In Canada, add 7% GST (#R129786448). On subscriptions outside the United States, add $12 per year for foreign postage. All foreign orders must be paid in U.S. funds. Make checks payable to:

Ⓢ **SAGE Publications, Inc.** • P.O. Box 5084 • Thousand Oaks, CA 91359 • (805) 499-0721　　**T5686**